W9-ABI-636

The Poets Laureate

Also by Kenneth Hopkins

LOVE AND ELIZABETH: poems
42 POEMS
POOR HERETIC: poems
COLLECTED POEMS, 1935–1965
POEMS ENGLISH AND AMERICAN
AMERICAN POEMS AND OTHERS

WALTER DE LA MARE
PORTRAITS IN SATIRE
ENGLISH POETRY: A SHORT HISTORY
THE POWYS BROTHERS

THE CORRUPTION OF A POET
A TRIP TO TEXAS

LLEWELYN POWYS: A selection from his writings
EDMUND BLUNDEN: A selection from his writings
H. M. TOMLINSON: A selection from his writings
WALTER DE LA MARE: A selection from his writings
SELECTED POEMS OF JOHN COWPER POWYS
THE ENGLISH LYRIC
THE POETRY OF RAILWAYS
etc.

A health to poets! all their days

May they have bread, as well as praise.

—THOMAS PARNELL

The Poets Laureate

BY *Kenneth Hopkins*

BARNES & NOBLE

BOOKS

10 East 53d St., New York 10022

(a division of Harper & Row Publishers, Inc.)

DALE H. GRAMLEY LIBRARY
SALEM COLLEGE
WINSTON-SALEM, N. C.

PR
505
H 69
1966

Copyright © 1954, 1966, 1973 Kenneth Hopkins

Third edition, revised and enlarged, published in the U.S.A. 1973 by
HARPER & ROW PUBLISHERS, INC.
BARNES & NOBLE IMPORT DIVISION

ISBN 06 492973 6

Printed in Great Britain by
Redwood Burn Limited, Trowbridge & Esher

To

E. LEWIS BARTON
of Fleet Street E.C.4

9-76

CONTENTS

I *The Poets Laureate*

II *Selections from the Works of the Poets Laureate*

PREFACE

THERE HAVE been five books on the Laureateship before this one; they are: *The Lives of the Poets-Laureate* by Wiltshire Stanton Austin, Jun., and James Ralph, 1853; *The Poets Laureate of England* by Walter Hamilton, 1879; *The Laureates of England* by Kenyon West,* 1895; *The Poets Laureate of England, their History and their Odes* by W. Forbes Gray, 1914; *The Laureateship, a Study of the Office of Poet Laureate in England with some account of the Poets* by Edmund Kemper Broadus, 1921.

Of these works, all long out of print, only the last is of value today, for the earlier studies are incomplete and in places inaccurate, being grounded in part on insufficient information. Professor Broadus (he was Professor of English at the University of Alberta when his book was published) gave detailed attention to the origins of the office of poet laureate and gathered a great deal of new material on the subject, but he wrote for the scholar and the specialist; my own purpose has been to offer an account of the Laureateship and its holders to the general reader, who is interested perhaps more in personalities than in what Dr. Johnson somewhere calls "remote inquiries." Professor Broadus gives more technical history than I do—his sixty closely argued pages on the origins of the Laureateship I cover in six—and I give more anecdote and quotation than he does.

I owe thanks to the librarians of Trinity College, and Gonville and Caius College, Cambridge, for furnishing information, and to Mr. Barney Blackley, Professor Edmund Blunden, and the late Professor V. de Sola Pinto for reading the manuscript and making helpful suggestions. I owe a further special debt to Mr. John H. Harvey for lending me his scholarship in areas where I was a stranger, and another to Mr. A. B. Gourlay. I gratefully remember the courtesies of John Masefield and C. Day Lewis, during their terms of office; and I am also particularly grateful to Mrs. Jill Day-Lewis for reading my chapter on her husband.

For the use of copyright material I have to make the following acknowledgements: Poems from *The Poetical Works of Robert Bridges* 1936, ©1936 Oxford University Press, by permission of the

---

*"Kenyon West" was the nom de plume of Frances Louise Morse Howland (1855–1944), the only American historian of the Laureates, and a minor novelist and miscellaneous writer who is now generally forgotten.

DALE H. GRAMLEY LIBRARY
SALEM COLLEGE
WINSTON-SALEM, N. C.

Clarendon Press, Oxford; poems by John Masefield, The Society of Authors as literary representative of the Estate of John Masefield; *The Times* newspaper for three "laureate" poems by Masefield; poems by C. Day Lewis, A. D. Peters and Co.; poems by Sir John Betjeman from *Collected Poems*, John Murray (Publishers) Ltd.

Southrepps,   Kenneth Hopkins
Norfolk
30 June 1973.

I

The Poets Laureate

DALE H. GRAMLEY LIBRARY
SALEM COLLEGE
WINSTON-SALEM, N. C.

1

Before the Laureateship: Jonson and Davenant

POETRY is very nearly as old as language, and from the remotest antiquity it has been employed to celebrate the deeds and virtues of the great. It has counselled in sorrow, rejoiced in fortune, triumphed in victory and mourned in defeat. By poetry we remember the names of kings dead five thousand years ago, their tombs long since crumbled, their very cities obliterated. The word of a king may determine life or death, but the word of a poet gives immortality.

It is a little surprising, therefore, that the notion of keeping a salaried poet permanently on the royal household staff seems to have occurred to none of the kings of antiquity. Many individual poets have received honours, pensions, gifts and patronage from the monarchs they served, but until the reign of Charles II in England there was nothing closely comparable with our office of Poet Laureate. In no age, and no country, until the death of Sir William Davenant on April 7th, 1668, was the passing of one court poet considered the occasion for the appointment of another with the same duties and the same emolument. It was left for the nation that has produced the greatest poetry of the world to establish the highest office to which a professional poet can aspire. And to this office, on April 13th, 1668, John Dryden was appointed.

One cannot, however, begin quite so baldly as that, especially as the Patent formally issued on August 18th, 1670, confirming Dryden in office, mentions specifically certain of his 'predecessors,' including 'Sir Geoffrey Chaucer, knight,' 'Sir John Gower, knight,' and several others, some of whom were not even poets.

Dryden's patent of 1670 appointed him Historiographer Royal and served to confirm the existing Laureateship appointment. It bestowed on him the several rights and privileges formerly enjoyed by those who held either of the offices before him, but with magnificent vagueness forebore to notice that 'Sir Geoffrey Chaucer, knight' (to look no further) had been born, and in due course had died, some three hundred years earlier, when neither office was an established Royal appointment. This vagueness extended to the titles given in the document to Chaucer and Gower.

The fact was, Davenant had succeeded to the Laureateship in a somewhat casual fashion after Ben Jonson died; and Ben Jonson had acquired it—rather vaguely—for services to James I. And before Jonson the word 'laureate' meant all kinds of different things in connection with the honouring of poets, except the thing we are concerned with here: a definite appointment to a definite post.

Since ancient times the laurel or bay leaf has been the crown for poets, and numerous references occur in the accounts of celebrated mediaeval poets of the crowning with laurel which was their reward for some special work, or for general eminence. The divine Petrarch was thus honoured at Rome in 1341, and there are other recorded cases.

Accordingly, it had always seemed reasonable to speak of a poet who had achieved distinction as 'laureated,' and naturally enough poets who enjoyed the notice of kings and great nobles were sometimes called 'laureate' by contemporary commentators. In addition to this, certain University degrees were associated with the laurel. The best-known case of confusion arising from these university laurels is that of John Skelton, who was 'poet laureate' at both Oxford and Cambridge in the late fifteenth century. Some early writers on the history of English poetry spoke of Skelton as though he held a royal laureateship, and to some extent the tradition persists to this day, although poets with a stronger title are forgotten.

For example, there was Bernard Andreas, who enjoyed an annuity of ten marks under Henry VII and is described as 'Poet Laureate' in the bill granting this sum. This poet—who was a blind Augustinian friar—wrote Latin verses on a number of 'official occasions' and also held the title Historiographer Royal, which he justified by writing a history of the reign of Henry VII.

These poets, and a number of others, do not properly come into a study of the office of Poet Laureate. Chaucer, we know, held appointments under the Crown; Spenser received £50 a year from Queen Elizabeth. These and similar misleading circumstances have caused the beginnings of the Laureateship to be confused in some accounts, but an examination of the evidence reveals the true genesis of the office as we know it today.

BEN JONSON

On February 1st, 1616, a patent was issued granting to Ben Jonson a pension of 100 marks, and this pension was clearly in recognition of his services as a poet. For ten years previously he had been furnishing the long series of magnificent entertainments which contain so much of his finest lyrical work—the masques, beginning with *The Masque of Blackness* in 1605 and continuing in a splendid series until 1634. Before that, in 1603 Jonson was associated in the pageantry devised for James's coronation and again, a few days later he provided verses for the opening of the king's first parliament. Accordingly, in 1616 Jonson had already done much to deserve favour and reward at the king's hands; but, whereas such reward might have taken the form of a single grant, it is significant that it did not. It took the form of a *permanent stipend*, and to this yearly 100 marks a long line of succeeding laureates owe their salaries.

These early 'laureate' verses of Jonson's were not unworthy of the office they virtually inaugurated. Jonson preaches a little sermon on the duties of a king, under the fine sounding title, 'A Panegyre, on the Happie Entrance of James, our Soveraigne, to His first high session of Parliament in this his Kingdome, the 19 of March 1603:'

> . . . *He knew that those who would with love command*
> *Must with a tender (yet a steadfast) hand*
> *Sustain the reins, and in the Check forbear*
> *To offer cause of injury, or fear;*
> *That kings, by their example, more do sway*
> *Than by their power; and men do more obey*
> *When they are led, than when they are compelled.*
> *In all these knowing arts our Prince excelled* . . .

Jonson's patent of 1616 was replaced in 1630 by another in which Charles I increased the pension granted by his father from 100 marks to £100, and added for good measure the famous 'one Terse of Canary Spanish wyne yearely' to be paid out of the King's own cellars. This second patent was not secured without a hint from Jonson, as the 'Humble Petition of Poore Ben' demonstrates. After remarking that James gave him a pension, the poet says this has caused envy among his

fellow poets and suggests that he could better put up with their envy if
they had something more to be envious of:

> *Please your Majestie to make*
> *Of your grace, for goodnesse sake,*
> *Those your* Fathers Markes, *your* Pounds;
> *Let their spite, (which now abounds)*
> *Then goe on, and doe its worst . . .*

It is one thing to have a pension, but quite another to collect it.
Jonson was not the only poet to suffer from promises that did not
always bring fulfilment with them; but he was one of the most
articulate in protesting. Dryden complained by letter when his pension
was in arrears, so did Shadwell, and Cowper made no official protest at
all when not a penny of his ever reached him.[1] Jonson, in 1630 lost
little time in reminding the appropriate officials of his rights:

> *What can the cause be, when the K. hath given*
> *His Poet Sack, the House-hold will not Pay?*
> *Are they so scanted in their store? or driven*
> *For want of knowing the Poet, to say him nay?*
> *Well, they should know him, would the K. but grant*
> *His Poet leave to sing his Household true . . .*

Perhaps the implied threat was enough—as was Dryden's when he
sent three famous lines to Jacob Tonson with the remark that 'He that
wrote these can write more.'

Although Jonson's greatest services to the Court were the masques,
he wrote a considerable group of occasional poems to the king and
queen—at the New Year, on the birth of a prince, and on great official
occasions. He was in no way obliged to do this by his patents of 1616
and 1630; the first merely records the services Jonson had done and
supposes that he would continue to do 'good and acceptable service';
and the second, although a longer document, adds nothing more
specific to the recipient's duties than that he is encouraged 'to proceed
in those services of his witt and penn which We have enjoined unto
him, and which we expect from him. . . .'

Jonson himself makes no claim to a Laureateship as we understand
the term. The title pages of the books published in his lifetime do not
even make Skelton's use of the title, and Jonson's references to himself
in relation to his office usually speak of 'the King's poet' as a servant in

---

[1] Cowper was not a Laureate, but he was granted a pension, at least on paper.

the sense that all subjects are servants, but not as the holder of a specified post. In *The Masque of Augurs* (1623) Notch, 'a Brewer's clerk,' says he hears neither 'the King's poet nor his architect have wherewithal left to entertain so much as a baboon of quality'—perhaps because pensions were in arrears again—and in *Neptune's Triumph* (1624) a character called, simply, 'the Poet' defines his own business about the Court.

'What are you, sir?' asks the king's Master Cook.

'The most unprofitable of his servants, I, sir, the Poet. A kind of Christmas ingine: one that is used at least once a year, for a trifling instrument of wit or so.'

It is a definition some of the later Laureates took to heart, when 'once a year' they were content to produce a laborious Ode or so in fulfilment of the letter of their duties. But it could not fairly be applied to Jonson himself, for he gave of his best in the masques which were his principal Court poems, and few of the 'official' Laureates can show a finer body of work performed in the course of their duty.

❖

SIR WILLIAM DAVENANT

Jonson died in August, 1637, but it was not until December, 1638, that a patent was issued to Davenant, his nominal successor as Laureate. In this patent nothing is said of Jonson, poetry, or for that matter of a 'terse of Canary Spanish wyne.' It merely states that 'in consideration of service heretofore done and hereafter to be done unto us by William D'avenant' that 'gentl' is to have an annual £100.

And Davenant's 'service heretofore done' consisted, as it happened, mainly in the provision of words for masques. In Jonson's last years his long association with Inigo Jones had been interrupted by a quarrel. Indeed, it is surprising that two men so strongly arrogant, individual and ambitious had not quarrelled irrevocably long before.

It was the business of Inigo Jones to devise the elaborate settings, costumes and engines that clothed the often extravagant business of the masques; and in some cases the words and songs were very subordinate to the gorgeous pageantry of costume, scenery, mime and music. Accordingly, in 1634 Jones by-passed Jonson and applied to Davenant for a 'script' and the result was *The Temple of Love*. This masque was performed by the Queen and her ladies on Shrove Tuesday, 1634, and not unnaturally as a result Davenant came to the notice of her majesty—and seems to have made a favourable impression. This success was followed and repeated in 1636 by *The Triumphs of the Prince d'Amour*, and was consolidated by the increasing reputation of Davenant's work for the legitimate stage.

Davenant, like Jonson (and for that matter, like most poets of the time, whether they had access to the Court or not) made use of royal and current events as themes for poems in which to celebrate his master's praises and in so doing to recommend himself to notice.

Before Jonson's death Davenant, in 'Madagascar,' had written a poem discussing the project, then under consideration, of sending Prince Rupert to conquer Madagascar. He also wrote a poem 'Upon His Sacred Majesty's Most Happy Return to His Dominions' after the Restoration and followed quickly with a poem 'To the King's Most Sacred Majesty.' He had been a faithful follower of the first Charles and had accompanied his widow into exile. But Charles II looked elsewhere for pensioners and although Davenant continued to hold such tenuous honour as his shadowy appointment offered, his pension lapsed with the downfall of Charles I.

Thus his collected *Works* in folio (1673) contains a portrait frontispiece in which he is seen wearing a laurel wreath, and a reference in the editor's preface to Davenant as 'Poet Laureate to two Great Kings.'

But neither success at Court, success in the theatre, nor the enjoyment of a pension may be considered evidence that a man has been appointed Poet Laureate. There is no direct documentary evidence that Davenant received such a title. There is a tradition, supported by remarks in the *Brief Lives* of John Aubrey and the *Athenae Oxoniensis* of Anthony à Wood, and by others writing later and probably influenced by these not always reliable authorities, that Davenant was, in fact, made Poet Laureate in Jonson's place. But Jonson himself had officially filled no such place.

If such poets as Skelton and Spenser may be called 'prelaureates,' perhaps Jonson and Davenant[1] may be called 'traditional laureates.' They all in various ways prepared for the coming of the first 'official' Laureate, John Dryden.

---

[1] For posterity Davanant's best "service heretofore done" lies in his *Gondibert* (1651) a curious unfinished epic in quatrains which had some influence (not wholly good) on later poets; and even posterity, I think, speaks of *Gondibert* more frequently than it reads it.

2

The First Laureate: John Dryden

IN 1668 John Dryden was thirty-seven and he had been before the
public as an author for a number of years. He was a man of good
Midland stock, born at Aldwinkle All Saints, Northamptonshire, on
April 9, 1631, and educated at Westminster and Trinity, Cambridge.
He inherited some slight income from his father (who died in 1654)
and at first leaving the university seems to have been content with
comparative idleness. He certainly did not turn early to letters; a
few schoolboy verses represent all he could do before the age of
twenty-seven—an age when, if W. J. Cory may be credited, 'one's
feelings lose poetic flow'; but Dryden's poetic flow was yet to
come.

He made a sure start with his 'Heroic Stanzas on the Death of
Cromwell'—originally, but less familiarly, 'A Poem Upon the Death
of His Late Highness Oliver, Lord Protector of England, Scotland and
Ireland' (1659). This is remarkable for its moderation and good sense
(a few prosodic excesses apart) and is, moreover, an accomplished poem
of which a practised poet need not have felt ashamed. Had Dryden in
the ten years or so since the wholly inadequate exercises of his schooldays, written verses which are now lost?[1]

It is possible; for the writing of poetry was a common occupation
for a gentleman, and the heroic stanzas show an easy familiarity not
inherent in the rather pedestrian 'Gondibert' stanza which Dryden
borrowed from Davenant:

> *He fought, secure of fortune as of fame,*
> *Till by new maps the island might be shewn;*
> *Of conquests, which he strewed where'er he came*
> *Thick as the galaxy with stars is sown.*

---

[1] Naturally he did a good deal of translating as school exercises: he remarks in a note to
his translations from Perseus '. . . I translated this satire . . . at Westminster; . . . it
and many other of my exercises of this nature in English verse, are still in the hands of my
learned Master, the Rev. Dr. Busby.

> *Nor was he like those stars which only shine,*
>   *When to pale mariners they storms portend;*
> *He had his calmer influence, and his mein,*
>   *Did love and majesty together blend.*

'After the Restoration this piece fell into a state of oblivion,' remarks
Sir Walter Scott, 'from which it may be believed that the author, who
had seen a new light in politics, was by no means solicitous to recall it.'

This was a reasonable attitude in a professional writer, as Dryden
shortly became. 'The King is dead—Long live the King' was a convenient slogan, especially if the dead king were only a Lord Protector.
But Dryden's enemies made telling use of the Cromwell stanzas a few
years later, reprinting them with heavily sarcastic comments as 'An
Elegy on the Usurper O.C. by the Author of *Absalom and Achitophel*,
published to show the loyalty and integrity of the Poet' (1681).

The Restoration gave a great impetus to letters by making the drama
once more a living vehicle for argument, propaganda and pure entertainment. It was the medium for almost every kind of writer, the one
likely way to fortune and fame in literature. Within a year or so one
of the crowd of dramatists jostling for attention was John Dryden, and
thereafter for nearly forty years he was a major force in the theatre.
But first he established himself as a poet.

Despite the work that may have preceded it, the Cromwell poem
was a trial of strength and from it Dryden proceeded to something
better. Perhaps, as George Saintsbury suggests, he was genuinely glad
to see Charles on the throne, despite the sincerity of his mourning for
Cromwell (for it is certainly sincere).

At all events, in 1660 appeared *Astraea Redux, a poem on the Happy
Restoration and Return of His Sacred Majesty Charles the Second*. It must
be admitted that the poem outshone Davenant's offering on the same
occasion, as well as foreshadowing the great Dryden of the years
ahead. *Astraea Redux* was succeeded in 1661 by *To His Sacred Majesty,
a Panegyric on his Coronation*, a poem which contains a number of lines
far above the merit usually found in such 'set' pieces. But there is no
evidence that Charles thought more highly of these praises than of the
many others he received. At least, they advanced Dryden in his reputation and probably helped to get him elected Fellow of the Royal
Society in 1662.

Dryden's first essay in the drama, *The Wild Gallant* was acted in
February, 1663. In his preface to the published play several years later
the author philosophically records its failure: 'I made the Town my

Judges; and the greater part condemned it . . . I doubt not but you will see in it, the Uncorrectness of a young Writer:[1] which is yet but a small Excuse for him, who is so little amended since. . . .' Nonetheless, the play was several times acted before the King, once in the critical presence also of Samuel Pepys who thought it 'so poor a thing as I never saw in my life almost . . . the King did not seem pleased at all. . . .' And Pepys could not determine which character was supposed to be the Wild Gallant. However, Dryden was neither the first dramatist nor the last to fail with his first play. There were better things to come.

From 1663 until 1694 Dryden was never far from the theatre, which provided most of his bread and butter. Those thirty-odd years produced as many plays,—some masterpieces and some mere journeywork, but nearly all interesting: for Dryden was too great a writer ever to be dull for long, however misguided we may now think some of those extraordinary works, the heroic plays, and the tagging of Milton's verses, and the operatic antics of King Arthur. Such works as *The Conquest of Granada* (1670), *Marriage A-la-Mode* (1672) and *All for Love* with its moving sub-title, *The World Well Lost* (1677) mark Dryden as the greatest dramatist of his age (and it was a great age). These are not plays for a mere lip-service commendation on the lecture platform; they are living works with a vitality that will outlast anything with which they were contemporary.

At the end of 1663 Dryden married Lady Elizabeth Howard, eldest daughter of the Earl of Berkshire; it was a marriage of ups and downs, but so are most marriages, and perhaps the Lady Elizabeth never quite got accustomed to being married to a man of genius. It is doubtful if these make the best husbands.

Dryden, moreover, had a reputation for taciturnity which is so persistent that in part at least it is probably deserved; indeed, he says as much himself: 'My conversation is slow and dull, my humour saturnine and reserved. In short, I am none of those who endeavour to break jests in company, or make repartees.' For this reason, perhaps, he was 'alarmed and amazed' when a jest was 'broke' upon himself. Someone translated a passage from one of his poems into Latin, caused it to be printed, and pasted the leaf into the bottom of an old hatbox. Dryden was then confronted with this evidence of his own plagiarism!

To trace Dryden's career as a playright, title by title, would require

---

[1] Dr. Johnson, with characteristic forthrightness, has an extension of this thought: 'The buyer has no better bargain when he pays for mean performances by being told that the author wrote them when young.'

a book rather than a chapter, and would entail reading, among some splendid things, a great quantity of remarkably dull bawdiness;[1] for with Dryden the smutty line is always contrived, and never spontaneous. This is one of several ways in which he was inferior to his enemy, Shadwell.

At the time of the Restoration Davenant was still active, and had some years yet to live. His work as Poet Laureate was the least of his preoccupations, and most of his attention was given to the theatre where, incidentally, he first introduced the device of moveable scenery. After his poems in recognition of the Restoration he wrote nothing directly addressed to the king or in support of his affairs, but in the same years Dryden, although also busy with other work—and the more busy by having his way still to make—found opportunity to produce several poems on national subjects. He was, in fact, doing what came to be considered the work of the Poet Laureate. These early 'laureate' poems included a *Satire on the Dutch* in 1662—which reappeared with slight modifications as the Prologue to *Amboyna, a Tragedy* in 1672; an epistle to the Duchess of York on the Duke's victory of June 3rd, 1665; and finally in 1667 the famous *Annus Mirabilis, The Year of Wonders, 1666. An Historical Poem.* This last is a long poem—over twelve hundred lines—which abundantly demonstrates Dryden's fittedness for the work of 'official poet.'

Accordingly, when Davenant died on April 7th, 1668, and it was at last officially recognised that he had held an appointment for which his death created a vacancy, Dryden was named within a week to succeed him with the given title of 'Poet Laureate.' This initial appointment was in the form of a warrant; and it was two years before his appointment to be Historiographer Royal provided an occasion for the issue of a formal Patent covering both offices.

In 1679 Dryden was the victim of an assault as the supposed author of *An Essay on Satyre* (which was, in fact, by the Earl of Mulgrave) in which among others the Earl of Rochester and the Duchesses of Portsmouth and Cleveland were attacked. One of these persons (usually

---

[1] I must, however, say one word in defence of *Limberham, or the Kind Keeper* (1678) which has generally been admitted to be beneath contempt by critics from Scott to Saintsbury. I have to confess I found it amusing; it is the nearest thing in Dryden to the special excellence of Shadwell as seen in (say) *Epsom Wells*. Dryden himself none the less has misjudged *Limberham*, for he says in the Dedication, 'I will be bold enough to say, that this Comedy is of the first Rank of those which I have written, and that Posterity will be of my opinion.' But George Saintsbury sums up the general opinion of posterity: '. . . this filthy stuff,' he says, '. . . as a play is by no means Dryden's worst piece of work; but in all other respects, the less said about it the better.' So I will say no more.

thought to have been Rochester) appears to have hired assistance, for one night as the poet passed through Rose Alley, Covent Garden, on his way home he was attacked and beaten by a group of masked men; nor did the offer of fifty pounds reward succeed subsequently in unmasking them or their employers. Thereafter most of the satirical attacks on Dryden taunted him with this mischance, as thought it were particularly disreputable to have cowardly enemies.

The Laureateship being now official, and Dryden its first holder, that poet lost no time in creating duties for himself and his successors. Nothing had been laid down for him, but—like the honest man he was —he considered the title to carry responsibilities. Henceforth, his pen was employed to support the King against his enemies at home and abroad in a series of magnificent poems that have remained for the general reader Dryden's chief contribution to literature. In the late seventeenth century King and Court were much nearer the heart of political controversy than was customary in later reigns, and Dryden had many opportunities to bring his pen to the King's aid. He was—as soon became apparent—a formidable satirist and in such poems as *Absalom and Achitophel* (1681) and *The Medal, a Satyre against Sedition* (1682) his full powers were displayed. Perhaps it was not without some consciousness of these powers in Dryden that the King authorised the original appointment. At all events, Charles secured a champion whom the other side could not match, despite some strenuous efforts by Shadwell, a poet unjustly underrated.

Absalom and Achitophel, the first and greatest of Dryden's major satires (and perhaps the greatest single satire in the language) was occasioned by the Earl of Shaftesbury's support of Monmouth's pretensions to succeed Charles as King—pretensions which later led to the Battle of Sedgemoor with its bloody consequences. Shaftesbury was implicated in the Popish Plot agitation, and was the bitter enemy of the Duke of York, who succeeded Charles II and became James II. It is a pity that the habit of quoting celebrated passages from long poems tends to direct attention away from them as a whole. Few 'purple passages' are more familiar than the character of Achitophel, beginning at line 150 of the poem, but how often is the reader encouraged to read the whole? Yet only by reading the whole (and it is but a thousand lines) can the full devastating force of Dryden's satire be appreciated.

This satire also gave Dryden an opportunity to retaliate upon the Duke of Buckingham, whose brilliant comedy *The Rehearsal* (1671)

had held Dryden and his works up to ridicule and first bestowed on
him the familiar name of Bayes,[1] which their enemies subsequently
applied to several future Laureates. Buckingham appears in *Absalom
and Achitophel* as Zimri, and can hardly have congratulated himself
upon the fact. *The Rehearsal*, however, contained much wholly justified
criticism of the absurd heroic plays, and indeed helped to kill them. Its
personal strictures on Dryden are less defensible: 'Not satisfied with
parodying some of the most familiar passages in Dryden's plays, the
Duke of Buckingham took considerable pains in teaching Lacy, who
performed *Bayes*, to mimic his author in his manner of reciting them.
Dryden was notoriously a bad reader, and had a hesitating and tedious
delivery, which, skillfully imitated in lines of surpassing fury and
extravagance, must have produced an irresistible effect on the audience.
The humour was enhanced by the dress, gesticulations and by-play of
the actor, which presented a close imitation of his original.'[2]

In *The Medal*, which followed, Dryden concentrated his attention
on Shaftesbury, who in 1681 had been imprisoned in the Tower and
prosecuted for high treason. Unfortunately for his enemies the Grand
Jury did not confirm the Bill and the Earl was released, whereupon his
supporters struck a medal with his head on the obverse, and the Tower
on the reverse, with the motto 'Laetamur' and the date of the Bill's
failure.

Joseph Spence in his *Anecdotes* gives an account of the poem's genesis
which some later critics have considered apocryphal. To me it seems
probable that there is a broad basis of fact in the story. 'It was King
Charles the Second' (Spence records, quoting 'a priest that I often met
at Mr. Pope's') 'Who gave Dryden the hint for writing his poem
called "The Medal." One day as the King was walking in the Mall, and
talking with Dryden, he said, "If I was a poet, and I think I am poor
enough to be one, I would write a poem on such a subject in the following manner:" and then gave him the plan for it. Dryden took the hint,
carried the poem as soon as it was finished to the King, and had a
present of a hundred broad pieces for it.' Perhaps the King's hint was
not very detailed; and perhaps the broad pieces were fewer; but that
the poem was conceived during a conversation in the Mall seems to me
perfectly possible. It had to be conceived somewhere, and why should
Dryden not discuss it with the King?

---

[1] Davenant, the existing 'laureate,' and other writers were also parodied, but Dryden
bore the brunt of the attack.
[2] Robert Bell, life prefixed to his edition of Dryden's poetical works.

At all events, the result was a poem which must have satisfied Charles that he had a redoubtable ally in his Laureate.

Despite his good services to the King, Dryden did not find Charles II any prompter at paying wages than Jonson had found James I, and to Dryden as to Jonson this was a serious matter, for both were professional men of letters—so far as such a thing then existed—depending for a living on the money their work brought in. And—as Matthew Prior has it in 'A Session of the Poets'—[1]

> *From Homer to D . . . . n it never was known*
> *That the Laureat had three Pence a Year of his own.*

In a letter which contains one of his most famous phrases Dryden made a dignified protest, directly at the delay in payment and by implication at the smallness of his salary. The letter is without superscription, but was no doubt addressed to the appropriate official, probably the Earl of Rochester, at the Treasury:

My Lord,

I know not whether my Lord Sunderland has interceded with your Lordship for half a yeare of my salary; but I have two other advocates, my extreme wants, even almost to arresting, and my ill health, which cannot be repaired without immediate retiring into the country. A quarter's allowance is but the Jesuites' powder to my desease; the fitt will return a fortnight hence. If I durst, I would plead a little merit, and some hazards of my life from the common enemyes; my refuseing advantages offered by them, and neglecting my beneficiall studyes, for the King's service: but I only thinke I merit not to sterve. I never apply'd myselfe to any interest contrary to your Lordship's; and on some occasions, perhaps not known to you, have not been unserviceable to the memory and reputation of my Lord, your father. After this, my Lord, my conscience assures me I may write boldly, though I cannot speake to you. I have three sonns growing to man's estate; I breed them all up to learning, beyond my fortune; but they are too hopefull to be neglected, though I want. Be pleased to looke on me with an eye of compassion: some small employment would render my condition easy. The King is not unsatisfied of me; the Duke has often promised me his assistance; and your Lordship is the conduit through which their favours passe: either in the Customes, or the Appeals of the Excise[2], or some other way, meanes cannot be wanting, if you please to have the will. 'Tis enough for one age to have neglected Mr. Cowley and sterv'd Mr. Butler; but neither of them had the happiness to live till your Lordship's ministry. In the meane time, be pleased to give me a gracious and speedy answer to my present request of halfe a year's pention for my necessityes. I am going to write somewhat by

[1] Not to be confused with Suckling's poem of the same name, written when Jonson's death left vacant the 'Laureateship.'
[2] A place later held by Addison.

his Majesty's command,[1] and cannot stirr into the country for my health and studies, till I secure my family from want. You have many petitions of this nature, and cannot satisfy all; but I hope from your goodness, to be made an exception to your general rules, because I am, with all sincerity,

Your Lordship's
Most obedient humble Servant,
John Dryden.[2]

This letter seems to have been written in mid-1683, and it is interesting to note that on December 17th of that year Dryden was appointed a collector of customs at London.

The satires apart, Dryden's purely 'laureate' poems—if by this is meant poems written in and arising from the office—are few and slight.

In 1685 the death of Charles II gave occasion for 'Threnodia Augustalis; a funeral pindaric poem, sacred to the happy memory of King Charles II.' The poem is not happy: 'it has neither tenderness nor dignity; it is neither magnificent nor pathetic,' Johnson wrote, adding, 'there is throughout the composition a desire of splendour without wealth.' Indeed, there is here little of the greatness that can often be seen even in the least of Dryden's pieces. There is nothing glorious about such a line as this, describing the King's corpse:

A senseless lump of sacred clay

into which, by medical skill, life is momentarily called back; which for five days the doctors struggle to maintain, but

> *The impregnable disease their vain attempts did mock;*
> *They min'd it near, they battered from afar*
> *With all the cannon of the medicinal war;*
> *No gentle means could be essay'd,*
> *'Twas beyond parley when the seige was laid:*
> *The extreamest ways they first ordain,*
> *Prescribing such intolerable pain,*
> *As none but Caesar could sustain:*
> *Undaunted Caesar underwent*
> *The malice of their art, not bent*
> *Beneath whate'er their pious rigour could invent:*
> *In five such days he suffered more*
> *Than any suffered in his reign before . . .*

[1] Probably, says Edmund Malone, a translation of *The History of the League*, which Dryden published in 1684. This work, from the French of Lewis Maimbourg, is described as 'Englished by his Majesties express command'—which doesn't save it from dullness.

[2] In the Dedication of *Cleomenes*, to Laurence Hyde, Earl of Rochester Dryden speaks, of the Earl's goodness 'even from a bare treasury' which suggests that this letter or similar appeals had met with success.

and—not surprisingly—he died. The whole poem—over five hundred lines—is an object lesson in uninspired bad taste, and confirms clearly enough the truth that even great poets cannot write well to order.

Dryden's maturer judgment on his late master is given in the preface to his opera *King Arthur; or, The British Worthy* (1691):

> If writers be just to the memory of King Charles the Second, they cannot deny him to have been an exact knower of mankind, and a perfect distinguisher of their talents. 'Tis true, his necessities often forc'd him to vary his councellours and councils, and sometimes to employ such persons in the management of his affairs, who were rather fit for his present purpose, than satisfactory to his judgment: but where it was choice in him, not compulsion, he was master of too much good sense to delight in heavy conversation; and whatever his favourites of state might be, yet those in his affection, were men of wit. He was easy with these, and comply'd only with the former: but in the latter part of his life, which certainly required to be most cautiously managed, his secret thoughts were communicated but to few; and those selected of that sort, who were *amici omnium horarum*, able to advise him in a serious consult, where his honour and safety were concerned; and afterwards capable of entertaining him with pleasant discourse, as well as profitable. In this maturest part of his age, when he had been long season'd with difficulties and dangers, and was grown to a niceness in his choice, as being satisfied how few could be trusted; and, of those who could be trusted, how few cou'd serve him, he confined himself to a small number of bosom friends. . . .

Elsewhere in the same Dedication he exclaims 'Peace be with the ashes of so good a King! Let his human frailties be forgotten; and his clemency and moderation (the inherent virtues of his family) be remembered with a grateful veneration by three kingdoms, through which he spread the blessings of them.'

In 1688—not long before his tenure of the office ended—Dryden wrote the last of his 'official' poems, 'Britannia Rediviva; a Poem on the birth of the Prince, born on the tenth of June, 1688.' This was James Francis Edward Stuart, afterwards the 'Old Pretender,' a prince with a sad destiny. Dryden's verses were a sad enough beginning for this young Prince of Wales and it was no misfortune to Dryden's fame (says George Saintsbury) that the Revolution left the verses out of print for the rest of the poet's life.

The Revolution had a more important effect on Dryden's fortunes than merely to make some of his verses unpopular. He found himself out of sympathy with the new King and Government, and they in turn found themselves well able to dispense with Dryden. He was deprived of his office and its advantages and a new Laureate was appointed. This was Thomas Shadwell.

Deprived of the income from his offices, which although doubtless irregular was at least something coming in to augment his slender private resources—and by now he had three sons to maintain—Dryden turned again to the stage, which he had for a time deserted. But his great days as a dramatist were behind him, and so were the days of popular success. He was obliged to work hard for every guinea.

Yet in some ways those last years were his best. He was nearly sixty when the loss of the Laureateship forced him, in effect, to start in business all over again; and he lived twelve years more. The great plays were already written, and the great satires, and the great didactic poems *Religio Laici* and *The Hind and the Panther*. It was unfortunate for Dryden's reputation for disinterestedness that the first of these was a defence of the Church of England, and the second an apology for the Church of Rome, into which he happened to be received about the time the Catholic James II came to the throne. But it is generally agreed that Dryden's change of heart, though opportune, was also sincere.

These works, and a huge body of journey work also lay behind; but the last years saw the bulk of the translations, and the publication of the interesting Miscellanies[1], and the incomparable *Fables*.

There was in England a tradition in translations going back to Chaucer and Lord Berners, and supported by the considerable names of Florio, Urquhart, North, Shelton, and others; there was a tradition, but not a system, and Dryden set himself characteristically to examine the problems of translation and formalise their use. With his translations he published also the method by which they had been made, in the preface to *Sylvae* (1685) in the preface to the *Fables* (1700) and elsewhere. These prefaces, which he was in the habit of prefixing to his works, contain the bulk of his prose writings, one or two prose translations excepted; and they provide one more reason for regarding Dryden as the greatest man of letters of his time. No previous writer—some isolated passages of Jonson excepted—had written English prose so lucid, so flexible, or so essentially 'ordinary.' Dryden wrote as though he were sitting with a few familiar friends, exchanging notes. He

---

[1] In these, too, Dryden was something of an innovator; nearly a century had passed since the last of the great Elizabethan anthologies, and the practice of collecting representative work by living poets into volumes of 'Miscellany Poems' had recently produced mainly ephemeral volumes. Dryden, and his publisher Tonson, revived it, and the six volumes of Miscellanies contain a wealth of interesting work otherwise largely inaccessible. Dryden took the work seriously: 'Since we are to have nothing but new,' he wrote to Tonson, 'I am resolv'd we will have nothing but good, whomever we disoblige!'

appears to be 'thinking aloud.' He is, with Southey, the supreme master of a sound yet eloquent 'prose of all work,' and he rescued English from the gorgeous and quite impracticable style which finds its extreme in Sir Thomas Browne.[1]

The Preface to the *Fables*, at the end of his life, and *An Essay of Dramatick Poesie*, his earliest considerable prose exercise, represent Dryden at his best as a critic; more than this, they are entertaining to read, and this is the true test: for to what use can the work be criticised that will not be read?[2]

The *Fables* appeared in a splendid folio in March 1700. In April, Dryden fell ill—he had long suffered from gravel, gout, and other diseases—and now the neglect of a poisoned toe occasioned his death, for he refused amputation until the matter was beyond remedy. The *Postboy* newspaper reported on April 30th that 'John Dryden Esq., the famous poet, lies a-dying.' The next issue of the same journal was able to record: 'Yesterday morning at three of the clock, John Dryden Esq., departed this life, who for his poetry &c. excelled all others this age produced.' After lying in state at the College of Physicians the poet was given a handsome funeral, and buried in Westminster Abbey on May 13th, 1700.

---

[1] Nothing is ever quite so simple as that! But adequately to discuss the development of English prose in a paragraph is impossible. My conclusion is broadly true, I believe; the reader who means to dispute it will doubtless first mug up the prose of Milton, Cowley, Lancelot Andrewes, Donne, Fuller, Bacon, and Miles Coverdale.

[2] This happy phrase I have doubtless borrowed from some better writer.

3

Thomas Shadwell

IN considering King William's Laureate many critics and most readers have been content to recall Dryden's stinging lines:

> The rest to some faint meaning make pretence,
> But Shadwell never deviates into Sense,

which—with many more in *Macflecknoe* and *Absalom and Achitophel*—give the unfortunate victim an immortality it is supposed his own works would not have won him. This is a singular case of poetic injustice, for Shadwell is a vigorous and intelligent writer, and his best plays give a picture of the manners of his day comparable with that given a lifetime earlier by Ben Jonson, whose disciple he was.

The life of Thomas Shadwell begins with a question: was he born in 1640 at Santon Hall, or in 1642 at Broomhill?

Santon Hall and Broomhill House were near Brandon, in Norfolk. Little now remains of either, but they were both connected with the Shadwell family, and there is evidence tending to confirm their several titles to have been the place of Shadwell's birth, together with other evidence that he was born in 1641.

Of Shadwell's education a little more is known. He had some private tuition, and he was then at the King Edward VI Free Grammar School, Bury St. Edmunds, from which he proceeded to Cambridge, matriculating at Gonville and Caius College on December 17th, 1656. His stay at the University, however, was brief, and he left without taking a degree, although he claims to have profited by his studies. When Dryden taunts him with small Latin and less Greek (in *Mac-Flecknoe*) Shadwell replies 'In Bury School in Suffolk, and Caius College in Cambridge, the places of my youthful education, I had not that reputation. . . .'[1]

Shadwell's father was a lawyer, and so in 1658 (on July 7th) we find the young man admitted to the Middle Temple, where if he studied Law

[1] Dedication to Sir Charles Sedley of *The Tenth Satyr of Juvenal* (1687).

he was strategically situated also to study the pleasures of the Town. When he began first to be interested in writing is not clear, but his interest in the theatre was early aroused, for a few years after his coming to London he married an actress, Anne Gibbs, who was employed with Davenant's company. This marriage took place within the years 1663–1666, but no exact date is known. We know pretty certainly that the same lady had married one Thomas Gawdy in 1662, but how and why she exchanged the first Thomas for the second we don't know; nor does it much matter. She appears to have been a good wife to Shadwell—'my beloved wife' he calls her in his will—and also a good actress, for her name appears against important parts in the cast lists of many plays from 1661 onwards as Anne Gibbs and as Mrs. Shadwell from 1668. When Shadwell's last play, *The Volunteer*, was post-humously published in 1693 his wife although she did not act in the play contributed a short prefatory letter to the Queen. The marriage seems to have been a happy one. There were four sons, John (who became Sir John, a distinguished physician) Charles (who edited his father's *Works*), George and William, and a daughter, Anne. There was perhaps another daughter, Sarah. It was in connection with his marriage that the rumour afterwards grew up that Shadwell was a Roman Catholic, not then a popular thing to be. He was married, said Nat Thompson, a writer busy with the scandals of the Popish Plot, 'by a Popish Priest . . . to which [accusation] he atheistically replied, "Come, damn Religion, let's drink. . . ." '[1] This reply seems to suggest that Shadwell was content to be married by any party competent to do the job, so only it were done. But although his writings display no Catholic bias, it is worth noting that when this accusation appeared Shadwell did not answer it. Yet—at that time—it was not the kind of accusation to leave unanswered.

It was natural for Shadwell to commence author with a play, for his wife must have brought the atmosphere of the theatre home with her, and in addition he was beginning to make friends among the men about town, some of whom were themselves dramatists. There was as yet no established 'profession' of letters, but generally speaking one who wrote for money could hope for little profit from non-dramatic work. It was in 1667 that Milton received his famous fee of £5 for *Paradise Lost*.

Accordingly, in 1668 appeared *The Sullen Lovers, or The Impertinents*,

[1] In a news-sheet, *The Loyal Protestant and True Domestic Intelligence*, January 11th, 1681–2.

a comedy acted by His Highness the Duke of York's servants and written by Tho. Shadwell. The play is founded on Molière's 'Les Fâcheux' but Shadwell carefully points out that he wrote much of it 'from a report' and before actually reading the French text. The play is duly notéd by Pepys:

> . . . to the Duke of York's playhouse at a little past twelve, to get a good place in the pit, against the new play, and there setting a poor man to keep my place, I out, and spent an hour at Marton's, my bookseller's, and so back again, where I find the house quite full. But I had my place, and by and by the King comes and the Duke of York; and then the play begins, called 'The Sullen Lovers; or, The Impertinents,' having many good humours in it, but the play tedious, and no design at all in it . . .

That was on May 2nd; a couple of days later he tries again (Sunday having intervened) this time with his sister for company: '. . . saw The Impertinents again, and with less pleasure than before, it being but a very contemptible play, though there are many little witty expressions in it. . . .' Pepys, in this instance at least, reflected the taste of the town, for he went yet again the following day and at last began to find the play entertaining. '. . . to see the folly how the house do this day cry up the play more than yesterday! and I for that reason like it, I find, the better, too. . . .'

Pepys saw the play again more than once after these attendances. By June he is calling it 'a pretty good play' and almost a year after the first production he says it is 'a play which pleases me well still.' Not a bad beginning for a new dramatist.

The Sullen Lovers, despite its French original, was in essence the work of the same Shadwell who later would write *Epsom Wells* and *The Squire of Alsatia*. Pepys found 'many good humours in it' and it was to Jonson, master of 'humours' that Shadwell looked for instruction. His preface affirms as much:

> I have endeavoured to represent variety of humours (most of the persons of the play differing in their Characters from one another) which was the practice of Ben Jonson, whom I think all dramatic poets ought to imitate, though none are like to come near. . . . He is the man of all the world I most passionately admire for his excellency in dramatic poetry. . . .

As for the writing of this particular play, Shadwell glances at the circumstances in his Epilogue:

> *The Itch of Writing Plays, the more's the pity,*
> *At once has seized the Town, the Court, the City.*
> *Among'st the rest, the Poet of this day*
> *By meer infection has produc'd a Play.*

After this promising start Shadwell became more and more closely identified with the theatre; play followed play, not always with complete theatrical success—'the silliest for words and design and everything, that ever I saw in my whole life,' writes Pepys of *The Royal Shepherdesse*, which is a harmless enough pastoral 'acted with good Applause' in Langbaine's phrase. But the cumulative effect of plays produced at regular and frequent intervals, whatever their individual merit, was to make Shadwell, in a few years, one of the best known writers of the time. He was a useful man to be associated with in business: 'the Playhouse had great Occasion for a Play,' he records in his preface to *The Libertine*, which accordingly he wrote in three weeks. Shadwell, like many another, was fond of boasting how little time his writings cost him, as if speed of composition ensured merit; but to a Playhouse having 'great Occasion' a tolerable, competent piece written in three weeks was worth more than a potential masterpiece produced after ten.

Shadwell's life, generally speaking, has now been told, for from the production of *The Sullen Lovers*, his first play, to the production of *The Scowrers*, the last he lived to see, he devoted himself to the theatre. His brief years as Laureate were incidental, and the cares of that office hardly troubled him. One or two pamphlets apart, he never ventured into general literature; he was not, as Dryden was, 'a man of letters of all work.' Dryden was critic, translator, historian, the master of half a dozen branches of literature; Shadwell was the master of but one, yet in that one he was not contemptible. His model, Jonson, might have acknowledged without shame the comedies *Epsom Wells*, *The Squire of Alsatia*, and *Bury Fair*.

These—and the majority of Shadwell's plays—are best when they most nearly conform to Jonson's manner in the great comedies—*Every Man in His Humour*, *Volpone*, *The Silent Woman*, *The Alchemist* and *Bartholomew Fair*. Shadwell, of course, has little tragic power, and his comedy is mainly rough and low. Yet it gives a vivid picture of certain aspects of late seventeenth-century life and manners. The first scene of act one of *The Squire of Alsatia* indicates at once the racy fare that Shadwell offers at his best. Belfond Senior, an eldest son with great expectations, is up from the country to sample London's delights; Shamwell, his cousin, a profligate man-about-town, undertakes to show them; and Cheatly, a complete rogue, profits from them both:

Enter Belfond Senior, meeting Shamwell

Belfond Senior. Cousin Shamwell, well met; Good morrow to you.

Sham. Cousin Belfond, your humble servant: what makes you abroad so early? 'Tis not much past seven.

Belf. You know we were bowsy last night: I am a lettle hot-headed this morning; and come to take the fresh air here in the Temple walks.

Sham. Well: and what do you think of our way of living here? Is not rich generous wine better than your poor hedge-wine stum'd, or dull March-beer? Are not delicate, well-bred, well dress'd women better than dairy-maids, tenant's daughters, or barefoot strumpets? Streets full of fine coaches, better than a yard full of dung-carts? A magnificent tavern, than a thatch'd ale-house? Or the society of brave, honest, witty, merry fellows, than the conversation of unthinking hunting, hawking blockheads, or high-shoo'd peasants and their wiser cattle?

Belf. O yea, a world adad. Ne're stir, I could never have thought there had been such a gallant place as London: here I can be drunk every night, and well next morning: can ride in a coach for a shilling as good as a Deputy Lieutenant; and such merry wags and ingenious companions—well, I vow and swear, I am mightily beholding to you, dear Cousin Shamwell: then for the women! Mercy upon us, so civil and well bred. And I'll swear upon a Bible, finer all of them than Knight Baronets' wives with us.

Sham. And so kind and pleasant!

Belf. Ay, I vow pretty rogues! No pride in them in the world; but so courteous and familiar, as I am an honest man, they'll do whatever one would have 'em presently; ah, sweet rogues: while in the country, a pies take 'em, there's such a stir with pish, fie, nay Mr. Timothy, what do you do? I vow I'll squeek, never stir I'll call out, ah hah—

Sham. And if one of 'em happen to be with child; there's straight an uproar in the country, as if the Hundred were su'd for a robbery!

Belf. Ay, so there is: and I am in that fear of my Father besides adad, he'd knock me i'th'head, if he should hear of such a thing: to say truth, he's so terrible to me I can never enjoy myself for him: Lord! what will he say when he comes to know I am at London? Which he in all his life time would never suffer me to see, for fear

I should be debauch'd forsooth; and allows me little or no money at home neither.

Sham. What matter what he says? Is not every foot of the estate entail'd upon you?

Belf. Well, I'll endur't no longer! If I can but raise money; I'll teach him to use his son like a dog, I'll warrant him.

Sham. You can ne'er want that: take up on the reversion. 'Tis a lusty one: and Cheatly will help you to the Ready: and thou shalt shine and be as gay as any Spruce Prigg that ever walked the street.

Belf. Well, adad, you are a pleasant man: and have the neatest sayings with you: *Ready*, and *Spruce Prigg*, and abundance of the prettiest witty words—but sure that Mr. Cheatly is as fine a gentleman as any wears a head: and an ingenious; ne'er stir, I believe he would run down the best scholar in Oxford, and put 'em in a mouse-hole with his wit.

Sham. In Oxford! ay, and in London too.

Belf. Goodsookers, Cozen! I always thought they had been wittiest in the Universities.

Sham. O, fie, cousin: a company of putts! Mere putts!

Belf. Putts, mere *putts*: very good, I'll swear, ha ha ha!

Sham. They are all scholar boys, and nothing else, as long as they live there: and yet they are as confident as if they knew everything, when they understand no more beyond Magdalen Bridge than mere Indians. But Cheatly is a rare fellow: I'll speak a bold word, he can cut a sham or banter with the best Wit or Poet of 'em all.

Belf. Good agen'. *Cut a sham or banter!* I shall remember all these quaint words in time: but Mr. Cheatly's a Prodigy, that's certain.

Sham. He is so; and a worthy brave fellow, and the best friend where he takes, and the most sincere of any man breathing.

Belf. Nay, I must needs say, I have found him very frank, and very much a gentleman, and am most extremely oblig'd to him and you for your great kindness.

Sham. This morning your clothes and liveries will come home, and thou shalt appear rich and splendid like thyself, and the Mobile shall worship thee.

Belf. The *Mobile*! That's pretty. (Enter CHEATLY)
Sweet Mr. Cheatly, my best friend, let me embrace thee.

Cheat. My sprightly son of timber and of acres: my noble heir, I salute thee: the cole is coming and shall be brought in this morning.

Belf. Cole? Why, 'tis summer, I need no firing now. Besides I intend
   to burn billets.
Cheat. My lusty rustic, learn and be instructed. Cole is in the witty,
   money. The Ready, the Rhino; thou shalt be Rhinocerical, thou
   shalt.
Belf. Admirable, I swear! *Cole! Ready! Rhino! Rhinocerical!*
   Lord how long may a man live in ignorance in the country!

"Tis a providence you are fallen into so good hands,' Shamwell
assures him, and so the tale proceeds. It is the sort of play that
brings its period to life more clearly than any social history; and
although it has not been revived for many years, it might well repay
revival.

At the time of his appointment to the Laureateship Shadwell, like
Dryden twenty years earlier, was already a professional man of letters,
which then meant a professional dramatist. In 1689, at 47, he was the
successful author of a dozen or more plays and of several pamphlets,
and he was known for as decided a Whig as Dryden was a Tory. It was
political differences that had made the break between them, after
Shadwell at the beginning of his career had been on good terms with
Dryden—'my particular friend, for whom I have a very great respect,
and whose writings I extremely admire. . . .'[1]

Dryden's publication of *The Medal* in 1682 soon led to a public
breach between the two dramatists, for *The Medal of John Bayes*
gathered in rough but vigorous couplets all the unpleasant things that
Shadwell could learn or invent about Dryden.

The name 'Bayes' had been given to the Laureate Davenant in *The
Rehearsal* when that satirical attack on contemporary drama had been
published in 1671, but Dryden's work was prominently attacked also
in the play and when in due course he succeeded to Davenant's place
his enemies passed the name on with the office. Frequently enough
where Dryden is meant, but not named, 'Bayes' is used to identify him,
in the copious pamphlet literature of the time.

Shadwell's poem is abusive without being witty. A good deal of the
abuse is unjustified or grossly exaggerated, and the whole performance
suffers from one fatal defect: it is boring. This criticism, however, it is
only fair to add was probably not valid at the time of publication.
Nothing so quickly loses its point as second-rate satire, but doubtless
The Medal of John Bayes once had sufficient life to amuse the Whigs.

[1] Preface to *The Humorists* (1671), his third play.

That it annoyed its victim was apparent enough; the poem appeared some eight weeks after *The Medal*, and all through the summer of 1682 Dryden had its success to gall him. In October 1682 he published his reply, *Macflecknoe*.

It is interesting to compare Shadwell's poem with Dryden's, for nothing could better illustrate the great advance made by Dryden in the use of the heroic couplet—which he brought to a perfection not surpassed by the greater polish achieved forty years later by Pope. What Pope gained in finish he lost in force. Dryden's couplet is the most perfect instrument for satire English verse has yet attained.

Shadwell, however (the accident of lesser genius apart) was working to an older theory of satire which stemmed back to the practice of John Donne and Bishop Hall a century earlier, when it was considered that rough sentiments ought to be uttered in a rough tongue.

'I do not think great smoothness is required in a Satyre,' Shadwell affirms,[1] 'which ought to have a severe kind of roughness as most fit for reprehension, and not that gentle smoothness which is necessary to insinuation.'

This theory led in practice to such uncouth verse as this:

> *Libeller's vile name then may'st thou gain,*
> *And moderately the writing part maintain,*
> *None can so well the beating part sustain,*
> *Though with thy sword, thou art the last of men,*
> *Thou art a damn'd Boroski with thy pen.*
> *As far from Satyr does thy talent lye,*
> *As from being cheerful, or good company.*

To a modern reader this mixture of half-truth and falsehood is neither entertaining nor instructive. Of Dryden it tells us nothing pertinent except to support the tradition that he was not 'good company'; and even of Shadwell no more than that his idea of satire was not ours.

The Medal of John Bayes does not repay close study, but it contains a few good strokes and one or two not ungenerous comments. Dryden could hardly be expected to like being called a 'cherry-cheek'd Dunce of fifty-three.' 'Thou never mak'st, but art a standing Jest,' refers nearly enough to Dryden's somewhat unsocial manner, and there is sufficient justification in the following lines to make them effective:

[1] Dedication to Sir Charles Sedley of his translation of Juvenal's *Tenth Satire* (1687). See also note on page 202.

> *Now farewell wretched mercenary Bayes,*
> *Who the King libell'd, and did Cromwell praise.*
> *Farewell abandon'd Rascal! only fit*
> *To be abused by thy own scurrilous wit,*
> *Which thou wouldst do, and for a moderate sum*
> *Answer thy Medal and thy Absalom.*
> *Thy piteous Hackney-Pen shall never fright us . . .*

The defiance in that last line was soon to be put to the test.

On the other hand, 'thou had'st a kind of Excellence in Rime,' Shadwell concedes:

> *In Verse, thou hast a knack, with words to chime,*
> *And had'st a kind of Excellence in Rime:*
> *With Rimes like leading-strings, thou walk'dst; but those*
> *Lay'd by, ay every step thou brok'st thy Nose.*
> *How low thy Farce! and thy blank Verse how mean!*
> *How poor, how naked did appear each Scene! . . .*

In this also there is some truth, for magnificent as the best work of Dryden is, there is poor enough stuff in the remainder, and it is consistently true that

> *Those who write in rhyme still make*
> *The one verse for the other's sake.*[1]

unless carried forward by great merit in the matter. As for the second part of the charge, any candid reader who looks into such a play of Dryden's as *Limberham* (1678) will marvel that a critic so acute could write a play so open to unanswerable criticism.

Dryden had more enemies than one, and if the Revolution was to deprive him of his office it was likely enough that the place would be filled by one of them; but that Shadwell should be the choice was doubly galling, for besides being the most persistent (he returned to the attack again and again) he was perhaps the smallest poet of them all. In his own time, and even by his friends, he was so little considered as a poet that the editors of his collected works did not trouble to include his occasional poems. The 1693 quarto issued soon after his death, and the 1720 edition edited by his son Charles contented themselves with presenting the plays.

On taking up his appointment (which incidentally was coupled for the last time with that of Historiographer Royal) Shadwell found himself the master of £300 a year and the traditional butt of Canary. He

---

[1] Samuel Butler, *Hudibras*.

had already himself been likened to something of the same shape by Dryden, who calls him a Tun . . . 'round as a globe and liquor'd every chink.' His fondness for the bottle and for good fellowship was shared by a later Laureate, Thomas Warton.

Of definite duties to go with this money and drink there were none. Dryden had lent his pen to the King's support and Shadwell was prepared to do the same in his turn; but Dutch William was less interested in literature than Charles II, and also less in need of support. There was no question of King and poet strolling in Pall Mall familiarly discussing the plan of a poem, and the poems Shadwell produced in justification of his appointment are few and poor.

The appointment had been made through the good offices of his patron, the Earl of Dorset. Dorset had already for some time allowed Shadwell a pension and perhaps he felt that this might as well be paid from the King's purse as from his own; pensions in those days, indeed, were more readily granted than paid. One of Shadwell's few surviving letters is a plea, in the familiar terms, for payment of arrears.

'My Lord, I presume to put your Lordship in mind of the last Christmas quarter which my wants force me to . . .' and so on. It is pleasant to record that at the time of his death Shadwell's salary was not in arrears, and in addition his dependents were paid the full salary for the year in which he died.

Dorset was frank enough in acknowledging that Shadwell was not exactly an obvious choice for the position, but he gave a reasonable answer to the suggestion that Shadwell was no great poet. 'I will not pretend to determine how great a poet Shadwell may be,' he is reported to have remarked, 'but I am sure that he is an honest man.' Two centuries afterwards a similar reasoning was still being used to excuse an apparently uninspired appointment, if Lord Salisbury's choice of Alfred Austin is any criterion.

Patronage apart, Shadwell had some small sheaf of verses to offer as specimens when Dryden's removal made the office vacant. He had written *A Congratulatory Poem on His Highness The Prince of Orange His Coming into England* which was by 'T.S. A true Lover of his Countrey,' and it says something for William's determination that in the face of such a tribute he did not turn tail.

> . . . *Let there be Light, th' Almighty Fiat run;*
> *No sooner 'twas pronounc'd, but it was done.*
> *Inspir'd by Heav'n, thus the great Orange said,*
> *Let there be Liberty, and was obey'd.*

> *Vast Wonders Heav'n's great Minister has wrought,*
> *From our dark Chaos, Beauteous Order brought:*
> *H' invaded us with Force to make us free,*
> *And in another's Realm could meet no Enemy.*
> *Hail Great Asserter of the Greatest Cause,*
> *Man's Liberty, and the Almighty's Laws:*
> *Heav'n greater Wonders has for Thee design'd*
> *Thou Glorious Deliv'rer of Mankind!*

Not long after the King's arrival he was followed by his Queen, and once again Shadwell joined in the chorus of welcome, with *A Congratulatory Poem to the Most Illustrious Queen Mary upon her Arrival in England.*

> . . . *She comes, She comes, the Fair, the Good, the Wise* . . .[1]

The new King required all holders of office to swear allegiance, and, among those who refused to do this was John Dryden. Accordingly, within a few weeks of these tributes being published Shadwell had his reward. On March 9th, 1688–9 a Warrant was issued 'to sware Thomas Shadwell Esqr into the place and quality of poet-Laureat to His Matie.'

Shadwell had but three years more of life before him. His few official poems include an *Ode on the Anniversary of the Queen's Birth* (April 30th, 1689) and another for the King's birthday the following year. In 1691 he returned to celebrating the Queen's birthday, and on New Year's Day, 1692 he produced *Votum Perenne, A Poem to the King on New Year's Day*, the first and not the worst of a long line of New Year Odes by the Laureates of the succeeding hundred years. Shadwell also recorded and celebrated the King's campaign in Ireland, with *Ode to the King on His Return from Ireland* and *On His Majesty's Conquests in Ireland, made immediately after the Victory at Sea*, 1692. The 'victory at sea' was the action at La Hogue (May 19th, 1692) but Shadwell diplomatically discusses the King's own victory at the Boyne, two years earlier. The last poem to be mentioned is his *Ode for St. Cecilia's Day*, written in 1690 for the celebration then customary. This poem is far below the great St. Cecilia odes[2] of Dryden, but it is not contemptible.

Shadwell's health was poor for a year or two before his death. In the preface to *Bury Fair* (1689) he records 'eight months painful sickness'

---

[1] This is reminiscent of another bad line, in Oldham's elegy on the death of Miss Katherine Kingscourt:

> *She did, she did, I saw her mount the sky!*

[2] Yet another St. Cecilia Ode—by William Hawkins (1781)— may have given a hint to Wordsworth, for it contains the reiterated phrase 'daughter of the voice of God' so effectively used in Wordsworth's *Ode to Duty.*

and a year later he refers again to long sickness. Part of his trouble was gout, from which he had been a sufferer for some years, no doubt as a result of convivial nights and days with Sir Charles Sedley and his set. On November 19th, 1692 he took opium, as his habit was, to relieve the pain: but the dose was a fatal one, and on the following day he died.

The Laureate was buried in St. Luke's, Chelsea (the old parish church) and his funeral sermon was preached by the young Nicholas Brady, then minister of St. Catherine Cree in the City. Shadwell had interested himself in Brady, and by influence with Dorset, the Lord Chamberlain, had caused Brady's play, *The Rape*, to be acted. Brady found in his dead friend the usual excellences that funeral sermons commonly celebrate, and even the overdose of opium was not frowned upon: 'His Death seized him suddenly, but could not unprepared, since (to my certain knowledge) he never took his dose of opium, but he solemnly recommended himself to God by prayer, as if he were then about to resign up his Soul into the Hands of his faithful Creator. . . .'

4

Nahum Tate

THE world of letters in the seventeenth century was a small one and it was natural for the Laureates to be men drawn from a comparatively restricted circle. The poets living when Shadwell died—Dryden apart—were mainly employed in the drama, and included none whose fame then or now rested on any considerable body of fine poetry. The prolific Sir Richard Blackmore had written *Prince Arthur, an heroick poem in ten books*, to which he had obligingly added an index. But even thus early in his career nobody took him seriously except himself. Pomfret, whose talent for fine-sounding emptiness might have been noted, had not yet published the work which made his name. Prior, after Dryden the best living poet, was busy with more important affairs. Congreve, who might have made a satisfactory Laureate, was overlooked.[1] The choice fell upon Nahum Tate. I cannot discover that anybody has ever been enthusiastic over Nahum Tate; it seems that from birth he was the kind of man who survives in footnotes. 'Who knows whether the best of men be known, or whether there be not

[1] Congreve would have been Dryden's choice of a successor:

> *Oh that your brows my laurel had sustained,*
> *Well had I been deposed, if you had reigned:*
> *The father had descended for the son;*
> *For only you are lineal to the throne.*
>
> —To My Dear Friend Mr. Congreve on his
> Comedy call'd *The Double Dealer*.

Dryden goes on to complain that Shadwell and Rymer were given respectively the Laureateship and the office of Historiographer Royal; but when the verses were published Shadwell was already dead. These lines addressed to himself in *The Mourning Muse of Alexis, a pastoral lamenting the death of our late Gracious Queen Mary of Blessed Memory* (1695) suggest that Congreve entertained no very high opinion of his own laureate pretensions:

> *Wert thou with ev'ry Bay and Lawrel crown'd,*
> *And high as Pan himself in Song renown'd,*
> *Yet wou'd not all thy Art avail to show*
> *Verse worthy of her Name, or of our Woe.*

Congreve might have made a respectable Laureate in the eighteenth century manner, but we may well be satisfied to have his comedies instead.

more remarkable persons forgot, than any that stand remembered in the known account of time?' asks Sir Thomas Browne, and it is a question the pertinence of which is confirmed by such persons as Tate, his collaborator Nicholas Brady, his successor Nicholas Rowe, and a few more whose names have survived from that period. The early 18th century, we feel, cannot have been so dull as all that. The best judgment I have found on Tate comes from the antiquary William Oldys, who describes him as 'a free good-natured fuddling companion.'

Nahum Tate was Irish, the son of Dr. Faithful Teate, and he was born in Dublin in 1652. 'Tate,' it is usual to point out, is the Irish way of pronouncing 'Teate'; but I have not learned when Tate himself made the change—perhaps he did not consciously change, for at that time spelling was no very exact science. I have nowhere found him called Teate, which serves to prevent confusion with his father, who was a poet even more minor than his son, and the author of *Ter Tria*, a poem which discusses the Trinity at some length.

At sixteen Tate entered Trinity College, Dublin, and at twenty he graduated B.A. Soon after this he crossed to England but little is recorded of his activities until in 1677 he published his *Poems*. This collection made no stir then, although it was reissued with additions in 1784, and it has certainly not since improved its former reputation. All the same, it is a creditable collection for a young man's first book; if it contains little 'poetry' it displays some wit, some originality and invention, and comparatively few real blemishes. It is a great deal more readable than its author's next work, the play *Brutus of Alba, or the Enchanted Lovers*, in which Betterton played in 1678.

This is a tragedy, the story of which was furnished by Geoffrey of Monmouth and much of the settings and situations by Virgil. Tate supplied the words and took the credit: 'The Play tonight is new, the Poet too,' remarks the Prologue, adding prophetically, 'But Critics, 'spite of Fate, will play the Devil.'[1]

The beginning of *Brutus* is rather in the manner of *The Tempest* but this promise dies on the second page and thereafter Tate is on his own. The Dedication to Shadwell's patron the Earl of Dorset marks the commencement of a long association, for Tate seems to have turned often enough to that nobleman in the succeeding years, and in due course Dorset was to bestow the Laureateship on him.

---

[1] Lamb, however, found a few lines from *Brutus* fit for inclusion in his *Specimens of the English Dramatic Poets* (1808). He adds no comment upon them.

The following year *The Loyal General* was acted, with a prologue by
Dryden:

> *If yet there be a few that take delight*
> *In that which reasonable men should write,*
> *To them Alone we Dedicate this Night* . . .

The Loyal General was followed by an adaptation of Shakespeare's
Richard the Second in which 'every scene (was) full of respect to Majesty
and the dignity of Courts; not one altered page but what breathes
loyalty.' Unfortunately, this view was not generally held and the
authorities suppressed the play on the second night. This sad experience
with Shakespeare as collaborator did not deter Tate, and in the same
year (1681) he produced *King Lear*. He was now securely launched in
the theatre.

The main difference in the two *Lears* (poetry apart) lies in the happy
ending which Tate supplies and Shakespeare most certainly does not.
Tate's version is altogether more satisfactory for most of the characters,
including Cordelia, who marries Edgar. In the process of revision Tate
dispenses with the Fool and incidentally with some of the greatest
tragic poetry in the world. This would now be condemned yet there
have been respectable critics on Tate's side.

Of these, Addison was not one: '*King Lear* is an admirable tragedy
. . . as Shakespeare wrote it,' he remarks in *The Spectator* (No. 40)
'but as it is reformed according to the chimerical notion of poetical
justice, in my humble opinion it has lost half its beauty.' Not much
commendation there; but it is worth noting that the passage was
written in 1711, thirty years after Tate's play first appeared. The play
was by then established in the theatrical repertory, a fate not common.
Over fifty years later, long after Tate and Addison were both dead,
the play was alive and finding a defender in Johnson. And Johnson was
considering it beside Shakespeare's original:

> 'A play in which the wicked prosper, and the virtuous miscarry,
> may doubtless be good, because it is a just representation of the
> common events of human life; but since all reasonable beings
> naturally love justice, I cannot easily be persuaded, that the observa-
> tion of justice makes a play worse; or, that if other excellencies are
> equal, the audience will not always rise better pleased from the final
> triumph of persecuted virtue.
>
> 'In the present case the public has decided. Cordelia, from the
> time of Tate, has always retired with victory and felicity. And, if my

sensations could add anything to the general suffrage, I might relate, I was many years ago so shocked by Cordelia's death, that I know not whether I ever endured to read again the last scenes of the play till I undertook to revise them as editor.'[1]

The weakness of Johnson's case, of course, lies in his phrase 'if other excellencies are equal.' The poetry in Shakespeare's *Lear* represents one of the great peaks in the world's dramatic literature, and leaves Tate completely at a loss. But 18th century audiences went to the play not only to hear poetry, and if they found the 'entertainment value' of Tate's version greater they were entitled to prefer it. At all events, prefer it they did for over a hundred years.[2]

So late as 1808 Leigh Hunt, writing in *The Examiner*, could give an approving nod at Tate for omitting the Fool, 'which is now out of date,' even while he condemned the play 'as it was altered by Tate, who was altered by Colman, who was altered by Garrick ' Lamb thought *Lear* unactable: '. . . the Lear of Shakespeare cannot be acted. . . . Tate has put his hook in the nostrils of this Leviathan, for Garrick and his followers, the show-men of the scene, to draw the mighty beast about more easily. A happy ending!—as if the living martyrdom that Lear had gone through—the flaying of his feelings alive, did not make a fair dismissal from the stage of life the only decorous thing for him.'

It should be noted that from the Restoration till the mid-nineteenth century it was unusual for Shakespeare to be acted from an original text. Garrick's version of *The Taming of the Shrew*, for example, kept the stage for nearly a hundred years. Among probably a hundred plays adapted from Shakespeare, Tate's *Lear* was the most successful with players, audiences, and even for a time with readers. It is not much, but it is something.

It would be tedious to discuss all Tate's plays—his adaptations from other Elizabethans were less successful than the *Lear*—but it is amusing to note that in his turn he was 'adapted'—and not merely by Colman and Garrick as Hunt reported.

In 1684, was acted, and in 1685 was published, *A Duke and No Duke*, Tate's most successful essay in comedy. The play was not original, being fairly closely based on Sir Aston Cokain's *Trappolin Suppos'd a Prince*

---

[1] General Observations on the Plays of Shakespeare (1765): in Johnson's *Shakespeare's Works*.

[2] 'The general suffrage,' however, was not quite general. Thomas Warton, in the course of three papers discussing *Lear* in *The Adventurer* (December 4th, 15th, 1753, and January 5th, 1754) never so much as glances at Tate's version. Richardson's reference in *Clarissa* also is hardly 'suffrage.'

(1658) but it was a lively piece which met with some success. It is also the only play by Tate that is still tolerable to read. The plot concerns one Trappolin, a low person of Florence, who by magic is made to look and speak like the great Duke of Tuscany, Lavinio, who is away in foreign parts. Trappolin, taken for the Duke, gives orders that throw the court into confusion, especially when the real Duke turns up and issues counter-orders. Various court officials are in and out of prison like jacks-in-the-box for a scene or two while the rival Dukes go about behaving in a Grand Ducal manner without actually meeting; until the magician, his revenge accomplished, turns Trappolin back to his normal appearance—without, however, apprising him of the change, which is brought home to Trappolin only when the orders he gives are no longer obeyed. No doubt my brief synopsis is somewhat confusing, but then so is the plot of an eighteenth century farce.

The interesting thing about this unimportant piece is that one Robert Drury thought it suitable to turn into an opera of sorts, which was sung without success in 1732 under the title *The Devil of a Duke*, or *Trapolin's Vagaries*. A few years earlier John Thurmond had, with similar non-success, tried the thing as a pantomime, and a little later the Scottish poet Allan Ramsay (who had genius enough to know better) added some new songs and gave Scotland a version. So late as 1826 T. J. Dibdin's *The Duke and The Devil or, Which is Which*? was to be seen at Sadlers Wells. Generally speaking, it is Tate rather than Cokain from whom these adaptors borrow. Perhaps that accounts for their failure.

The considerable success of *King Lear*, and the qualified success of one or two other plays encouraged Tate to continue in the drama, while leaving him time for other work. Like his friend Dryden (though to a smaller extent) Tate was a writer of all work. In the period—nearly forty years—that he spent as a professional author he produced, besides nearly a dozen plays, a formidable mass of occasional verse which nobody had since had the courage to collect into a definitive edition. His translations alone would fill a volume, and include, besides the assistance he gave to Dryden in his version of Virgil, an 'attempt in English' of *Syphilis: or, a Poetical History of the French Disease*, 'written in Latin by Fracastorius.'

Girolamo Fracastoro[1] is perhaps not often read now in Latin or

---

[1] Girolamo Fracastoro (1483–1553) was an eminent physician and poet, born at Verona. His friend Scaliger thought him the best poet in the world next to Virgil, and Bayle, after remarking that the poet would have been better employed in curing the disease, goes on to call *Syphilis* an 'incomparable poem.' Tate's translation does not appear to have made Fracastoro's name a household word in English.

English, and least of all, it is to be hoped, by sufferers from the French disease. Even Tate admits his treatment to have been superseded, for in the Dedication to Mr. Hobbs (Surgeon to his Majesty) he speaks of

> *Numbers that yield (Alas!) too just survey*
> *Of Physick's growth and Poetry's decay;*
> *That show a generous Muse impair'd by me,*
> *As much as the Author's Skill's out-done by thee.*

The last reflection was probably a comfort to His Majesty.

The poem itself is quaint and interesting, and affords one more example of Tate's pleasant habit of not keeping always to familiar paths. Here is a passage indicating a recommended diet for the afflicted person:

> *I hold nor Cucumber nor Mushrooms good*
> *And Artichoke is too salacious Food:*
> *Nor yet the use of Milk would I enjoin,*
> *Much less of Vinigar or eager Wine,*
> *Such as from Rhaeta comes, and from the Rhine;*
> *The Sabine vintage is of safer use,*
> *Which mellow and well-watered fields produce:*
> *But if your banquets with the Gods you'd make*
> *Of Herbs and Roots the unbought dainties take;*
> *Be sure that Mint and Endive still abound,*
> *And Sowthistle, with leaves in Winter crown'd,*
> *And Sian by clear fountains always found;*
> *To these add Calamint and Savery,*
> *Burrage and Balm, whose mingled sweets agree,*
> *Rochet and Sorrel I as much approve:*
> *The climbing Hop grows wild in every Grove,*
> *Take Thence the infant buds, and with them join*
> *The curling tendrels of the springing Vine,*
> *Whose arms have yet no friendly shade allow'd*
> *Nor with the weight of juicy clusters bow'd.*
> *Particulars were endless to rehearse,*
> *And weightier Subjects now demand our Verse.*

The patient or his advisors are left to decide how these remedies are to be applied.

The work which stands with the 'improvement' of *King Lear* as the most celebrated of Tate's undertakings is his versification of the Psalms. This, entitled *A New Version of the Psalms of David*, first appeared in 1696, and was quickly followed by enlarged editions. The book was an immediate and complete success and soon congregations all over the country were singing the new Psalms.

These Psalms were partly the work of Nicholas Brady,[1]—and 'Tate and Brady' very soon ousted for ever the formerly popular 'Sternhold and Hopkins.' To sing David's version of the Psalms seems to have occurred to no-one. Among the Tate and Brady Psalms were a number which are still in use as hymns, notably 'As pants the hart for cooling streams,' 'Through all the changing scenes of life,' and 'Have mercy, Lord, on me, as Thou wert ever kind.' To these were added several original 'psalms' and hymns, including 'While Shepherds watched their flocks by night.' Although the poems were not separately signed, it is usual to assign the best of them—including 'While Shepherds watched' —to Tate. Somewhere embedded in these psalms also is the familiar phrase 'an untimely grave.'

Tate was one of the least original of contemporary dramatists and his best plays are those in which he leaned most heavily on some existing theme or text; but in an age when to 'alter' Shakespeare or adapt Moliere was taken as a matter of course, it was not unreasonable for a writer of small talent to avail himself of such aids as came to his hand.[2] Accordingly, in 1692, he had a respectable reputation, based mainly on his plays including the version of *King Lear*. He had also written a couple of commemorative poems to mark the loyalty a right-thinking poet ought to pay to the monarch in power, and had published a considerable body of miscellaneous poems,[3] including a continuation of Dryden's *Absalom and Achitophel* into which the Master himself had written a couple of hundred bitter lines attacking Settle and Shadwell.

In his Preface Tate obligingly indicates for the student's convenience, the place of this contribution: 'that Part beginning Page 13, Line 17, *Next these, a Troop of busie Spirits press*, and ending Page 18, Line 18, *To talk like Doeg and to write like thee*, containing near two hundred verses, were entirely Mr. Dryden's composition. . . .'

---

[1] Nicholas Brady (1659–1726) was another Irishman (he was born at Bandon, Co. Cork). He was at Westminster, Christ Church, and Trinity, Dublin, where he graduated. He became Prebendary of Cork and was active at the time of the troubles in 1690, when he persuaded the authorities not to burn the town of Bandon and later represented the townspeople's grievances to Parliament. He settled in London, where Shadwell became his friend and gave him some literary assistance. Among his works is a translation of the *Aeneid*. He held the livings of Richmond and Clapham.

[2] 'Now Poets are turned Cobblers: they vamp and mend old plays,' remarks a character in John Lacey's *Sir Hercules Buffoon* (1684).

[3] In which occasionally he found invention apt to flag. Half-way through *A Poem On the Promotion of Several Eminent Persons in Church and State* (1694) he actually admits defeat.

> *Next, were my Strength proportion'd to my Zeal,*
> *I'd sing the Guardian of the Privy-Seal.*

The poem suffers as sequels usually do; the necessary element of novelty is absent, and the first fire has died. That the poem is not equal to the first part does not indicate that in Dryden's hands it would have been much more successful. The joke was getting stale. As it is, Tate has some telling passages and a few happy phrases. The lines that introduce Dryden's own are not without a rude force:

> *Next him, let railing Rabsheka have place,*
> *So full of zeal he has no need of Grace;*
> *A Saint that can both Flesh and Spirit use,*
> *Alike haunt Conventicles and the Stews:*
> *Of whom the question difficult appears,*
> *If most i'th' Preacher's or the Bawd's arrears.*
> *What caution cou'd appear too much in him*
> *That keeps the Treasure of Jerusalem!*
> *Let David's Brother but approach the town,*
> *Double our Guards (he cries) we are undone;*
> *Protesting that he dares not sleep in's bed,*
> *Lest he should rise next morn without his head.*

One of the pleasantest occasions in Tate's life must have been when he was invited to supply an Ode for the first centenary of the founding by Queen Elizabeth of Trinity College, Dublin. To return to his old College as Poet Laureate, not so many years after leaving Dublin with no particular prospects, probably gave Tate as much satisfaction as the performance (to music by Purcell) of his centenary verses—*An Ode upon the Ninth of January, 1694–5, the First Secular Day since the University of Dublin's Foundation by Queen Elizabeth, by Mr. Tate.*

An account of the occasion is preserved by that indefatigable journalist John Dunton, in *Some Account of My Conversation in Ireland* (1699). 'In the afternoon, there were several Orations in Latin spoke by the Scholars in praise of Queen Elizabeth and the succeeding Princes; and an Ode made by Mr. Tate (the Poet Laureate), who was bred up in this College. . . . After this Ode had been sung by the principal Gentleman of the Kingdom there was a very diverting speech . . .' No doubt a diverting speech went down well after this sort of thing, even if set by Purcell and sung by Gentlemen:

> *Great Parent, hail! all hail to Thee*
> *Who hast the last distress surviv'd,*
> *To see this joyful day arriv'd;*
> *The Muse's second Jubilee.*

Another Century commencing,
    No decay in thee can trace,
Time, with his own law dispensing,
    Adds new charms to every grace,
That adorns thy youthful face.

After War's alarms repeated,
And a Circling Age completed,
    Numerous offspring thou dost raise,
    Such as to Juverna's praise,
Shall Liffey make as proud a name,
    As that of Isis, or of Cam.

As a personality, Tate eludes us; he seems to have made no very
great impact upon his contemporaries[1] and references to him are neither
very frequent nor very illuminating. 'A person who died in 1763, at
the age of ninety, remembered him well, and said he was remarkable for
a downcast look, and had seldom much to say for himself,' says the
compiler of *A New and General Biographical Dictionary* ('A New
Edition,' 1784) adding 'with these qualities, added to a meagre countenance, it will not appear surprising that he was poor and despised.'
The younger generation of writers had little time for him; and no
doubt Dryden's death was a severe blow. Addison, as we have seen,
found nothing good to say for Tate's *Lear*, and Pope refers unflatter-
ingly to him in his *Epistle to Dr. Arbuthnot*:

And he, who now to sense, now nonsense leaning,
Means not, but blunders round about a meaning;
And he, whose fustian's so sublimely bad,
It is not poetry, but prose run mad:
All these, my modest satire bade translate,
And own'd that nine such poets made a Tate.

In the *Dunciad*, more justly because more accurately, Pope finds a
happy phrase for Tate's condition:

O! pass more innocent, in infant state,
To the mild limbo of our father Tate.

---

[1] Swift notes this in his 'Dedication to Prince Posterity' of *A Tale of a Tub*. 'There is
another,' he says, 'called *Nahum Tate*, who is ready to make oath, that he has caused many
reams of verse to be published, whereof both himself and his bookseller (if lawfully
required) can still produce authentic copies, and therefore wonders why the world is
pleased to make such a secret of it.' Tate's poem on Tea ought not to go unnoticed,
although it contains an extraordinary amount about gods, goddesses, kings and queens
and almost nothing about tea. However, 'I must honestly acknowledge,' he tells us in the
preface, ''tis to this (despicable) tea-leaf that I owe Recovery out of a weakly Con-
stitution from the very Cradle   ..'

To have written so much where no obligation existed would alone have seemed a virtue, and the poems themselves were thought well enough:

> *The* British *Laurel by old* Chaucer *worn,*
> *Still* Fresh *and* Gay, *did* Dryden's *brow adorn,*
> *And that its lustre may not fade on Thine,*
> *Wit, Fancy, Judgment,* Tate, *in thee combine* . . .[1]

Tate's laureate poems (to which might be added a few of an 'official' nature written before he was appointed, or as it were in addition) would fill a fair size volume. They include New Year and Birthday Odes, poems on the deaths of Queen Mary and Queen Anne, and poems on victories by sea and land. These last are the most unrewarding: for, as Saintsbury has noted,[2] from the death of Drayton to the appearance of Campbell, nobody, and least of all the poets of the early eighteenth century, seems to have had any notion how to write a war song. If, however, Tate's work is read alongside the similar work of his contemporaries—the 'resident Frenchman,' Peter Motteux, for example, a great versifier of public events (he wrote a New Year Ode in 1694) or Richard Duke,[3] or Thomas Yalden, or a dozen others—it will be found that the laurel sits as justly on his brow as it would on any.

It was these poems, rather than Tate's works as a whole, that Southey appears to have had in mind when he remarked[4] 'Nahum Tate, of all my predecessors, must have ranked the lowest of the Laureates if he had not succeeded Shadwell.'

This point of view would have puzzled Tate's contemporaries. The Laureate had still no specific duties and could write or not write as the fancy took him when some national occasion for verse presented itself. Even the New Year and Birthday Odes which were by now more or less an institution were not necessarily the work of the Laureate. To

---

[1] Commendatory verses by 'R.B.' in Tate's *Panacea, a Poem Upon Tea* (1700).
[2] Collected Essays and Papers, Vol. I: 'English War Songs.'
[3] Typical is the opening of Duke's 'On the Death of King Charles the Second':

> *If the indulgent Muse (the only cure*
> *For all the ills afflicted minds endure,*
> *That sweetens sorrow and makes sadness please,*
> *And heals the heart by telling its disease)*
> *Vouchsafe her aid, we also will presume*
> *With humble verse t' approach the sacred tomb;*
> *There flowing streams of pious tears will shed,*
> *Sweet insense burn, fresh flowers and odours spread,*
> *Our last sad offerings to the royal dead!*

Each reader may choose for himself which of these poets had the most 'indulgent' Muse.
[4] Life of Cowper.

'rank the lowest of the Laureates' by reason of the insipidity of a few official poems might have seemed a hard fate for the author of *King Lear*, the busy translator and satirist, the successful dramatist and poet.

Unlike his predecessor (who had little time to show his Laureate quality before he died) Tate was a voluminous Laureate during three reigns. At his appointment shortly after Shadwell's death, William and Mary were still reigning; these sovereigns Tate outlived and his position was confirmed by their successor, Anne, and her confirmation was in its turn confirmed by George I, after which it was Tate's turn to die, which he did on July 30th, 1715. His term of office lasted, therefore, rather more than twenty-three years and included such potentially stirring events as the victories of the great Duke of Marlborough and the union of England and Scotland. Tate ejaculates upon them all without producing anything likely to enhance their inherent fame. He has the singular power of making a famous victory look fatuous—a power which was exercised also by some of his successors.

By the accident of serving as Laureate in three successive reigns Tate saw several changes in the status of his appointment. When he followed Shadwell it was with a Patent in identical form with the single difference that as he was made Laureate only, and not Historiographer Royal (which was conferred on Thomas Rymer) his fee is £100 and not £200. However, the 'butt or pipe of Canary' is safely bestowed. The accession of Queen Anne made it necessary for his appointment to be confirmed by the new sovereign, and this was duly done, but with a comparatively informal document issued by the Lord Chamberlain. This was the first step towards divorcing the Office from the greater State Offices, and making it a more personal one. The 'King's Poet' was becoming the King's responsibility and in 1710 the Laureate's pension was made chargeable to the Lord Chamberlain's department. At the Queen's death (August 1st, 1714) Tate was once more technically 'out of a job' but the new King showed no inclination to effect a change and in due course his loyal poet rewarded him with a Birthday Ode in which the first George is found to have every kingly virtue enjoyed by his predecessors.

Tate's own life was now closing, rather miserably. He had had his triumphs, but he had survived them, or at least he had survived the money they had afforded. He took refuge from his creditors, choosing for this purpose the Mint; and here, surrounded by money no doubt, but unable to lay hands upon it, on July 30th, 1715, he died. His 'mild limbo' now is a tomb in St. George's, Southwark.

5

Nicholas Rowe

'MR. Nic. Rowe is made poet laureat in the room of Mr. Tate, deceased. This Rowe is a great Whig, and but a mean poet.' In recording this Thomas Hearne[1] was doing Rowe rather less than justice, for in 1715 the new Laureate had an impressive list of achievements to offer besides the bait of being 'a great Whig.'

Rowe, like the previous Laureates, was primarily a dramatist; and like them, he was badly served by his immediate biographers, so that an adequate tale of his life is now not easily told, despite the careful researches of Professor J. R. Sutherland. What the art of biography owes to Mason and Boswell may easily be understood by reference to the so-called 'lives' that preceded them (Boswell's debt to Mason is seldom recognised although he himself acknowledged it). There are a few exceptions, but in the main, seventeenth century accounts of the great, even when written by friends and contemporaries, are inaccurate and cursory. Thus Dr. James Welwood at 'Mr. Rowe's request in his last sickness' furnished some account of the poet as preface to the posthumous publication of the translation of Lucan, and before this Stephen Hales had prefixed a note to *Musarum Lachrymae, or Poems To the Memory of Nicholas Rowe, Esq. By Several Hands.* (1719). Other near-contemporary accounts include T. Cibber's in his *Lives of the Poets*, and Dr. Johnson's in his *Lives*. What all these authorities give us of solid fact can be summarised in a page; and they contradict one another.

Nicholas Rowe was born at Little Barford, in Bedfordshire, on June 20th, 1674. His father was a lawyer, John Rowe, whose family had been settled in Devonshire for generations, and it was perhaps the comparative nearness of Little Barford to London that prompted Mrs. Rowe to lie-in there at the house of her father, rather than in 'dull Devonshire.'

Nicholas proved a forward child at school, first at Highgate and later

---

[1] *Reliquiae Hearnianae*. Contemporary estimates of Rowe place him in a respectable position. I confess a preference for Tate.

at Westminster, where 'poetry was his early bent and darling study.'
These early poems (T. Cibber adds) 'were produced with so much
facility (they) seemed to flow from his imagination, as fast as from his
pen.'[1]

By the time Rowe was old enough to leave Westminster his father
had advanced in his profession to the rank of Serjeant-at-Law, and he
naturally proposed the same career for his son. In 1691 Rowe was
admitted to the Middle Temple, and in 1696 he was called to the Bar.
But John Rowe, before ever he had the chance to practice as a Serjeant,
had died and although Nicholas did not at once give up his studies
(and may even have practised after he was called) the encouragement to
remain in the Law must have been considerably less after his father's
death, especially as his mother had died years before. With the modest
income his father had left him, and with pleasant Temple chambers,
Rowe returned once again to poetry, his 'darling study.'

In 1698 he married Antonia Parsons and the following year his son
John was born.

For the next year or two we know comparatively little of Rowe's
activities; it was now, perhaps, that he practised Law. He makes no
appearance in letters until 1700 when his first play, *The Ambitious Step-
mother* was staged at Lincoln's Inn Fields. This tragedy had a friendly
reception and was afterwards published with an interesting dedication
to the Earl of Jersey, in which Rowe discusses the difficulties of a be-
ginner: 'I was led into an Error in the writing of it, by thinking that it
would be easier to retrench than to add: but when I was at last necessit-
ated, by reason of the extreme length, to cut off near six hundred Lines,
I found that it was maim'd by it to a great disadvantage.' Perhaps the
lines cut were superior to those retained.

Just as Shadwell in commencing dramatic author proclaimed
Jonson as his model and master, so now Rowe affirmed his indebted-
ness to an original: but the hero for him is Otway—'The famous Mr.
Otway who succeeded so well in touching, and must and will at all
times affect people, who have any tenderness or humanity.' Rowe,
equipped with a smaller genius, could not attain the dramatic heights
upon which strode the magnificent muse of Otway, but in his degree
he was as much a credit to that chosen model as was Shadwell to his.
Rowe touched people of tenderness and humanity genuinely and sometimes deeply, for two generations.

---

[1] Cibber's phrasing is basically from Welwood, but for once rather pleasantly improved
in the borrowing.

In his second play, the famous *Tamerlane*, Rowe took the opportunity to demonstrate his 'great Whiggishness,'for his all-conquering hero was admittedly intended for King William III. Unfortunately the King could afford no better encouragement to the play than to die most inconsiderately about the time it was staged. Even in the face of this rebuff the piece found favour, and was for many years produced annually on the anniversary of William's first landing in this country.

Early in 1703 Rowe produced *The Fair Penitent*, the first of his 'good' plays. Like most early eighteenth-century plays, (and nearly all late seventeenth-century) it was based on an obscure original, in this case Massinger's *The Fatal Dowry*. Gifford, that most partizan of editors, attempted to demonstrate that Rowe deliberately stole his plot, expecting not to be detected, but to the less biased reader this seems unlikely. Rowe at least affords one line which is not indebted to Massinger and has become, if not a familiar quotation, at least a quotation:

> *Is this that haughty, gallant, gay Lothario?*

These tragedies added to Rowe's standing and gave some justification to the critic who remarked in 1702, 'Considering the degeneracy of our present poets, Mr. Rowe has the fairest pretence to succeed Dryden in tragedy of any of his brethren, excepting none.'

Having demonstrated what he could do, Rowe now displayed the characteristically human trait of attempting something different. He wrote a farce called *The Biter* which was universally condemned. 'It had a six Days run,' Downes records, 'and the six Days running it out of Breath, it Sicken'd and Expir'd.'[1] Johnson says that Rowe himself was well pleased with the piece: 'He is said to have sat in the house laughing with great vehemence, whenever he had in his opinion produced a jest. But finding that he and the public had no sympathy of mirth he tried at lighter scenes no more.'[2]

There seems some excuse for Rowe, despite the failure of this essay in fun, for he was not a naturally doleful man although he wrote best on gloomy subjects. 'His conversation was pleasant, witty, and learn'd,' Welwood records, adding that 'his inimitable manner of diverting and enlivening the Company, made it impossible for anyone

---

[1] *Roscius Anglicanus* (1708).
[2] Johnson, *Life of Rowe*.

> *Ev'n thy famed* Biter *had not half a tooth*

remarks an anonymous contemporary critic.—*A Lash for the Laureate* (1718).

to be out of humour when he was in it.' Lord Oxford's secretary, Lewis, told Spence that Rowe was 'of a comely personage, and a very pretty sort of man.', and Pope, when Spence quoted a weak epigram and remarked that he had supposed Rowe too grave to write such things, cried out 'He!—why he would laugh all day long! he would do nothing else but laugh!'

Be that as it may, after *The Biter* Rowe prudently returned to tragedy and in 1705 he produced *Ulysses*, now perhaps the least readable of his plays. It is interesting to turn over the pages with Stephen Phillips in attendance: the two poets, separated by two hundred years from one another and by some thirty centuries from their original, approach the subject with a grave nicety and deliberation, apparently unaware that the story is essentially *alive*—is 'front page news,' urgent and sensational.

Rowe at least was more successful with history nearer home, and in his next three plays, *The Royal Convert* (1707), *Jane Shore* (1714) and *Lady Jane Gray* (1715) he returned to English history—though the first, about 'Hengist, King of Kent' has about as much historical truth as *King Lear*, and rather less poetry.

In 1709 Rowe published his edition of Shakespeare and added the first life of that poet. It was a pioneer work, and open to much criticism in the light of later scholarship, but it was nonetheless an important enterprise, performed in a workmanlike manner, and it directed attention to Shakespeare's own text at a time when his plays were acted only in adaptations by the Restoration dramatists.

Another of Rowe's enterprises was a translation of Claudius Quillet's *Callipaedia*, a poem on the art of begetting beautiful children. 'If the author' (says Rowe) 'ever leans towards Indecency in a description Part, he first begs Pardon, or excuses it by the necessary relation it bore to his Scheme, which must have been deficient without that Description. However, in the *English*, the Terms of Art have so shadow'd those Parts, that they will be intelligible only to Physical Readers. . . .' I can testify to the exact truth of this statement.

Rowe's appointment to the Laureateship[1] a few days after Tate's death seems to have met with little criticism. He was, after all, a writer

---

[1] Rowe held at various times a number of minor appointments, of which 'Surveyor of Landwaiters' sounds the most interesting. It was perhaps in connection which something of the kind that Rowe once waited upon my lord Oxford (as Spence records it) and was advised to learn Spanish. Rowe hurried off and did so, doubtless expecting at least to be appointed Ambassador to the Court of Spain. He returned and announced to Lord Oxford that he had mastered the language. 'Then, Sir,' replied Oxford, 'I envy you the pleasure of reading *Don Quixote* in the original!'

of established reputation, and he had many friends in high places. The most sustained attack on him was the anonymous *A Lash for the Laureate* (1718) which gets off to a good start by calling him 'this Bay-dress'd Poetaster,' but the poem is political rather than personal in its satire, and was occasioned by Rowe's prologue for Cibber's *The Non-Juror*. It has one telling couplet, which might well be applied to others besides Rowe:

> *The Ass of Aesop in his Lyon's Skin,*
> *Tho' Laureate outward, was but Rowe within.*

Dorset, who had been concerned in the fortunes of Dryden, Shadwell and Tate, was now a power no longer, and the Duke of Bolton was Lord Chamberlain. Rowe took the oath on August 12th, 1715. Dutifully on the following New Year's Day he produced his first Ode, but George I was not in England to hear it performed; he was tasting the delights of his native Hanover.

His three years in office gave Rowe little opportunity to shine as official poet; the King was hardly an heroic figure, and the times were peaceful. The 'fifteen rebellion was over and Rowe gave it but a passing glance in his first Ode:

> *Faction, Fury, all are fled,*
> *And bold Rebellion hides her daring Head.*

Neither he nor his king were present to see Rebellion put her head forth again in 'forty-five.

Rowe was, moreover, nothing if not a dramatic poet; he needed the larger canvas provided by five acts. Failing these, he needed the extended compass of epic. 'Occasional poetry must often content itself with occasional praise,' Johnson remarks and it is a judgment with which Rowe would have agreed. In one of his Dedications he speaks of 'my own inconsiderable Pretensions to Verse,' and those pretensions are seen at their least considerable in the Laureate poems, and the handful of other short pieces.

In his last important work, however, Rowe displayed his best strength. This was the translation of Lucan's *Pharsalia*, published by the second Mrs. Rowe after the Laureate's death.

The idea of an English Lucan was not new, and Tonson, who printed Rowe's version magnificently in folio in 1718, had formerly projected a translation by several hands but (as Johnson puts it) 'this design, as must often happen when the concurrance of many is necessary, fell to the ground, and the whole work was afterwards performed by Rowe.'[1]

It was performed greatly to the Doctor's satisfaction: 'The version of Lucan is one of the greatest productions of English poetry; for there is perhaps none that so completely exhibits the genius and spirit of the original. . . . The *Pharsarlia* of Rowe deserves more notice than it obtains, and as it is more read will be more esteemed.'[2]

Rowe apparently considered it the Laureate's duty to perform something more than the yearly Odes; for in her preface to the translation of Lucan his widow writes:

> While my deceased Husband was engaged in the following long and laborious Work, he was not a little supported in it by the Honour which he proposed to himself of Dedicating it to Your Sacred Majesty . . . he expressed to me his Desire that this Translation should be laid at Your Majesty's Feet as a mark of that Zeal and Veneration which he had always entertained for Your Majesty's Royal Person and Virtues.

This was tactful, if not completely true (for Rowe had been engaged on Lucan for twenty years, off and on, and certainly long before George I was his 'Sacred Majesty') but at the same time it suggests that Rowe felt that a great translating enterprise could be laid at the King's feet as appropriately as might an original work. The 18th century was a great age of translation, and Rowe's *Lucan* was one of its first important monuments.

The King seems to have taken some notice of the Lucan (though

---

[1] *Life of Hughes.* John Hughes (1677–1720) translated the tenth book, which was later published in his Works. He was a friend of Rowe, and gave him some assistance with the Laureate poems, as this letter to him testifies:

'Covent Garden, Oct. 22, 1716.

Dear Sir,

As you were so good formerly to promise me a little of your poetical assistance, you can never give it me at a time when it will be more useful than now. I beg you will be so good as to think of some words for Mr. Eccles and the new year. The entertainment is not to consist of above half an hour in time at most. Three or four airs, with some little recitative between, is what the composer will be glad of. I need not tell you, you are the fittest man in the world for this occasion, by your equal knowledge of music and poetry. I will only beg you now, for friendship's sake, to have compassion on, dear Sir,

Your most affectionate and faithful humble servant,
N. ROWE.'

Another similar helper was George Jeffreys (1678–1755) who furnished an Ode for the New Year, 1719, which appears in the works of both Rowe and Jeffreys. Jeffreys says 'Written at the Request of Mr. Rowe, Poet Laureate'; Rowe (who was dead when it appeared) says nothing of its authorship. Naturally, the rival texts differ; so the interested reader may take his pick. The editor of the *Correspondence of John Hughes* remarks that Jeffreys supplied the 1720 Ode for Eusden, 'his former collegian'; if he did, he deserves more credit for friendship than for poetry.

[2] *Life of Rowe.*

probably not to the extent of reading it, for George was no lover of letters). At all events he granted the poet's widow a pension of £40 per annum.

There was now some fifty years tradition behind the Laureateship. The Poet Laureate was news by virtue of his office and apart from purely personal considerations. Accordingly, when Rowe had been taken ill most of the newspapers recorded the fact and reported on the progress of his illness. 'Nicholas Rowe, Esq., Poet-Laureat to his Majesty, and Surveyor of the Land Waiters, lies so dangerously ill at his House on Covent Garden that his Life is despair'd of,' said *The Weekly Journal or British Gazeteer* on November 8th, 1718. It was a month, however, before *The Original Weekly Journal* recorded (December 6th) 'Nicholas Rowe, Esq., Poet-Laureat . . . was yesterday given over by his Physicians.' And so, at the early age of 44, he died and was buried in Westminster Abbey, 'close by the side of old Parr, who was 152 years of age when he died' and 'over against Chaucer. . . .'

One of the executors was Alexander Pope, and some lines of his were intended for the Laureate's monument:

> *Thy relics, Rowe, to this fair urn we trust*
> *And sacred, place by Dryden's awful dust:*
> *Beneath a rude and nameless stone he lies,*
> *To which thy tomb shall guide inquiring eyes.*
> *Peace to thy gentle shade, and endless rest!*
> *Blest in thy genius, in thy love too bless'd!*
> *One grateful woman to thy fame supplies*
> *What a whole thankless land to his denies.*

Altered and extended (perhaps by another hand) the verses were afterwards inscribed on the elaborate monument which may still be seen in the Abbey.

6

Laurence Eusden

DRYDEN had brought to the office of Poet Laureate a great name, and he had adorned it with great poems. Since Dryden lesser poets had contributed smaller poems until the place had gathered only the traditions that mere age brings. For fifty years one or another had held the title, enjoyed the salary, and drunk the sack. It was time for another important poet to bring authority to the Laureateship if the office were not to continue no more than a minor place in the royal household.

Looking back across two hundred years we can see who were then the living giants (they were a small company) but people on the spot lacked our advantage of historical perspective. The appointment went to Laurence Eusden, thus ensuring for him a sort of immortality, since he cannot be left out of the list of Laureates although he is seldom admitted to the list of English poets.

Laurence Eusden was then thirty, which makes him the youngest of the Laureates on his appointment. He was born in 1688 at Spofforth in Yorkshire, where his father, another Laurence, was rector. The family was of Irish stock. Eusden was sent to St. Peter's School, York, and from thence to Trinity College, Cambridge, where he did well. In 1712 he became a Fellow of his college, and a sublector. He began to publish poems here and there: some verses addressed to Richard Bentley, then Master of Trinity; several competent translations from or into Latin and Greek; various occasional pieces, and a set of verses for the Cambridge Commencement.

The *Verses Spoken at the Public Commencement at Cambridge* were described by Austin and Ralph in *The Lives of the Poets-Laureate* (1853) as 'purient lines, which we dare not quote.' It occurred to me that perhaps the passage of a hundred years might have made them more acceptable, but on examining them I had some difficulty in detecting the bits to which those earlier historians took exception. I found this, which may encourage the proprietors of a popular contemporary journal:

> *And* Punch *is merry twice at least a year*

and another couplet which shows a proper perspective in the writer upon questions of love as opposed to literature:

> *My Lawrel'd Hopes I willingly resign,*
> *Give me but* Flavia—*take the tuneful* Nine.

For the rest, the poem is mainly a dissertation upon women's fashions.

Eusden's poems are generally dull, but so is a great deal of minor verse of the eighteenth century. At least they afford an occasional felicitous phrase; the last of these four lines, for example, from his *Hero and Leander*:

> *The barren Beach and Seas she round survey'd,*
> *And hop'd her Lover in the Dark had stray'd:*
> *But ah! too soon she spy'd him, where he lay*
> *A Lump of beautiful, tho' breathless Clay.*

It was worth reading the four hundred and fifty that went before to come upon that last line in the end.

Although no doubt Eusden practised poetry in order to enjoy its pleasures for their own sake, he has also the customary eighteenth century eye to the main chance. If one's college Master were Bentley there was nothing to be gained by addressing civil couplets to Boyle. It was also better for a poem offered to the newly acceded king to discuss his virtues, rather than to dwell too kindly on those of his predecessors. Accordingly, in *The Royal Family!—A Letter to Mr. Addison on the King's Accession to the Throne*, Eusden has things to say about George I which must have gratified that monarch (if they came to his notice) in ratio to his credulity. This poem (Mr. Addison's *Spectator* duly noted) contained many 'noble and beautiful Strokes of Poetry.'

In the same year (1714) Eusden published a translation into Latin of Halifax's poem on the Battle of the Boyne, prefixing to it an English poem in which he invited the noble Lord's attention to his efforts. Lord Halifax would perhaps have been a useful patron, but about this time he very inconveniently died without having afforded any solid recognition of Eusden's tribute. The hopeful poet had to look elsewhere for preferment and he chose the Duke of Newcastle, a

younger man apparently in excellent health. Eusden wrote a handsome Epithalamium for this nobleman's wedding to Lady Henrietta
Godolphin.

Not long after his marriage the Duke became Lord Chamberlain,
and very soon after that Rowe died. Even before the official announcement of his successor the word was circulating that Eusden would
succeed to the Laureateship, though not to Rowe's other offices. In
recording Rowe's death the *St. James's Evening Post* added: 'It is said that
he will be succeeded . . . by Mr. Eusden, a gentleman of great
learning and merit.' On December 16th the same journal was able to
confirm its own prophecy by announcing that 'Laurence Eusden Esq.,
is made Poet Laureat.'

In a recent biography,[1] Mr. Peter Smithers suggests that this appointment might perhaps have come through Addison's recommendation;
both Rowe and Eusden were numbered among his friends, and it
appears likely enough that the death of the one might have afforded
him an opportunity to advance the other. Eusden had addressed a
number of verses to Addison, including a tribute to *Cato*, and had
contributed to *The Spectator*.

By dying in December Rowe disobligingly left his successor with
only a couple of weeks in which to produce his first New Year Ode.
The task proved to be well within Eusden's powers; no doubt he
approached his first ode a good deal fresher than he was when he set
pen to paper for the writing of his last, a dozen years later: for every
18th century laureate's biggest difficulty was the finding of new ways
in which to express the old compliments. This first ode appears not to
have been printed.

'Eusden was a person of great hopes in his youth,' Gray later wrote
to Mason, and this character of him seems to serve up till the time of
his appointment to the Laureateship. The unfriendly references to him
in various pamphlets and poems, mainly occur after he became if not a
public figure (for he was never that) at least the holder of a public
office. The wide world beyond his immediate circle was not aware of
Eusden until he became Laureate, and then his smallness (even judged
by the standards, not very elevated, of Rowe and Tate) became
apparent. Naturally the satirists attended to him. But the greatest of
them, Pope, was at pains to point out after Eusden's death that 'the
allegory [a reference in *The Dunciad* apparently to Eusden] evidently
demands a person dipped in scandal and deeply immersed in dirty

[1] The Life of Joseph Addison. *Oxford*, 1954.

work, whereas Mr. Eusden's writings rarely offended but by their length and multitude.'[1]

The worst Pope said of Eusden was mild enough compared with what he said of others:

> *Know, Eusden thirsts no more for sack or praise,*
> *He sleeps among the dull of ancient days,*

and even this was among the additions to the *Dunciad*.

The most vigorous of Eusden's early critics (for by the time Pope glanced at him he had been laureate ten years) was the Duke of Buckingham—Pope's friend Sheffield, not Dryden's enemy Villiers—with his poem *The Election of a Poet Laureat in* 1719 (usually called *A Session of the Poets*, which was a popular title used by a number of writers after Suckling's original). Buckingham's poem followed the customary pattern, mentioning most of the living poets and assessing in a line or two their title to the laurel; and then he neatly brings in his twist—for he was writing *after* the appointment:

> *At last in rush'd Eusden, and cry'd 'Who shall have it,*
> *But I, the true Laureat, to whom the King gave it?'*
> *Apollo beg'd pardon, and granted his Claim,*
> *But vow'd, Tho' till then, he ne'er heard of his name.*

It has been customary in writing of Eusden to call him names, and writers on the Laureateship in particular have been severe in their censure: 'contemptible' is almost the least of their epithets for him, and yet it is difficult to understand why. It would be a poor lookout for most of us if we were judged by the figure we made in someone's satires. We don't judge Johnson by a few vigorous lines in Churchill, nor Addison by the 'Atticus' of Pope, nor FitzGerald by Browning's sonnet. Perhaps too much has been made of Eusden's appearance in the *Dunciad* because he makes so few appearances elsewhere. He was the least 'public' of the Laureates, and seems to have been very little known outside his immediate circle, even after his appointment; it is this which gives point to Buckingham's lines.

If Pope, the most waspish of satirists, could let Eusden down lightly, perhaps he was not so contemptible a fellow after all. Another savage contemporary was Swift, and it is surely significant that his *Directions*

---

[1] Perhaps Byron took this remark as a precedent when he accused a later Laureate, Southey, of writing more prose and verse 'than anybody knows'; but on the score of bulk Byron had justification, whereas Eusden's output was, in fact, rather slender whatever its other faults might have been.

for a Birth-day Song, Oct: 30, 1729 is almost good-humoured in its
oblique glances at Eusden, though sarcastic enough where the King is
concerned; and the principal satire is directed at birthday odes as such:

> 'Tis not deny'd that when we write,
> Our Ink is black, our Paper white;
> And when we scrawl our Paper o'r'e,
> We blacken what was white before.
> I think this Practice only fit
> For dealers in Satyrick Wit:
> But you some white-lead ink must get,
> And write on paper black as Jet:
> Your Int'rest lyes to learn the knack
> Of whitening what before was black . . .

Another near-contemporary reference to Eusden's appointment
which illustrates the difference in reputation between that Laureate
and his predecessors occurs in Thomas Cooke's *Battle of the Poets* (1725)
where Eusden is called 'a laurelled Bard, by Fortune rais'd, by very
few been read, by fewer prais'd.' The same might be said of Thomas
Cooke,[1] incidentally.

Cooke's lines are worth quoting at length, and the whole poem
merits the attention of 'the curious'—that 'excellent anonymous company whose attention, for which nothing is too remote, keeps life in a
thousand authors otherwise dead to the world's regard.'

> Eusden, a Lawrel'd Bard, by Fortune rais'd,
> By very few been read, by fewer prais'd;
> From place to place, forlorn and breathless, flies,
> And offers bribes immense, for strong Allies.
> In vain he spent the Day, the Night in vain;
> For all the Laureat, and his Bribes, disdain.
> With heart dejected he returned alone,
> Upon the banks of Cham, to make his moan;
> Resolv'd to spend his future days in ease,
> And only toil in Verse, himself to please;
> To fly the noisy Candidates of Fame,
> Nor ever court again so coy a dame.

The suggestion that Eusden offered bribes is interesting, in view of a
note by the editor of the *Correspondence of John Hughes*, who says the

---

[1] Thomas Cooke (1702–1746) was the translator of Hesiod who (said Johnson) presented
Foote to a club 'in the following singular manner: "This is the nephew of the gentleman
who was lately hung in chains for murdering his brother".'

1720 New Year Ode was written by George Jeffreys. The Ode does not appear in Jeffreys' Works, and may have been confused with the one he certainly wrote for Rowe. But there, for what they may be worth, are two separate suggestions that Eusden sought to farm out his labours; perhaps the new Laureate was accustomed to the sort of collaboration more common in Elizabeth's day than George's, as John Lacy satirically infers in *The Steeleids* (1714) when he remarks that the three poets Tickell, Gay and Eusden share two muses between them.

No doubt Eusden's small contemporary reputation lay in the fact that he was not a dramatist, for the drama was still the surest path to fame, nor a satirist, in the noisy hurly-burly of name-calling. After his appointment he contended himself with punctiliously affording his two odes a year and left the pursuit of general fame to others. The years of his tenure offered nothing of outstanding interest as a theme for his pen, except a death or two; George II's moment of martial splendour came long after Eusden had left this mortal scene. He made nothing notable to mark the death of Marlborough, and left Newton to be nobly mourned by another.[1] The 'great hopes of his youth,' in so far as they referred to hopes of poetic achievement, were gradually dissipated in the task of making a translation of Tasso, which he left in manuscript at his death. Some time in the 'twenties he took orders and became Chaplain to Lord Willoughby de Broke, and later Rector of Coningsby, Lincs.—where, later, the poet Dyer held the living.

Eusden died on September 27th, 1730. A month later, his Ode for the King's Birthday was performed,—on October 30th. The news of the Laureate's death reached the capital on October 31st.

A number of needy poets began to wonder about the vacant place.

---

[1] James Thomson, whose admirable tribute *A Poem Sacred to the Memory of Sir Isaac Newton*, has never received adequate recognition.

7

Colley Cibber

'IN the year 1730, there were many Authors, whose Merit wanted nothing but Interest to recommend them to the vacant *Laurel*, and who took it ill, to see it at last conferred upon a Comedian. . . .' So wrote Colley Cibber in his autobiography, and he gives a lively glimpse of the rough-and-tumble that went on among the crowd of poets to whom a pension of £100 represented a fortune.

Colley Cibber, a man of almost sixty when Eusden died, was certainly not an obvious choice for the office. He was a very indifferent poet, as he knew. This certainly set him apart from his rivals, who were indifferent too, and unaware of it. But he was at least a man of some standing: a celebrated actor, a successful dramatist, the manager of a theatre.

It was his play *The Non-Juror* (1718) with its brisk satire on the Jacobites which now, over twelve years later, brought him the Laureateship. This Cibber himself tells us: 'I have reason to think,' he wrote in *An Apology for the Life of Colley Cibber* (1740) '. . . (however unequal the Merit may be to the Reward) that part of the bread I now eat, was given me, for having writ the *Nonjuror*.'

Cibber was the son of Caius Gabriel Cibber, the sculptor, who is best remembered now for his graphic bas-relief at the base of the Monument in London (a work of art which is being allowed to perish amid the varied and unattractive vapours of Billingsgate Market). Colley, his eldest son, was born in London on November 6th, 1671. His schooling, he tells us, he got at the free school, Grantham, which was near the home of his mother's family, the Colleys, from whom he got his unusual first name.

At school he seems to have been somewhat unpopular; his fellows called him 'a pragmatical bastard,' although he earned a holiday for the whole school by writing a coronation ode for James II. He had just previously written a 'funeral oration' for Charles II and thereby been raised to the top of the class, 'a preferment dearly bought' for it increased his unpopularity, especially as the master used to take him for rides on horseback while the other boys plodded away at their lessons.

Having reached the top form at Grantham, at sixteen Cibber tried to get into Winchester College, without success (his younger brother Lewis later fared better, when old Cibber presented a statue of the Founder to the College, about the time—doubtless by a coincidence—of his son's application).

It was decided to send Colley straight to Cambridge, and arrangements for this were in the making when the Revolution began. The elder Cibber was at Chatsworth, working for the Earl of Devonshire. Colley therefore joined himself to a troop raised by the Earl and spent the winter under arms without being put to the inconvenience of fighting. After the disturbance had subsided he remained in the Earl's service with some prospect of advancement and accompanied that nobleman to London, where the attractions of the theatre soon overcame him. Despite opposition from his parents he left the old master for a new; but to this one he gave over fifty faithful years of service.

He joined Betterton's company at the Theatre Royal as a probationer, (unpaid, as the custom was) and by one of those characteristic accidents which seemed typical of his life, at length got himself on the payroll: he was playing a small part and stumbled over some lines in a scene with Betterton. At the end of the performance Betterton ordered him to be fined five shillings, only to be told that the young player had no salary. 'Then put him down ten shillings a week and forfeit him five!'

Cibber records somewhat sadly that he could never aspire to great heroic parts because of an ineffectual voice and presence, although it was his youthful ambition to play hero opposite Mrs. Bracegirdle. He soon became a successful actor, nonetheless, and in 1694 he played in a command performance of Congreve's *The Double Dealer*, before the Queen. But the theatre then as now was a competitive profession and Cibber never attained to the first rank as an actor, except in certain somewhat restricted types of comedy parts.

However, he went forward happily enough, with spells of good fortune to offset the other sort. In 1693 he married Katherine Shore, daughter of the king's Sergeant Trumpeter and for some years the lady eked out their income by acting, though she was never so celebrated as her daughter-in-law, Susannah.

In 1695 the death of the Queen provided the occasion for Cibber's first published exercise in authorship, and in June he put out his *Poem*

on the Death of Our Late Sovereign Lady Queen Mary. Her majesty had
then been dead six months, and the cream of the market for elegies had
already been taken by Congreve and others, including a certain S.O.
whose tribute begins thus auspiciously:

> *Albion's hard Fate with equal Tears I mourn,*
> *Ye Muses! Will ye to your Seats return?*

after which, secure of an audience, the indifferent work proceeds.

Cibber's biographer R. H. Barker[1] remarks that 'the Poem conclu-
sively demonstrates that the future laureate of England had no talent
for verse,' but in fairness it must be added that none of the crop of
elegies was conspicuous for poetic merit although the Queen's death
was sincerely mourned. The important thing for Cibber was that he
had commenced author, and like any sensible author he now forgot
this work and proceeded to the next—his first play, *Love's Last Shift.*[2]
This comedy was successfully produced, and appeared in print in
February, 1696.

For the next thirty years Cibber's life was wholly in the theatre, as
actor, author, and manager.

Although he acted successfully in many plays, his own and those
of others, and although for a certain type of comedy (the thing he did
best) he was unmatched among his contemporaries, it was as a theatre
manager that he filled the greater part of the best years of his working
life—simultaneously with acting and writing.

About 1700 Cibber became associated with Christopher Rich, the
principal manager of Drury Lane. This was the rival theatre to Betterton's company at Lincoln's Inn Fields, with which, however, Cibber's
connection was now severed; his plays had been put on at Drury Lane.
Rich was a difficult man to get on with, but Cibber appears to have
worked amicably enough with him for several years—years of unrest
in the London theatre-world, with constant bickering between the
companies, between Betterton (who finally retired), Vanbrugh and
Congreve, who succeeded him, and the Drury Lane group. Finally in
1706 Cibber joined the new company at the Haymarket and Rich
began to specialise in elaborate musical entertainments and almost
ceased to provide 'straight' plays. Cibber's new associate was Owen
Swiney, a man today little remembered but then a great power in the
theatre.

---

[1] *Mr. Cibber of Drury Lane* (New York, 1939).
[2] Which in a French translation is said to have been titled *La Dernière Chemise de
L'Amour.*

Three years later after further bickering between the rival companies in which both addressed appeals to the Lord Chamberlain desiring him, in effect, to put the other down, Swiney proposed a scheme whereby his principal actors—Cibber, Thomas Doggett and Robert Wilks (and as originally suggested, Mrs. Oldfield)—should become partners in the management. Doggett took the view that there was not much to be said for having women in business, and to this Mrs. Oldfield unexpectedly agreed: so she accepted a guaranteed salary of £200 a year, plus a benefit, and left the men to their management. For twenty-odd years, despite ups and downs, the partnership kept going under this arrangement, or slight modifications of it, first at the Haymarket and later at Drury Lane.

During those years, with varying fortune but the balance on success, Cibber's plays were staged, Cibber's voice was heard on the boards, and Cibber's will swayed the policies of the London theatre. Like most men who exercise power, he made enemies; and one of these was Alexander Pope.

In 1717 Cibber accepted for Drury Lane the farce *Three Hours after Marriage*, written by Pope, Gay, and Arbuthnot. Various living persons (including Cibber himself) were caricatured and no doubt Cibber hoped that this topicality would save an otherwise rather indifferent piece. He played Plotwell, the character based on himself. Despite this the play failed in a storm of hisses, which after its withdrawal continued in the pamphlets. Cibber goodhumouredly accepted this reverse and shortly afterwards, while playing Bayes in *The Rehearsal*, introduced topical references to the recent failure. Pope was present at this performance and went behind in a rage to threaten Cibber and Cibber in his turn told Pope what he thought of him. Pope sent Gay the next night to chastise the actor-manager, and the actor-manager pulled the author's nose. It is a great pity things of that sort so seldom happen today—or, if they do (for one occasionally hears rumours) that they are hushed up. So far as Cibber was concerned, the incident was closed; and Gay makes no further distinguished appearance in the matter; but Pope's spleen was easier aroused than escaped. For the moment he lay in wait.

Cibber's next contact with the world of poetry—as opposed to that of the play—came at the end of the same year, when his play *The Non-Juror* was a great success and ran for sixteen nights.[1] For this Nicholas Rowe, then poet laureate, wrote a lively Prologue, for which

[1] Eighteen, says Cibber.

he was rewarded in due course by the satire, *A Lash for The Laureate*. In his autobiography twenty years and more later, Cibber adds to our scanty knowledge of Rowe the information that Congreve and the Laureate entered into a friendly rivalry for the favours of Mrs. Bracegirdle.

The scuffle with Pope and the business of Rowe's prologue were Cibber's most interesting contacts with the world of letters at this time. His theatrical affairs (including many quarrels) provided good copy for the lesser lights of Grub Street, especially for Nathaniel Mist, who ran *Mist's* (or *Fog's*) *Journal*, and was ever at Cibber's heels. Once, Mist announced that Cibber was dead, and that night at the theatre when he appeared many people took him for his own ghost.

So, busy in his world, Cibber came to the age of fifty-nine, and Laurence Eusden died. For a week or two after the death of Eusden was made public the vacant laurel seemed likely to go to Stephen Duck, the 'Thresher Poet.' *The Weekly Register* of October 31st, in announcing Eusden's death, added 'we are credibly inform'd that he will be succeeded, as Poet Laureate, by that Surprising Genius, Mr. Stephan Duck, the Wiltshire Thresher.'

Mr. Stephen Duck's genius was, in fact, surprising enough. Although by failing in his candidature he has, properly, no place in these pages, a paragraph or two can do no harm.

'Honest Duck,' as Crabbe called him, was born in 1705 at Great Charlton, Wilts, the son of poor parents. He was given some schooling but the schoolmaster complained that he learned 'too fast' so his mother removed him from school 'lest he should become too fine a gentleman for the family that produced him.' He became a farm labourer, but he continued to study as chance allowed; he even worked overtime in order to save enough money to buy books, and in writing an account of him at the time of his appearance in London, Joseph Spence was able to record his favourite books: 'Milton, the *Spectator*, and Seneca were his first favourites; *Telemachus*, with another piece by the same hand (the *Demonstration of the Being of a God*), and Addison's *Defence of Christianity* his next.' After reading, writing: and the young labourer began to make verses. These came to the notice of neighbouring gentlemen, and so in due time reached the ears of the Queen.

Queen Caroline invited the poet to Windsor, gave him £30 a year, made him first a yeoman of the guard and then librarian of her 'select library at Richmond, called Merlin's Cave' and encouraged him to take orders. His poems were published after having enjoyed the distinction of pirated editions, and as all this happened in 1730 it seems not unreasonable that this 'comet of a season' appeared likely for the Laureateship.

Writing to John Gay a few weeks after Eusden's death, Swift recorded that 'the vogue of our few honest folks here is, that Duck is absolutely to succeed Eusden in the Laurel, the contention being between Concanen[1] or Theobald, or some other hero of the *Dunciad*.' Lewis Theobald was a critic rather than a poet although like many another he had written verses from time to time. It was his strictures on Pope's edition of Shakespeare that brought him the uneviable distinction of a leading role in the *Dunciad*, then (1730) as much the centre of controversy as on its first appearance two years earlier—in truth, it might almost be said that the history of the Dunciad 1728–1744 is virtually the history of English poetry in that period, a few isolated peaks apart.

But, critic or poet, Theobald like most writers of the time, was in need of patronage. In a letter to Warburton he thus describes the progress of his candidature:

> . . . You remember well, that Mr. Cotesworth was the gentleman who gave Mr. Eusden his Lincolnshire Rectory; and, as consequently, he was the person who had the earliest notice of Eusden's death, the account no sooner reached us, but the women spurred me up to put in for the withered laurel. Accordingly, I with Lord Gage attended Sir Robert Walpole; was commanded by him to attend at Windsor; had his warmest recommendation to the Lord Chamberlain; nay, procured these recommendations to be seconded even by his Royal Highness: and yet, after standing fair for the post at least three weeks, had the mortification to be supplanted by Keyber. But, as the vacancy has been so supplied, I think I may fairly conclude, with Mr. Addison's Cato,

> *The post of honour is a private station . . .*

Theobald's comparatively philosophical account of his non-success was written, of course, after the appointment. The general opinion beforehand inclined to support Duck's chances (whatever its view of his deserts) but on October 29th the *St. James's Evening Post* reported a new contestant in the field: 'We hear that Mr. Cibber opposes Mr. Stephen Duck for the Place of Poet Laureate to His Majesty . . .' and this came at a time when the Thresher Poet was away in the country

---

[1] Matthew Concanen (1701–1749) a minor poet and pamphleteer who appeared in the *Dunciad* and survived to be attorney-general of Jamaica, which appears to give point to Dryden's remark, 'the corruption of a poet is the generation of a statesman.'

attending the death-bed of his wife, and so consequently unable to do any lobbying on his own behalf.

The new candidate came in for his share of ridicule, though it is doubtful if many people took his chances seriously. Pope wrote in the *Grub Street Journal* (November 12th):

> Shall royal praise be rimed by such a ribald,
> As fopling C . . . r or attorney T . . . d?
> Let's rather wait one year for better luck;
> One year may make a singing swan of Duck.
> Great G—! such servants since thou well canst lack,
> Oh! save the salary and drink the sack!

A whole chorus of disapprobation followed, especially from the disappointed contenders and their supporters.[1] But on November 19th the *Grub Street Journal* reported that Cibber had indeed been appointed —and added that it didn't believe this report. But it was true: the Duke of Grafton had not forgotten his friend.

As for Stephen Duck, he continued to enjoy her majesty's patronage and wrote poems progressively more conventional and less meritorious, including a specimen of a laureate Ode 'humbly inscribed to the Poet Laureate,' and various not conspicuously superior serious Odes for the Queen's birthday.[2] These, with his poem *On the Marriage of His Serene Highness The Prince of Orange*, and several others, show that he would have had little difficulty in being at least as bad a Laureate as Cibber. On the other hand, *The Thresher's Labour*, with its sober and realistic account of the life of a farm labourer, and parts of his other earlier poems, show what can be done by even an untutored poet, writing about what he knows. A somewhat similar experience was to befall Robert Bloomfield a lifetime later, though Bloomfield's success was more permanent, and his end less lamentable. Duck took Orders in 1746, became Rector of Byfleet in 1753, and in 1756 drowned himself.

Cibber, like so many of his fellow Laureates, took office just in time to begin work on an Ode. First he appeared at Court: 'On Thursday

---

[1] One of the few friendly notes was struck by Benjamin Victor:
> Let empty journals weekly rail;
> May all dull bards repine:
> If wit unequall'd shou'd prevail,
> The laurel's justly thine.

[2] The Queen was a patron of poets in her fashion; she had another volunteer laureate in Richard Savage, whom she pensioned with fifty pounds a year in exchange for an annual Ode. Cibber was vexed.

(Dec 4) Colley Cibber Esq., the famous Comedian and Comic Author, was at Court, and had the Honour to Kiss His Majesty's Hand (on his being appointed Poet Laureat in the Room of the Rev. Mr. Laurence Eusden, Deceased) and was graciously received.' (*Appleton's Weekly Journal*, Dec. 5). In due course the New Year Ode was performed, and whatever its effect on George I (who went to sleep if he had any sense) it was heartily derided by the public at large, despite one or two occasional beauties like this:

> Behold in ev'ry Face imperial Graces shine
> All native to the Race of George and Caroline;
> In each young Hero we admire
> The blooming virtues of his Sire;
> In each maturing Fair we find
> Maternal charms of softer kind.

The wits were at once in full cry and parodies, lampoons, epigrams and the like crowded all the papers.[1] Colley Cibber joined in, as he records in his autobiography, with a set of verses ridiculing himself in the *Whitehall Evening Post*, which he kept anonymous until *An Apology for the Life of Colley Cibber* came out in 1740. To general day-to-day satire he was indifferent, and the only antagonist he ever answered carefully and at any length was Pope.

At the time of his Laureate appointment Cibber was preparing to retire from active work in the theatre. His last play of importance, *The Provok'd Husband*, based on a piece left unfinished at his death by Vanbrugh, was staged with great success in 1728, and thereafter his increasingly rare theatrical excursions consisted of prologues or epilogues to other men's plays, with one or two musical trifles and the very unpraiseworthy *Papal Tyranny in the Reign of King John*,[2] which was nevertheless able to keep the stage ten nights with the real *King John* of Shakespeare playing under Garrick a couple of streets away. This was in 1745, however, and our concern is with the years following 1730.

---

[1] 'A Compliment to *Colley* must be a Rarity indeed!' as the Laureate remarked later, in *The Egotist, or* Colley *upon* Cibber (1743).

[2] Cibber's other excursion into making Shakespeare acceptable to a civilized age was *The Tragical History of Richard III* (1700), in which is buried perhaps the only line of Cibber's that anyone now remembers:

> Catesby: My Liege, the Duke of *Buckingham* is taken.
> Gloster: Off with his Head—so much for *Buckingham*.

The line would have commended itself to Dryden.

Cibber's only formidable antagonist was, and had always been, Pope; for a few quips by Fielding in *Tom Thumb* seem on the whole not to have upset the Laureate, and although Fielding made a number of satirical references to Cibber elsewhere, especially in the opening of *Joseph Andrews*, Cibber took no sustained public exception. With Pope, however, the case was otherwise.

Their quarrel began with the luckless staging of *Three Hours after Marriage*, as above mentioned, in 1717. After this there was a reconciliation of a sort: Cibber had subscribed to Pope's *Homer*, and Pope soon after their green-room scuffle sent along four guineas for seats for *The Non-Juror*. Thereafter, Pope slipped a sly gibe at Cibber into his works from time to time: for example, not long after seeing the *Non-Juror* he put out his satirical pamphlet, *The Plot Discovered or a Clue to the Comedy of the Non-Juror*, which, despite some hard things, Cibber ignored. A few years later Pope renewed the attack, this time with several digs at Cibber in *The Art of Sinking in Poetry* and the first version of the *Dunciad* (1728), and again in 1735 in the *Epistle to Dr. Arbuthnot*. There were other pin-pricks, none of them very sharp, but cumulatively effective. Cibber, preparing his autobiography, decided to reply.

An Apology for the Life of Colley Cibber appeared in 1740, and was a great success, as it deserved to be. This lively and eccentric book engages the reader's sympathy for Cibber from the start, and the old actor-manager draws an excellent likeness of himself, warts and all: he displays his failings as candidly as his merits, and at the same time gives a remarkable picture of the stage through forty crowded years.

He discusses Pope at some length, affirms that he has no personal quarrel with the satirist, and indeed that he greatly admires his works; even the attacks on himself can be explained, he says, by the fact that he is a prominent public figure—a much more interesting object for satire than some obscure scribbler or other—and after all Mr. Pope wants his works to circulate. 'My face and name are . . . known, (and) right or wrong, a lick at the laureate will always be a sure bait . . . to catch him little readers.' Pope's reply was to insert new references to Cibber in the *New Dunciad* of 1742 and Cibber sat down to answer in earnest. He wrote his celebrated pamphlet, *A Letter From Mr. Cibber to Mr. Pope, Inquiring into the Motives that Might Induce Him in His Satyrical Works, to be so Frequently Fond of Mr. Cibber's Name.* (1742).

This long title led into a lengthy but still good-humoured expostulation which made a great noise in the Town, and penetrated with loud rumbles to Bath, Tunbridge etc. Indeed, it arrived in Tunbridge to find Mr. Cibber already in residence, as Benjamin Victor[1] records: 'Cibber's *Letter to Pope* was brought down there (to Tunbridge) by a gentleman of my acquaintance, who favoured me with the reading it that afternoon—in the evening of that day, going on the walks, to return the letter to my friend, I had the pleasure of finding him with the author of it—the gay blooming COLLEY, just arrived from London! As unexpected as welcome! well, we passed that night happily together. . . .'

Pope apparently passed his nights with the pamphlet less happily. When he first heard of it, he was casual enough: 'God knows when I shall find time to read it,' he wrote to Lord Orrery; but Joseph Richardson (Johnson records) was present when he did find time:

'I have heard Mr. Richardson relate, that he attended his father, the painter, on a visit, when one of Cibber's pamphlets came into the hands of Pope, who said, 'these things are my diversion.' They sat by him while he perused it, and saw his features writhing with anguish; and young Richardson said to his father, when they returned, that he hoped to be preserved from such diversion as had been that day the lot of Pope.' The satire in this first letter, and in two others which followed in 1743 and 1744 is inherently so reasonable that a fair answer could not easily be written—as Cibber says, 'Even the Malicious, though they may like the Libel, don't always believe it.' The same letter (the first) incidentally contains an amusing echo of a celebrated trifle of Pope's, the little epigram

> *I am his highness's dog at Kew;*
> *Pray tell me, sir, whose dog are you?*

when Cibber asks, 'And so, if I am the King's Fool, now, sir, whose Fool are you?'

And so we come to a strange irony: Cibber, by a reasoned tone throughout and by advancing sound arguments and fair criticisms, was left clearly the victor; perhaps the only antagonist who could say the

[1] Benjamin Victor (1703–1778) was Deputy Manager to Thomas Sheridan at the Smock Alley Theatre, in Dublin. He wrote 'Birthday Odes' for the Court in Dublin, and when the Duke of Dorset resigned the Lord Lieutenancy in 1755 he got Victor's name put on the Viceregal establishment as 'Poet Laureate of Ireland.' Victor wrote (and, which is worse, published) nineteen Odes for the King's or the Queen's birthdays. He was much distressed at one stage when it seemed likely that Cibber's nominee, the bricklayer poet Jones, might be appointed Laureate in Ireland; but the danger passed and so did Jones, as we shall see. For Cibber the Irish Laureate—thinking him, no doubt, an 'elder brother in the Muse'—had always a high regard. He calls him the 'poetical king of Great Britain' (which he wasn't) and 'an able newsmonger' (which he was).

same after twenty years of Pope's emnity. But Pope, who came off entirely second best, is supposed by posterity to have quite destroyed the luckless Cibber; and posterity supposes this, because it reads the *Dunciad*; and, generally speaking, has never even heard of the *Apology*, and the *Letters to Mr. Pope*.

In 1744, with Warburton's assistance, Pope brought out the final text of the *Dunciad*, in which he replaced Theobald, the original 'hero,' by Cibber—carelessly omitting to alter passages which suited Theobald very well, and had no proper application to Cibber. It scarcely mattered: the most brilliant of eighteenth century satires went on its way, carrying with it a cardboard puppet loaded with ridicule whom readers for the next two centuries were, in the main, perfectly content to accept for Cibber.

As for Cibber himself, even now he continued to stand outside the battle. One of his supporters showed him a new poem attacking Pope, and Cibber advised him to persuade the writer not to publish it as it might give undue distress to a sick man;[1] and in fact a week or two later Pope died. Cibber had the last word he had promised Pope he intended to enjoy, and sent an Epitaph to *The Gentleman's Magazine*.

For thirteen years more Cibber produced his New Year and Birthday Odes—on one occasion after seeking Johnson's opinion. Johnson 'made some correction, to which he was not very willing to submit.' Towards the end Cibber recommended the bricklayer-poet Henry Jones as his successor in a letter to the Duke of Grafton, but the Laureateship was not for Jones and in due course he was run over by a cart in St. Martin's Lane.

Cibber himself died,[2] apparently of old age, on December 11th, 1757, and was buried in Grosvenor Chapel, South Audley Street—a wholly enchanting little church in which to be buried.

---

[1] The go-between here was Benjamin Victor, who replied 'Mr. *Pope* was seen in London, on Saturday last, in Mr. *Cheseldon's* chariot, and though in a bad state of health, it is the general opinion, he will outlive the summer.' The general opinion was wrong.

[2] A discussion of Cibber's remarkable family would be irrelevant here, but it may be well to add that the well known 'Lives of the Poets' usually cited as by Cibber are by Theophilus Cibber, the old man's son—or so the title page affirms. In actual fact, the best part of the work was written by Robert Shiels, at a time (Johnson says) when T. Cibber was in prison for debt. For those who enjoy these excursions into dead controversy, it may be added that *The Monthly Review* for May, 1792, says the opposite; and Boswell very impartially prints both versions.

8

William Whitehead

IT is customary to lament that Thomas Gray declined the Laureate-ship left vacant by Cibber's death. 'Here at last,' runs the argument, 'was the first chance since Dryden of the office falling to a great poet.' Something like this may have been in the Duke of Devonshire's mind when, as Lord Chamberlain, he caused the offer to be conveyed to Gray, for he proposed that the New Year and Birthday odes should no longer be an obligation on the Laureate. But Gray refused, and I think rightly; for by temperament he was quite unsuited to the office.

The incident, however, is worth telling in some detail for the light it throws on the characters of those concerned. 'The best of all Johns,' as Gray called him,—Lord John Cavendish—had been the poet's friend for a number of years and it was he, perhaps, who prevailed upon his elder brother the Duke to offer the Laureateship to Gray. The offer itself was made through William Mason, formerly Lord John's tutor, and himself an intimate friend of Gray. It was an interesting situation, for Mason was also a poet, the author of works more admired than admirable. But the Duke of Devonshire's patronage of Mason took the form of securing for him an appointment as one of the King's Chaplains.

Gray's letter of refusal is well known, but I reproduce it again for the characteristic comments it contains on previous Laureates. It is dated December 19th, 1757.

Dear Mason,

Though I very well know the bland emollient saponaceous qualities both of sack and silver, yet if any great man would say to me, 'I make you rat-catcher to his Majesty, with a salary of £300 a year and two butts of the best Malaga; and though it has been usual to catch a mouse or two, for form's sake, in public once a year, yet to you, sir, we shall not stand upon these things,' I cannot say I should jump at it; nay, if they would drop the very name of the office, and call me Sinecure to the King's Majesty, I should still feel a little awkward, and think everybody I saw smelt a rat about me; but I do not pretend to blame anyone else that has not the same sensations; for my part I would rather be serjeant trumpeter or pinmaker to the palace. Nevertheless I interest myself a little in the history of it, and rather wish

somebody may accept it that will retrieve the credit of the thing, if it be
retrievable, or ever had any credit. Rowe was, I think, the last man of
character that had it. As to Settle, whom you mention, he belonged to my
lord mayor, not to the king. Eusden was a person of great hopes in his
youth, though at last he turned out a drunken parson. Dryden was as dis-
graceful to the office, from his character, as the poorest scribbler could have
been, from his verses. The office itself has always humbled the professor
hitherto (even in an age when kings were somebody), if he were a poor
writer by making him more conspicuous, and if he were a good one by
setting him at war with the little fry of his own profession, for there are
poets little enough to envy even a poet-laureat . . .

(The remainder of the letter concerns other matters).

It was another Cambridge man, and another friend of Mason's, to
whom the laurel now fell. This was William Whitehead, a native of the
university city, where his father had been a baker, though perhaps not
a wholly prosperous one. The elder Whitehead's trouble seems to have
been an inclination to neglect the bakery for frivolous and non-
productive pursuits: 'he spent his time chiefly in ornamenting, rather
than cultivating a few acres of land near Grantchester, which still goes
by the name of Whitehead's Folly.' So Anderson wrote in 1793, but
since then so many other follies have passed over Cambridge that this
one has been obliterated.

The future Laureate was born in February, 1715, and received his
early education at a 'common school' in Cambridge, removing thence
to Winchester College when he was fourteen. He was a quiet, studious
boy with some talent for acting; he played a female part in the College
production of Terence's *Andria*, and in Addison's *Cato* he played
Marcia with 'great applause.' He was so fond of poetry that he usually
showed up a great deal more than the lesson required, but his verses
were always in English, which perhaps hindered him in learning Latin
and Greek. It seems, however that the master thought the verses so
good that he excused the writer for employing the wrong language.
These excellent verses have not survived, and neither has the next
success of Whitehead's muse, although it brought him a guinea.

In 1733 the Earl of Peterborough took Pope along to inspect the
College, and while there asked the poet to propose a subject for the
boys to compose verses upon: Pope suggested 'Peterborough' and the
Earl bestowed ten guineas to be competed for. No doubt those of the
boys who had heard of this aged warrior were able to say something
of the splendid military prowess he had displayed thirty years or so
before most of them were born; and the rest perhaps took refuge in

elaborate Personification, which the 18th century so well knew how to employ to disguise poverty of thought or invention.

Six single guineas were given in prizes, one of them to Whitehead, and the remaining four were laid out on a set of Pine's *Horace* for the library. One other result of this encounter with Pope was that young Whitehead set to work to translate the first book of the *Essay on Man* into Latin; perhaps the only time when he waived his habit of always composing in the vulgar tongue. The Latin version remained unpublished.

'His school friendships were usually contracted either with noblemen or gentlemen of large fortunes,' remarks Anderson,[1] adding that this was not snobbery but merely an indication that Whitehead, like all right-thinking persons, needs must love the highest when he saw it. Unluckily, these important acquaintances availed him nothing when he applied to go on from Winchester to New College: 'through the force of superior interest' he was prevented from getting in to the Oxford college, and he returned home sadly to Cambridge.

His father had died soon after the boy went to Winchester, and this now enabled him to get into Clare Hall as a sizar, for a few places were reserved for the orphan sons of Cambridge citizens. This was in 1735, and the following year gave him occasion for a poem on the marriage of the Prince of Wales, which was duly followed by one celebrating the birth of a young prince in 1738; these poems were included in the collection issued at Cambridge. The prince survived to become George III.

Whitehead now settled down at the University, and in 1742 he became a Fellow of Clare Hall. He began to make a small but respectable reputation as a poet as his first considerable poem, *The Danger of Writing Verse* (1741) reached a wider circle than his immediate friends. It can still be read with interest, if not pleasure, by anyone with time to spend on small poetry; here are a few specimen lines:

> Say, can the bard attempt what's truly great,
> Who pants in secret for his future fate?
> Him serious toils and humbler arts engage,
> To make youth easy, and provide for age;
> While lost in silence hangs his useless lyre,
> And tho' from heav'n it came, fast dies the sacred fire.[2]

[1] Robert Anderson, *The Poets of Great Britain* (1793).
[2] The point is made more effectively by Johnson in his *Life of Collins*: 'A man doubtful of his dinner, or trembling at a creditor, is not much disposed to abstracted meditation, or remote inquiries.'

It now began to be necessary for Whitehead to think of his own future fate, even at the risk of losing the sacred fire. He could not remain indefinitely a Fellow of Clare Hall, with no other employment; moreover, to remain a Fellow at all he must take Orders, and this he was thinking of doing when he received an offer to become tutor to the son of the Earl of Jersey. This lad, Viscount Villiers, was then ten years old, and for companion to him another lad named Stephens was added to the household. Villiers grew up to become a prominent 'Maccaronie' and Stephens became a general; in the meantime their education gave Whitehead a pleasant job in an Earl's household and left him with time to cultivate the Muses as well as the nobility. He put out various small poems, and in February, 1750, his play *The Roman Father* appeared at Drury Lane. This tragedy was based on the *Horace* of Corneille and was so far successful that it was made the subject of a comprehensive *Comparison Between the* Horace *of Corneille and the* Roman Father *of Mr. Whitehead*, in which after some fifty tedious pages Whitehead is allowed the victory. Meanwhile Whitehead was turning from the couplet as popularised by Pope and debased by his imitators, to Milton as a model. *An Hymn to the Nymph of Bristol Spring* (1751) is quite competent blank verse of the pedestrian sort:

> *O for a* Shakespeare's *pencil, while I trace*
> *In Nature's breathing paint, the dreary waste*
> *Of* Buxton, *dropping with incessant rains*
> *Cold, and ungenial; or its sweet reverse*
> *Enchanting* Matlock, *from whose rocks like thine*
> *Romantic foliage hangs, and rills descend*
> *And Echoes murmur.* Derwent, *as he pours*
> *His oft obstructed stream down rough cascades*
> *And broken precipices, views with awe,*
> *With rapture, the fair scene his waters form.*

I am tempted to continue this tour of the 18th century spas, Cheltenham, Scarborough, Tunbridge and the rest, but as Whitehead remarks a little later, '*Avonia* frowns! and justly may'st thou frown, O Goddess, on the Bard, th' injurious Bard . . . who idly roves.'

In 1754 Whitehead's second successful tragedy, *Creusa* was acted at Drury Lane 'with applause.' This play is based on the *Ion* of Euripides; it has the rather frigid competence of the lesser tragedies of its time—a time which came right at the end of a prolific period in the drama and just as the taste for verse tragedy of this kind was failing.

'I have seen *Creusa*,' Horace Walpole wrote to John Chute, 'and more than agree with you: it is the only new tragedy that I ever saw and really liked. The plot is most interesting, and though so complicated, quite clear and natural. The circumstance of so much distress being brought on by characters, every one good, yet acting consistently with their principles towards the misfortunes of the drama, is quite new and pleasing. Nothing offended me but that lisping Miss Haughton, whose every speech is inarticulately oracular.'

Writing a lifetime later, Thomas Campbell said *Creusa* was then 'seldom read, and never acted' but that it was 'by no means destitute of dramatic feeling and conception . . . with bold and sometimes interesting alterations (to the *Ion*).'

Almost immediately after its initial success Whitehead set off for the Continent with his pupils. He had now added Viscount Nuneham to his train and for two years he led his charges in a leisurely progression through Flanders, Germany, Austria, Italy, Switzerland and Holland, bringing them safely back, together with material for a book of *Elegies*, in the autumn of 1756. During his absence, by Lady Jersey's influence, he had been appointed Secretary and Registrar of the Order of the Bath. *Elegies, with an Ode to the Tiber, written abroad*[1] appeared early in 1757. It contains four pieces, one each addressed to his two Viscounts (Nuneham he calls 'noble Youth,' the other 'My Villiers') one written at a Convent and addressed to nobody in particular, and the Tiber ode. While this small quarto (price one shilling) was circulating, Cibber died.

Whitehead's qualifications as a poet were at least as respectable as those of Mason and somewhat bulkier than those of Gray. Among his contemporaries there were better poets, but there were also worse. The Duke of Devonshire seems to have spent little energy after the failure of his overture to Gray, in seeking out a successor to Cibber, probably because the aged George II was not the man to think this small office important. The influence of Jersey (with that of Harcourt added, perhaps) was quite sufficient to secure the place for Whitehead, and in a very short time after Cibber departed the new laureate was at work. His first Ode was for the King's fifty-fifth birthday, for the waiving of such things was a concession offered only to Gray. Mason, indeed, recommended that Whitehead farm the work out to indigent

[1] 'He published among them,' say the authors of *The Lives of the Laureates*, 'some lines to a sick friend, the perusal of which could by no means have accelerated his convalescence.' As I cannot identify these lines in the copy that lies before me I cannot discuss the truth of this criticism.

versifiers, 'and reserve his own pen for certain great occasions that might occur, such as a Peace or a Marriage . . .', but this Whitehead preferred not to do; his Odes were all his own, and so much the worse for that, according to Johnson, one of the few critics to prefer Cibber's work to Whitehead's: 'Cibber's familiar style was better than that which Whitehead has assumed. *Grand* nonsense is insupportable.'

Johnson was speaking (the passage is in Boswell) in 1763. The New Year Ode for that date contains 'grand nonsense' of this nature:

> At length th' imperious lord of war
> Yields to the fates their ebon car,
>   And frowning quits his toil;
> Dash'd from his hand, the bleeding spear
> Now deigns a happier form to wear,
>   And peaceful turns the soil.
> Th' insatiate furies of the train,
> Revenge, and Hate, and fell Disdain,
>   With heart of steel, and eyes of fire,
> Who stain the sword which honour draws,
> Who sully virtue's sacred cause,
>   To Stygian depth retire.

In 1757 the Laureateship was nearly a hundred years old and some of the balance was shifting; it was no longer an appointment in which the holder was expected to take up his pen against the other side— Whig or Tory as the case might be—in his sovereign's defence and for the support of Government. If the provision of two odes a year was still an obligation, it was at least not an irksome one; that such odes were indifferent verse was taken now for granted; Walpole once re-remarked of a poem of Whitehead's, that it contained 'not more poetry than is necessary for a Laureate.' There was not much unpleasant publicity, and the office could be a rather stagnant but not unattractive backwater for an unambitious poet to lie in undisturbed. Faction still fought battles in Grub Street, but there was no need for the Laureate to be involved unless by his own choice. Whitehead, a conscientious laureate, if not a great one, contented himself for the next twenty-eight years in writing the necessary odes as well as he knew how, and in willingly giving offence to no one.

Accordingly, no one took offence, very much, except Charles Churchill, who was the type of professional satirist who chooses a subject for its possibilities, regardless of whether or not any injury has been given. Whitehead intended no harm to Churchill, but Churchill thought the Laureate a suitable recipient now and again for a blow from the cudgel. Probably his chief offence was in not being Paul Whitehead, for Paul—one of the most scurrilous of contemporary satirists— was very acceptable to Churchill (and to hardly anybody else).

Churchill—right or wrong—was always readable, and his attacks on Whitehead contain some pretty strokes which Whitehead amiably admits:

> . . . *Churchill strings,*
> *Into some motley form his damn'd good things,*

he writes, and he comes out of the affair with credit, just as Cibber by his manly good humour gets the better of the far cleverer Pope.

Whitehead himself would have agreed that such of those 'damn'd good things' as referred to himself—or specimens of them—ought not to be left out of an account of the Laureateship, especially as at the end of his life Whitehead could write that he had

> *liv'd to see*
> *Churchill forgot, an empty shade like me.*[1]

References to Whitehead are scattered all through Churchill's vigorous poems. In *The Prophecy of Famine* (1763) he calls the Laureate's tone 'dull and unvaried' (which it wasn't) and in *Independence* (1764) he joins Mason's name with Whitehead's, calls them 'little, piddling Witlings,' remarks that they are given to self-admiration and 'drawl out measur'd prose, which They call verse.' The most sustained attack, however, is in the book three of *The Ghost* (1762–63)—the poem, incidentally in which Johnson receives a knock or two.

> *Come, METHOD, come in all thy pride*
> *DULLNESS and WHITEHEAD by thy side,*
> *DULLNESS and METHOD still are one,*
> *And WHITEHEAD is their darling Son . . .*

(Here follows a passage praising the infamous Paul Whitehead, which we can afford to miss)

> . . . *HE, who in the Laureat chair,*
> *By Grace, not Merit planted there,*
> *In awkward pomp is seen to sit,*
> *And by his Patent proves his Wit;*

---

[1] But Churchill is not quite forgotten: my friend Mr. Edmund Blunden keeps an eye on the preservation of his fame.

> *For favours of the Great, we know,*
> *Can Wit as well as rank bestow,*
> *And they who, without one pretension,*
> *Can get for Fools a place or pension,*
> *Must able be suppos'd, of course*
> *(If reason is allow'd due force)*
> *To give such qualities and grace,*
> *As may equip them for the place.*
>
> *But HE—who measures, as he goes,*
> *A mongrel kind of tinkling prose,*
> *And is too frugal to dispense,*
> *At once both Poetry and Sense,*
> *Who, from amidst his slumb'ring guards,*
> *Deals out a Charge to Subject Bards,*
> *Where Couplets after Couplets creep*
> *Propitious to the reign of sleep,*
> *Yet ev'ry word imprints an awe,*
> *And all his dictates pass for law . . .*

This passage sufficiently demonstrates how far the satire of the mid-eighteenth century falls below that of Dryden. Shadwell had cause to be disturbed, when Dryden assailed him; Whitehead was not so seriously injured by Churchill's shafts. The joke about dullness after nearly a century was wearing thin. Austin and Ralph call these sarcasms 'too savage,' but consider the criticism juster than that directed at Shadwell by Dryden and at Cibber by Pope. I confess to an opposite opinion: for example, Churchill accuses Whitehead of being dull and monotonous, but in fact he is the reverse. Often his lines are lively enough to call Prior to mind, and no poet who can be compared with Prior can be called dull.

The 'charge to subject bards' mentioned is a capital example of Whitehead's lighter manner. Churchill took it too seriously, perhaps because a line or two formed a cap he found would fit himself; but to suggest that Whitehead was pompously giving advice, from his exalted position as Laureate, to his less favoured brethren is absurd. This poem—*A Charge to The Poets* (1762)—is a half-humorous, half-serious examination of the poet's job and status, and refers back to *The Danger of Writing Verse*, an allied poem published over twenty years earlier (when Charles Churchill was ten years old). The theme appealed to Whitehead, and a variant of it appears again in his posthumous *Pathetic Apology for All Laureats, Past, Present, and to Come* which first appeared in Mason's *Memoir* of Whitehead.

These good humoured pieces need have provoked nobody; and that they provoked Churchill (the *Charge*, anyway) is to my mind merely evidence that Churchill was looking for somebody to fight. No-one can possess a talent like his without wanting to exercise it, and the fact that his attacks on Whitehead are not in his best manner suggests to me that they are 'manufactured' rather than the result of a strongly felt resentment.

Although Whitehead betrayed no great dismay at Churchill's attacks they had some effect on his fortunes, for about this time Garrick refused a tragedy. The tragedy was in fact never produced, and never printed; it remains nameless—unless, indeed, it was the *Oedipus* completed and published by Mason after Whitehead's death. Garrick was especially sensitive to Churchill's satire, although it had not fallen upon himself; the influence of *The Rosciad* was enormous, and Garrick had no desire to provoke an antagonist so powerful. That, at least, is the only explanation that has ever been offered for the fate of the tragedy, and it is supported by the fact that Whitehead's next play, a farce, *The Trip to Scotland* was acted without his name as author. This was in 1770, and in 1776 Whitehead again put out a work anonymously—*Variety, a Tale for Married People. The Goat's Beard*, (1777) his last separate publication, provoked a reply, *The Asses Ears* which is perhaps the feeblest attack ever launched at a Laureate. It is wholly contemptible and contains not a single line worth a second glance; indeed one wonders why it was written and who read it.

Whitehead also had his supporters, including Horace Walpole's acquaintance, the amiable Richard Owen Cambridge. The author of *The Scribleriad* might be thought a competent judge; at all events, in his *Epistle to Mr. Whitehead on his being made Poet Laureat* he begins without unnecessary preamble:

> *'Tis so—tho' we're surpriz'd to hear it:*
> *The laurel is bestow'd on merit.*

Most of the poem, however, somewhat tactlessly discusses the new laureate's funeral and ends with an exhortation to teach his fellow poets the job before he goes, no doubt in order to secure a competent succession:

> *O! teach us, ere you change the scene*
> *To Stygian banks from Hippocrene,*
> *How free-born bards should strike the strings,*
> *And how a Briton write to kings.*

Whitehead and Cambridge were good friends and addressed verses to one another; both also wrote poems under the title *The Danger of Writing Verse* without in the least abating their own practice of the art.

Whitehead had some status at Drury Lane, apart from the success of his plays produced there, for Garrick employed him as a reader of plays, especially in cases where he wanted another opinion to supplement his own. The system was much resented by playrights, who sometimes thought Whitehead's views of no great value; among these malcontents was Goldsmith.

Late in 1767 Goldsmith went along to Garrick with his comedy *The Good Natur'd Man* in his hand, but the great actor suggested all sorts of modifications before he would put the play on. Goldsmith would not alter. Garrick would not take the play unaltered. There was discussion, argument, many letters were written; Goldsmith needed the money, as always, and at last he made concessions. But by this time Garrick had thought of further objections. He suggested calling in Whitehead as 'arbitrator.'

John Forster, who tells the story, seems to sympathise with Goldsmith, although I cannot see why the Doctor should have objected to the suggestion. After all, he had never previously written a play, and Whitehead was the successful author of two or three. Anyhow, as Forster says, 'a dispute of so much vehemence and anger ensued, that the services of Burke as well as Reynolds were needed to moderate the disputants. Of all the manager's slights of the poet, this was forgotten last. . . .' Personally I think the slighted party was the Laureate; we are not told that he was allowed to have any friends in the matter, and to be involved in a dispute with Burke 'as well as Reynolds' can have been no light matter.

Another formidable antagonist was Gibbon who attacked the birthday Ode for 1758 (Whitehead's first official task) for inaccuracy. With more optimism than accuracy the Laureate traces the king's lineage back to one Othbert or Ottoberto, who 'about the year 993' was engaged in certain enterprises in Northern Italy from whence he proceeded into Germany and founded George's royal line—according to Whitehead. Not so, remarked Gibbon, placing the ancient prince in Tuscany and attributing to him somewhat different enterprises. Referring to the poem as 'one of the annual odes which still adorn or disgrace the birthdays of our British Kings,' the historian remarks that 'the poet may deviate from the truth of history, but every deviation ought to be compensated by the superior beauties of fancy and fiction.'

In 1774 Whitehead put out his collected works in two volumes, with a refreshingly short and characteristically modest preface:

> Most of the pieces contained in these volumes have already had their fate with the public; and would probably never have been collected in the manner in which they now appear, if the author had not imagined that his character as Laureate obliged him in some measure to revise and correct them. If in their present state they have any degree of real merit belonging to them, they will support themselves. If they are so unfortunate as to want it, they will naturally sink into the oblivion they deserve.

This, despite obvious differences, always reminds me of the brief and memorable preface Coventry Patmore wrote for the collected edition of his poems. To the 1774 edition Mason, after Whitehead's death, added a third volume to which he prefixed his *Memoir*; this appeared in 1788.

Whitehead himself did little after the collected edition appeared; he sent out *Variety* in 1776 and *The Goat's Beard* in 1777, both anonymously and for the rest contended himsef with punctiliously providing his two Odes a year, which were duly printed in successive *Annual Registers*.

He lived in Charles Street, Grosvenor Square, quietly enjoying his friendships with the great, until April 14th, 1785, when as he asked his servant to give him his arm he suddenly ceased to breathe. His death was as unexpected, and as simple as that. He was buried in the same church—South Audley Street Chapel—as Cibber, and there presumably (for there is nothing to mark their graves) they both still lie.

Whitehead, in his long series of official Odes, did his best to teach how a Briton should write to kings. His tone is neither servile nor flattering; he avoids domestic politics and speaks rather of world affairs, and Britain's place in them. The quarter century of his term of office included Wolfe's victory and death at Quebec, the war with America (which admittedly gave little scope for an official British poet),[1] and such things as a king's funeral, his successor's Coronation, and a royal wedding. Whitehead was no Drayton, no Campbell; and such an event as the victory at Quebec, which might have produced

---

[1] Early in the war there was a sort of victory at Bunker's Hill (June 17th) and it was perhaps to this that Walpole referred in a letter to Lady Ossory (August 3rd): '. . . [at Nuneham I found] Mr. Whitehead, the Laureate, too, who, I doubt, will be a little puzzled, if he has no better a victory than the last against Caesar's next birthday. There was a little too much of the *vertere funeribus triumphos* for a complimentary ode in the last action.' Whitehead apparently thought so, too; his Birthday Ode for 1775 keeps well away from the subject of America.

from those poets another *Agincourt*, or another *Battle of the Baltic*, did
no more than inspire such lines as these:

> *Thee, Glory, thee through climes unknown*
>   *Th' adventurous chief with zeal pursues;*
> *And Fame brings back from every zone*
>   *Fresh subjects for the British Muse.*
> *Tremendous as the ill-omen'd bird*
> *To frighted France, thy voice was heard*
>   *From Minden's echoing towers.*
> *O'er Biscay's roar thy voice prevail'd,*
> *And at thy word the rocks we scal'd*
>   *And Canada is ours.*

This is no way to report bloody battles, and no one will say they had
rather have written that poem than taken Quebec; but it must be remembered that *for its purpose within a convention* such verse was suitable.
A little later in the same Ode (for 1761) George III makes his first
appearance. To my way of thinking the note here is at once incredulous
and despairing, but no doubt in this I am at fault:

> *—And who is he, of regal mien,*
>   *Reclin'd on Albion's golden fleece,*
> *Whose polish'd brow, and eye serene*
>   *Proclaim him elder-born of Peace?*
> *Another GEORGE! . . .*

George II's 'blooming Heir,' as Whitehead calls him later.)
It is easy enough to enjoy a joke at the expense of a laureate ode, but
in the main Whitehead did very well. There is dignity, for example, in
the beginning of the New Year Ode for 1760:

> *Again the sun's revolving sphere*
> *Wakes into life th' impatient year,*
>   *The white-wing'd minutes haste:*
> *And, spite of Fortune's fickle wheel,*
> *Th' eternal Fates have fix'd their seal,*
>   *Upon the glories of the past.*
> *Suspended high in memory's fane,*
>   *Beyond even Envy's soaring rage,*
> *The deeds survive, to breathe again,*
>   *In faithful History's future page.*
> *When distant times shall wond'ring read*
>   *Of Albion's strength, of battles won,*
> *Of faith restor'd, of nations freed . . .*

Whitehead was the first Laureate to 'speak for England' and not for a court faction, a political party, only. If his voice was poetically undistinguished, this was not his fault. He valued and respected his office, and discharged it to the best of his powers.

9

Thomas Warton

WHITEHEAD'S death was 'sudden and without a groan,' Mason tells us—adding that he left a Birthday Ode unfinished. The King's Birthday was to be celebrated on June 4th, so once again a new Laureate, whoever he might be, would have to set to work at once to justify his appointment.

There was little delay in making it, and on April 26th the name of Thomas Warton was announced. This formidable man of letters had written a number of verses on royal occasions, and although we do not know much about the secret history of this appointment (we don't, for example, hear of many unsuccessful applicants)[1] it is apparent that Warton was thought a safe man. Writing to Bishop Percy a few weeks later, Dr. Michael Lort said, 'T. Warton was made Poet Laureate, as some say, at the King's own motion; others say Sir Joshua Reynolds mentioned him to the Lord Chamberlain.'

It would have been reasonable, certainly, for Reynolds to have lent his aid, for he had been mightily pleased with the verses Warton had written in praise of his work at New College; so pleased, indeed, that he asked for the general term 'artist' to be removed and his own name inserted, for—as he wrote to Warton at the time (May, 1782), 'It is not much to say that your verses are by far the best that ever my name was concerned in. I am sorry therefore my name was not hitched in, in the body of the poem. If the title page should be lost, it will appear to be addressed to Mr. Jervais.' Accordingly Warton took steps

---

[1] Except the excellent John O'Keeffe, who tells us in his *Recollections* (1826), 'On the demise of Whitehead, I had an interview with Lord Salisbury (then Lord Chamberlain), in Arlington-Street, and asked him to make me poet-laureate. With much complacency he told me, he had not the smallest objection; but that he had previously given his promise to another. This was the learned Dr. Warton. So I put in no more claims for the Daphne wreath. Mr. Pye deservedly succeeded Warton; and my son's school-fellow at Westminster, Robert Southey, is now adorned by, and adorns the laurel.' Lord Salisbury had some reason for complacency, if he reflected on the respective merits of John O'Keeffe and Thomas Warton. O'Keeffe's *Recollections* are full of delightful things, but like Cibber and Richard Cumberland in his own time (not to come nearer than that) he writes better autobiography than poetry.

to ensure, in later editions, that no one could mistake for whom the praise was intended, and this he was the more easily able to do because to insert the word Reynolds in the appropriate place did not affect the rhythm. Professor Broadus suggests that Warton might have enlisted Horace Walpole's help, but I think this less likely, as Walpole's friend and cousin the Earl of Hertford had ceased to be Lord Chamberlain in 1783. Although there is no direct evidence that I know of to indicate what Warton's intentions were, I am inclined to think the offer reached him from without, unsought.

For Thomas Warton was not a particularly ambitious man; nor was he a man particularly in need of preferment. He was quite happy in his life at Oxford, where he was the typical Don of his period—fond of food, wine, conversation, leisure, and perfectly willing, if pressed, to give an occasional lecture.

This had been his life for some forty years, and the Laureateship could bring little accession of dignity or wealth; he would think it a pleasant distinction unsought, but one hardly worth actively seeking.

Thomas Warton was the second son of the Rev. Thomas Warton, Vicar of Basingstoke, and master of the ancient grammar school in that town. At Basingstoke, in 1728, Thomas was born, and there he was brought up and educated mainly by his father, until at sixteen he was admitted to Trinity College, Oxford. His elder brother, Joseph, went to Winchester College, and subsequently became Headmaster.

Young Tom took early to poetry and at the age of nine sent to his sister 'the first production of my little Muse,' a translation from Martial:

ON LEANDER'S SWIMMING OVER THE HELLESPONT TO HERO

When bold Leander sought his distant Fair,
(Nor could the sea a braver burthen bear)
Thus to the swelling wave he spoke his woe,
Drown me on my return—but spare me, as I go.

At eleven, we learn from his biographer, Richard Mant, in 'the excessive cold winter of 1739–40 . . . he would quit the family fireside, and retire to his chamber, and there apply himself assiduously to his books, not as a task, but an amusement.' It was the beginning of a life spent almost wholly in the company of books, most of them open, and three or four of them simultaneously in process of being read. Warton was to stand with Southey as the best-read of the Laureates, and indeed between them they must have read practically everything ever written; or so it would seem to the ordinary mortal.

Old Thomas Warton, although he 'had the character of a very honest, ingenious, and good-natur'd man,' was not particularly wealthy. He had formerly (1718–1728) been Professor of Poetry at Oxford, where in 1719 he had very boldly preached 'a Jacobite sermon,' and had triumphed in the subsequent proceedings against him. The worst that came out of this incident was the enmity of Nicholas Amhurst, who attacked him here and there in print and called him 'squinting Tom of Maudlin.' His Jacobite leanings led him to write some verses addressed to 'James III,' Thomas Hearne tells us, and a satire on George I called *The Turnip Hoer*, occasioned by the King's suggestion that St. James's Park should be turned into a turnip field. These verses have not survived, and were apparently never printed.

The Poetry Professor was not much inclined to profess his own poetry—after his death his papers were found to include enough original verse to fill a fair-size volume, but his sons had never seen or heard a line of it. The old man died in 1746 leaving no money and a quantity of debts. It was in order to discharge these that Joseph Warton proceeded to print his father's poems by subscription, and about the same time he wrote to his brother at Oxford: 'Do not doubt of being able to get some money this winter; if ever I have a groat, you may depend upon having twopence.' The brothers were always firm friends, and indeed were very similar in temperament, and in the course their lives took.

Old Thomas Warton's book is so rare, and his fame so small, that I am tempted to leave young Thomas at Oxford awaiting twopence while I copy a few of his father's verses; for although it cannot have influenced the brothers much, since they were writing verse long before they ever saw it, this work of their father's is the product of a mind remarkably similar to those of his sons.

ASTROPHIL TO HIS SON, AGED SEVEN MONTHS

> *O Thou! with whom I fondly share*
> *My faithful* Stella's *Love, and Care,*
> *To thee 'tis giv'n to tumble o'er*
> *Thy absent Sire's poetic Store,*
> *(With eager hands these Lines to seize*
> *And tear, or lose 'em, as you please,)*
> *Thou too from Pedantry art free,*
> *And I can safely sing to thee.*

> *What tho' thy Age no Skill can boast,*
> *In one small Round of Follies lost;*
> *Yet ev'n thy Joys, and Tears, and Strife,*
> *Act all the World in little Life.*
> *Alike Man aims at all he can,*
> *And Imitation teaches Man:*
> *—But then has Man his Play-things too?—*
> *—Yes sure—Amusements all allow,*
> *And are more serious Fools—than thou.*
> *We differ, only in th' Intent*
> *As idle, but less innocent.*

Also in these *Poems on Several Occasions* we find one of the earliest (perhaps the very earliest) of the 18th century imitations of Spenser, several Odes which anticipate the manner of Gray, a line or two which may have given a hint to Johnson—'All human Race, from *China* to *Peru*, Pleasure, howe'er disguised by Art, pursue,'—and some *Verses Written After Seeing Windsor Castle* which recall one of Joseph's stories of his brother as a child.

The two brothers went with their father to see Windsor Castle, and old Tom was much concerned to notice an apparent lack of interest in young Tom. 'Thomas goes on,' he said sadly to Jospeh, 'and takes no notice of anything he has seen !' But Joseph 'in maturer years made this reflection: "I believe my brother was more struck with what he saw, and took more notice of every object, than either of us." ' His great interest in ancient architecture in later years came at a time when such studies were very unusual; he would go off during vacations scrambling over the ruins of old castles, and measuring abbeys, and exploring cathedrals, with indefatigable interest. Some of the earliest written appreciation of Gothic in English appears in his *Observations on The Faerie Queene* (1754; but the 'gothic essay' was added in the 2nd edition, 1762.)

In 1747 Warton took his B.A., and in the same year he entered into Holy Orders. He became a Tutor in his college, though perhaps not a very efficient one; Lord Eldon wrote years later: 'Poor Tom Warton! He was a Tutor at Trinity; at the beginning of every term he used to send to his pupils to know whether they would *wish* to attend lectures that term." This willingness to fulfil obligations without undue inconvenience to himself no doubt also explains why he is said to have had only two sermons for all occasions—one by his father, and one out of a book.[1]

[1] Probably apocryphal; another authority credits him with at least three.

His academic career proceeded smoothly; he was M.A. in 1750, Fellow of his College in 1751, B.D. in 1767. In 1757 he succeeded Mr. Hawkins of Pembroke College[1] as Professor of Poetry, an office which, like his father before him, he held for the usual ten years. In 1785—a little before succeeding to the Laureateship—Warton was elected Camden Professor of History at Oxford. Thus his career had been progressively successful in the academic world.

The new Laureate had not made the composition of poetry his primary concern in authorship, but in one way or another it had been his main study; his observations on Spenser's *Faerie Queene* (1754) had been followed by editions of the Greek Anthology (1766) and of Theocritus (1770) and in the year of the Laureateship by his edition of Milton's *Minor Poems*, as truly a landmark in Miltonic criticism as the *Observations* were in Spenserian. Then there was the great *History of English Poetry*, the three volumes of which appeared 1774–1781. This gigantic undertaking was never completed and the existing work breaks off in Elizabeth's reign before the appearance of the greater part of English poetry. This book led Warton into the most serious of his literary scrapes—a far worse affair than any satire occasioned by the Laureateship.

Joseph Ritson, an able scholar but a most unamiable man, very quickly put out a volume of critical emendation and comment,

---

[1] It seems a pity for William Hawkins to appear and disappear thus so briefly; he was a person of importance in his day. Let us rescue a mild specimen of his Muse from oblivion:

TO A WORM WHICH THE AUTHOR ACCIDENTALLY TRODE UPON

> *Methinks thou writhest as in rage;—*
> *But, dying reptile, know,*
> *Thou ow'st to chance thy death!—I scorn*
> *To crush my meanest foe.*

> *Anger, 'tis true, and justice stern*
> *Might fairly here have place.—*
> *Are not thy subterraneous tribes*
> *Devourers of our race?*

> *On princes they have richly fed,*
> *When their vast work was done;*
> *And monarchs have regail'd vile worms,*
> *Who first the world had won.*

> *Let vengeance then thine exit cheer,*
> *Nor at thy fate repine:*
> *Legions of worms (who knows how soon?)*
> *Shall feast on me, and mine.*

His other poems include a *Rapsody in Praise of the Particles*—written long before Browning learned to 'dock the smaller parts o' speech,' and a number of not unlively pieces besides. All this labour is forgotten now as though it had never been, and Mr. Hawkins of Pembroke with it.

expressed in terms of violent contempt and abuse. His *Observations on the three first volumes of the History of English Poetry: In a familiar letter to the author* (1782) lists one hundred and sixteen errors, some of considerable magnitude. Maliciously, he ordered the *Observations* to be printed 'in the size of Mr. Warton's History,' as 'extremely proper to be bound up with that celebrated work, to which they will be found a very useful appendix.' And in private letters he exulted over his victory: 'I have at last put my libel upon Warton into the hands of a bookseller,' and, later, 'What say you to my scurrilous libel against Warton?'

Warton himself said little, but the public condemned the pamphlet for its violence; such a work as Warton's, undertaken by one man, with no previous comparable history for guidance, must certainly contain errors. If temperately conveyed, criticisms would have been welcomed by any candid historian; as it was, Warton's credit was not particularly undermined and in later years Ritson is said to have repented of his illiberal tone.

Even these massive labours did not represent the end of Warton's prose works; he published biographies of Ralph Bathurst (1761) and Sir Thomas Pope (1772), various specimens of local history, some critical essays, and a number of trifles, including several lively essays in Johnson's *Idler*.

His poetry at the time of the Laureateship made a respectable collection, as might be expected from one whose Muse commenced operations at the age of nine. His first published poem had been an *Ode to a Fountain*, included in his brothers' *Odes on Various Subjects* (1746), and his first independent work the characteristically titled *Pleasures of Melancholy* (1747), which shows the young poet to have read much in Milton when most young men were reading Pope. Two years later *The Triumph of Isis* provided a modest triumph for its author.

Mason had recently published his *Isis, an Elegy*, a poem containing various strictures on the university, particularly for its alleged Jacobite sympathies during the '45 rebellion. Warton's reply 'excelled more in manly expostulation and dignity, than the poem that produced it did in neatness and elegance.' It was a gentlemanly contention on both sides and neither poet at first printed his poem in his collected works, until at last—nearly thirty years later—Mason said he hoped *The Triumph of Isis* was not to be allowed to remain out of print on his account, and Warton then put it into his next collection.

This performance, by a young man of twenty-one, was very

4

favourably received, and the learned Dr. King is reported to have left five guineas at the bookseller's 'if they would be of any service to the young man, that had written the poem.' Thus Warton did rather better financially by his first success than Whitehead had done.

At Oxford in his younger days Warton was not at all the studious small boy who sat in a cold chamber studying; he studied, true enough, but he also enjoyed to the full the pleasures of being young in a fine city. This gay life is reflected in those early poems which he included in *The Oxford Sausage*, an anthology which he put forth in 1764. Another light-hearted enterprise was the celebrated *A Companion to the Guide and a Guide to the Companion* (1760), which is an Oxford guide-with-a-difference; most guide-books content themselves with notes on colleges and antiquities; this one does not overlook the taverns and other places of resort popular with those who have examined tombs enough to be going on with. Finally in 1777 and 1791 Warton published collected editions of his poetry.

It is a pity Dr. Johnson did not live to see Warton's Laureate odes, for his opinion of them beside his remarks on those of Cibber and Whitehead would have been interesting. Johnson knew Warton well, and respected and esteemed him, although he once remarked that Tom Warton was the only man of genius he knew that was without a heart. The Doctor also wrote a little parody of Warton's later manner:

> *'Hermit hoar, in solemn cell,*
> *Wearing out life's evening gray;*
> *Smite thy bosom, sage, and tell,*
> *What is bliss? and which the way?*

Boswell. "But why smite his bosom, Sir?"

Johnson. "Why, to show he was in earnest," (smiling.)—He at an after period added the following stanza:

> *Thus I spoke; and speaking sigh'd;*
> *—Scarce repress'd the starting tear;—*
> *When the smiling sage reply'd—*
> *—Come, my lad, and drink some beer.'*

Boswell adds, 'I cannot help thinking the first stanza very good solemn poetry, as also the three first lines of the second. Its last line is an excellent burlesque surprise on gloomy sentimental inquirers. . . .'

When Warton was appointed, Mason himself was still alive, and he may have remembered the excuse made to him formerly when he was passed over, that 'being in orders, he was thought, merely on that account, less eligible for the office than a layman.' Warton, 'being in orders,' was nevertheless found eligible.

His Birthday Ode for 1785 duly appeared and met with little favour. George III was not used to this sort of thing:

> *. . . To Kings like these, her genuine theme,*
> *The Muse a blameless homage pays;*
> *To GEORGE, of Kings like these supreme,*
> *She wishes honoured length of days,* `
> *Nor prostitutes the tribute of her lays.*
>
> *'Tis his to bid neglected genius glow,*
> *And teach the regal bounty how to flow . . .*

It almost appeared that, after six weeks in office, the new Laureate was looking for an advance of salary. Richard Mant remarks that this first Ode was perhaps the poet's worst production. At all events, it was a godsend to the satirists, who as usual were waiting to have a word with the new Laureate.

Within a few weeks (for in the eighteenth century a book could be produced remarkably quickly) appeared *Probationary Odes for The Laureateship*, with a preliminary discourse by 'Sir John Hawkins, Knt.' This was Dr. Johnson's 'unclubbable man,' but his presence was part of the joke; he never wrote anything in his life so lively as the preliminary discourse. The *Probationary Odes* were the work of the authors of *The Rolliad*—French Laurence, George Ellis, Lord John Townshend, Joseph Richardson, Richard Tickell and others—and follow the tradition of the various 'sessions of the Poets' but with a new twist: each of the alleged candidates presents his own 'probationary ode'— and pretty bad they are, though mighty amusing. The worst is usually thought to be the one assigned to Thomas Warton (which happens to be his own genuine Birthday Ode). But the genuine Ode contains nothing so outrageous as this, for example:

RECITATIVE

Hog! Porker! Roaster! Boar-stag! Barbique!
Cheeks! Chines! Crow! Chitterlings! and Harselet new!
Springs! Spare-ribs! Sausages! Sous'd-lugs! and Face!
With piping-hot Pease-pudding—plenteous place!
Hands! Hocks! Hams! Haggis, with high seas'ning fill'd!
Gammons! Green Griskins! on gridirons grill'd!
Liver and Lights! from Plucks that moment drawn
Pigs' Puddings! Black and White! with Canterbury Brawn!—

TRIO

Fall to,
Ye Royal crew!
Eat! Eat your bellies full! Pray do!
At treats I never winces:—
The Queen shall say,
Once in a way,
Her maids have been well cramm'd—her young ones din'd like Princes!

FULL CHORUS—*accompanied by the whole* HOGGERY

For this BIG MORN
GREAT GEORGE was born!
The tidings all the Poles shall ring!
Due homage will I pay,
On this, thy native day,
GEORGE! by the grace of God, my rightful KING!!!

I rejoice especially in that magnificent line, 'Gammons! Green Griskins! on gridirons grill'd!' The supposed author of this Ode, Sir Joseph Mawbey, Bt., combined parliamentary duties with farming, and makes an appearance equally ridiculous in *The Rolliad*. It is a pity the *Probationary Odes*—and the rest of the *Rolliad* poems, for that matter—are not readily accessible, for they are full of good things. How many readers will sympathise with the opening of the Ode attributed to Sir Nathanial William Wraxall:

MURRAIN seize the House of Commons!
Hoarse catarrh their windpipes shake!

and how many with Lord Thurlow's robust opening:

DAMNATION seize ye all,
Who puff, who thrum, who bawl and squall!

Accompanying the Probationary Odes is the usual apparatus of discussion and explanation, with an appendix recording that the place went to the Rev. T. Warton, and a table of instructions supposed to have been issued with it for the guidance of the Laureate in the execution of his duties:

1st, THAT in fabricating the catalogue of Regal Virtues (in which task the Poet may much assist his invention by perusing the Odes of his several predecessors) you be particularly careful not to omit his Chastity, his skill in Mechanics, and his Royal Talent of Child-getting. . . .

2dly, It is expected that you should be very liberally endowed with the gift of Prophecy; but be very careful not to predict any event but what may be perfectly acceptable to your Sovereign, such as the subjugation of America, the destruction of the Whigs, life-long, &c. &c. . . .

until,

7thly, And finally, That it may not be amiss to be a little intelligible.

'This,' remarks a footnote, 'is an additional proof that Mr. Warton had not received the Instructions at the time he composed his said Ode.'

In addition to all this fun (in the main good-humoured) the book provides 'Thoughts on Ode Writing,' an essay supposedly by Warton, which is an admirable parody—though somewhat excessively exaggerated—on his critical prose writings, a 'Full and True Account of the Rev. Thomas Warton's Ascension from Christ-Church Meadow, Oxford' in a balloon, for the purpose of composing his first Ode a mile above the earth (Dr. Joseph Warton, protesting, having been left behind lest he be accused of lending his brother a helping hand with the rhyme-scheme) and a number of other squibs, in the course of which it is facetiously remarked 'in the example of a Whitehead's Muse, expatiating on the virtues of our gracious Sovereign, have we not beheld the best of Poets, in the best of Verses, doing ample justice to the best of Kings!'

Warton took office just at a time when the art of political satire was reviving. After the death of Pope in 1744 little really effective satire of the full-blooded sort appeared for nearly fifty years, the work of Churchill apart. The coarser satirists, like Paul Whitehead, were in the main feeble poets. The masters of light verse—Anstey, for example—were in the main feeble satirists. There was a good deal of pleasant light satire; Anstey's *New Bath Guide* is the obvious example, but this, and similar works, was more general than personal in application. The appearance of the *Rolliad* in 1784 began a new tradition which in its turn produced most of the best work of Peter Pindar, the *Anti-Jacobin*, such satires as *The Pursuits of Literature*, Gifford's *Baviad* and *Maeviad*, and a great many lesser things. Warton held the laureateship only five years, but it was long enough for most of the new generation of satirists to have a crack at him, though T. J. Mathias in *The Pursuits of Literature* rather goes out of his way to praise him.

'I always regret the loss of Thomas Warton,' Mathias says. 'In his various writings he is amusing, instructive, pleasant, learned and poetical. I never received information more agreeably from any modern writer than from Mr. Warton. His edition of Milton's smaller poems (an exquisite specimen of classical commentary, and worthy of his former observations on Spenser) leaves it a matter of unceasing regret that he never published the Paradise Lost and Regained. The want of the last volume of the History of English Poetry must for ever be lamented. I despair of any artists able to finish such a work, with so few imperfections, and with such various erudition.'

It was, however, for the various erudition that Mathias made his most telling shot at Warton. He quotes Falstaff ('H.IV.P.I.A.I.Sc.2.') 'I am as melancholy as a GIBBE CAT' and proceeds to mock the commentators: 'Dr. Johnson begins, "A Gibbe cat means *I know not why*, an *old* cat." Dr. Percy informs us next, that a Gib-cat in Northamptonshire, means a *He*-cat, which in some parts of England is called a *ram*-cat, and in Shropshire, a *tup*-cat. Then follow other wise criticks, and last of all appears Mr. Thomas Warton, who brings a train of *authorities* on this important question, showing *how* Gib is short for Gilbert, and Tib for Tibert; *how* Jack is appropriated to a horse, and Tom to a pigeon; *how* Chaucer, in his Romaunt de la Rose, mentions Gibbe our cat, to which Tib was synonymous, as it is at this day; *how* we read in "Gammar Gurton's Needle" (which is a right pleasant, witty, and merry comedy, written by Mr. S. Master of Arts) viz. "Hath no man stolen her ducks, or gelded GIBBE her cat?" Upon which Mr. Warton very *gravely* observes, "the composure of a cat is almost characteristick, and *I know not* (see Dr. Johnson's words above) whether there is not a *superior solemnity in* the gravity of a HE-CAT." '

All this is good fun and may have given the hint (for all books must have their origin somewhere) for Pye's *Comments on The Commentators of Shakespeare*, which appeared in 1807.

Not quite so good humoured were Peter Pindar's various 'licks at the Laureate,' although, as ever, he reserved his best strokes for the King, and the next-best for the politicians. The long *Ode upon Ode* with its (also long) 'apologetic postscript' has some amusing lines, but the best example of Peter's laureate satire comes in *Instructions to a Celebrated Laureate, alias The Progress of Curiosity, alias A Birth-Day Ode, alias Mr. Whitbread's Brewhouse.* '*Sic transit Gloria Mundi*,' runs the title page motto, translated as 'From House of Buckingham, in grand parade, to Whitbread's Brewhouse moved the Cavalcade.'

The poem begins with a 'serious expostulation'; 'come, Tom,' says the poet in effect, 'between ourselves, you don't really *mean* all that tosh you write, do you?'—

> But, *Thomas Warton, without joking,*
> *Art thou, or art thou not, thy Sovereign smoking?*
>
> *How canst thou seriously declare*
>   *That George the Third*
> *With Cressy's Edward can compare,*
>   *Or Harry?—'Tis too bad, upon my word:*
> *George is a clever King, I needs must own,*
> *And cuts a jolly figure on the Throne.*
>
> *Now thou exclaimst, 'God rot it! Peter, pray,*
> *What to the devil shall I sing or say?'*

'I'll teach thee how to make an Ode,' Peter promises, and launches into the famous visit to the Whitbread brewery:

> *. . . Full of the art of Brewing Beer,*
>   *The Monarch heard of Mister Whitbread's fame:*
> *Quoth he unto the Queen, 'My dear, my dear,*
>   *Whitbread hath got a marvellous great name.*
> *Charly, we must, must, must see Whitbread brew;*
>   *Rich as us, Charly; richer than a Jew.*
> *Shame, shame, we have not yet his Brewhouse seen.'—*
>   *This sweetly said the King unto the Queen . . .*

the visit goes itself splendidly:

> *. . . Now Mister Whitbread serious did declare,*
> *To make the Majesty of England stare,*
> *That he had Butts enough, he knew,*
> *Placed side by side, to reach along to Kew.*
> *On which the King with wonder swiftly cried,*
> *'What, if they reach to Kew then side by side,*
> *What would they do, what, what, placed end to end?'*
> *To whom, with knitted calculating brow,*
> *The Man of Beer most solemnly did vow,*
>   *Almost to Windsor that they would extend.*
> *On which the King, with wondering mien,*
> *Repeated it unto the wondering Queen.*

But it is much easier to start reading and quoting Peter Pindar than to stop.

His other large references to Warton are contained in *Brother Peter to Brother Tom* and in *Ode on No Ode*. In the first he says—with the good sense that underlies much of his banter—

> *Since truth belongs not to the Laureat trade,*
> *'Tis strange, 'tis passing strange, thou didst not flatter;*
> *Speak; in Light Money were thy Wages paid?*
> *Or was thy pipe of Sack half-fill'd with Water?*
> *Or hast thou, Tom, been cheated of thy Dues?*
> *Or hath a qualm of conscience touch'd thy Muse?*

Well, Warton certainly did not flatter; perhaps because he thought a conscientious Laureate best served the dignity of his sovereign, and of his office, by not doing so. But Peter goes on from this sensible point to one of his superb outrageous passages:

> *Thou might'st have praised for dignity of pride,*
> *Displayed not long ago among the Cooks—*
> *Searching the kitchen with sagacious looks;*
> *Wigs, christened scratches, on their heads he spied.*
>
> *To find a Wig on a* Cook's *head,*
> *Just like the Wig that graced his own,*
> *Was verily a sight to dread,*
> *Enough to turn a King to Stone!*
> *On which, in language of his very best,*
> *His Majesty his Royal ire express'd:*
>
> *'How, how! what? Cooks wear scratches just like me?*
> *Strange, strange! yes, yes; I see, I see, I see.*
> *Fine fellows to wear Scratches! Yes, no doubt;*
> *I'll have no more, no more, when mine's worn out.*
> *Hae! pretty, pretty, pretty, too it looks*
> *To see my Scratches upon* Cooks!

Warton himself had done something in the humorous way in his time, and in the way of satire; but he made no answer now beyond applauding 'the exquisite wit and humour' of the *Probationary Odes*. At the time of his appointment he was busily engaged on his studies in the text of Milton—his edition of the *Minor Poems* appeared in the year of his laureateship. This, and his lifelong devotion to Spenser, at a time when neither of these poets had been systematically studied, represents one of his best services to English literature; and if *Newmarket* (1751) and the *Oxford Sausage* contributions (lively enough though they are in parts) represent the full measure of his satiric powers, we need not regret that Peter and the others escaped his lash.

The King perhaps thought so, too. At all events, he is said to have encouraged Warton to edit further works by Milton. In fact, Warton projected a complete edition, but he died before it could be done. He left many notes, and a revised edition of the *Minor Poems* went through the press just before he died; but the unpublished notes were lost together with others supplied by J. Warton. When one considers what George III had suffered at Peter Pindar's hands his suggestion is seen to do him great credit. After all, he might have set his tame poet to the composition of an *Anti-Lousiad*.

For the four years succeeding his appointment Warton punctiliously supplied the requisite Odes. Then, in the autumn of 1788, when he was perhaps thinking of the forthcoming New Year Ode, the Laureate came up against a difficulty for which no precedent existed in the annals of his predecessors. His King went mad. It is hard for a Laureate to find anything suitable to say of a Sovereign who is insane and Warton took what may be described as evasive action. He maintained a discreet silence on January 1st, 1789, and no doubt hoped that by the time of the Birthday Ode the King would be better (as indeed he proved to be.)

The people preferred a King in his right mind, and Warton's Birthday Ode spoke for the whole nation. He pictures George's health as a fair landscape over which the shadow of a great storm passes, and continues:

> *Such was the changeful conflict that possest*
> *With trembling tumult every British breast;*
> *When Albion, towering in the van sublime*
>   *Of Glory's march, from clime to clime*
>   *Envied, belov'd, rever'd, renown'd,*
> *Her brows with every blissful chaplet bound;*
>   *When, in her mid career of state,*
>   *She felt her Monarch's aweful fate!—*
>   *Till Mercy from th' Almighty throne*
>   *Look'd down on man, and, waving wide*
>   *Her wreath, that, in the rainbow dyed,*
> *With hues of soften'd lustre shone,*
>   *And bending from her sapphire cloud,*
>   *O'er regal grief benignant bow'd;*
>   *To transport turned a people's fears,*
>   *And stay'd a people's tide of tears:*

Bade this blest dawn with beams auspicious spring,
With hope serene, with healing in its wing;
And gave a Sovereign o'er a grateful land
Again with vigorous grasp to stretch the scepter'd hand.

The popular delight at the King's recovery took the less literary form of loud huzzas, accompanied with a good deal of harmless merry making, and the Regency Bill, which had almost passed through Parliament, was discreetly allowed to lapse for the time being. But the new year again found no Laureate Ode, and this time the irrepressible Peter Pindar took the King's poet to task. The *Annual Register*[1] for 1790 records the lack of an Ode thus (and it will be noted that the Ode was 'omitted'; the account doesn't suggest that no ode was written. On the other hand, no 1790 Ode was ever subsequently published.):

> January 1st. This day there was no court either at Windsor or St. James's, as usual on New Year's Day, consequently the Laureate's ode was omitted. The New Year's Ode not being performed as usual has occasioned much speculation—It may not be unacceptable to our readers to give them the following passage from Mr. Gibbon's last volume of the History of the Decline and Fall of the Roman Empire: 'The title of Poet Laureat, which custom rather than vanity perpetuates in the English court, was first invented by the Caesars of Germany. From Augustus to Louis the muse had been too often false and venal; but I much doubt whether any age or court can produce a similar establishment of a stipendiary poet, who in every reign, and at all events, is bound to furnish, twice a year, a measure of praise and verse, such as may be sung in the chapel, and, I believe, in the presence of the sovereign. I speak the more freely, as the best time for abolishing this ridiculous custom is while the prince is a man of virtue, and the poet a man of genius.'

The *Register* then proceeds to print Peter's 'Ode on No Ode':

> *What! not a sprig of annual metre*
> *Neither from Thomas nor from Peter*
>   *Who has shut up the Laureate's shop?*
> *Alas! 'poor Tom's a-cold,' I fear;*
> *For sack 'poor Tom' must drink small-beer,*
>   *And lo!— of that a scanty drop! . . .*

Perhaps George is sick of being praised, Peter Pindar suggests, or perhaps he 'thinks the year boasts nothing worth recording.'

Worthy or otherwise, the events of 1789 were the last Warton had the chance of recording, for on May 21st, 1790, he died.

---

[1] The *Annual Register* writer marries part of a sentence in Gibbon's text (Vol. 4, Chapter LXX) with a footnote to it. The historian of Rome is discussing the poetic honours to which Petrarch aspired.

Tom Warton seems to have been a good fellow; some of the stories told about him effectively discredit Johnson's remark that he had no heart—and indeed his long friendship with the Doctor was only now and then mildly clouded, and who shall say that the fault lay with Tom? It was partly his influence that obtained for Johnson his M.A. at Oxford (a degree with which Johnson desired to grace the title page of his *Dictionary*, then about to be published) and in a number of other ways Sam had no reason to complain of Tom. He greatly enjoyed Warton's hospitality at Oxford, except perhaps on one occasion. The Professor of Poetry and the learned Lexicographer took a walk together into the surrounding meads and after a lengthy perambulation turned homewards: when the visitor found himself unable to keep up with Warton's swinging pace. So, perforce, from far in the rear he was obliged to cry out to him to stop, but even in this crisis he had the presence of mind to employ the Latin tongue.

Warton's fondness for a pot of ale was well known—indeed, he had written a popular poem called *A Panegyre on Oxford Ale*—and if he could sup this delicacy in the company of a group of bargees in a canal-side tavern his pleasure was complete. Like Johnson, he had no love for clean linen, either on himself or on others. But he did have a great love for martial music. Hartley Coleridge[1] records (but admits the story to be open to doubt) that on one occasion when Warton was not to be found anywhere a military band with fife and drum was despatched to play along the streets; and sure enough, from a low tavern to see the fun, appeared the Professor of Poetry.

He was apt to be discovered in peculiar situations. He was a frequent visitor to Winchester during Joseph's headmastership and became a great favourite with the boys,[2] whose exercises he would do—asking

[1] In the account of Mason in *Lives of Northern Worthies*. Another poet who couldn't resist the fifes and drums was W. J. Cory, who, when he was a master at Eton, would cease work as the Guards went by and cry out to his class, 'Brats, the British Army!' The red-coats were what did it, I think; we get a similar response in Wilfrid Blunt's superb sonnet on Gibraltar:

> . . . God! to hear the shrill
> *Sweet treble of her fifes upon the breeze*
> *And at the summons of the rock gun's roar*
> *To see her red coats marching from the hill.*

Khaki has killed romance; at all events I never noticed any public response when I passed by, in those carefree days when I was a lance-corporal.

[2] 'The Magnetism of Tom Warton draws many a youth into rhymes and loose stockings, who had better be thinking of prose and propriety; and so it is with his brother Joe. At School I remember we thought we must necessarily be fine fellows if we were but as absent and as dirty as the Adelphi of Poetry.'—Rev. Sir Herbert Croft to John Nichols, (Nichols's *Anecdotes*, 1786).

beforehand approximately how bad they ought to be. One such exercise was apparently not quite bad enough to be the work of the young scholar who was supposed to have produced it. The Headmaster sent for his brother, and asked him, in front of the boy, whether this were not really rather a good exercise. Tom agreed that it was. 'Worth half-a-crown?' asked Joseph. 'Certainly,' replied Thomas. So his brother made him give the boy half-a-crown.

On another occasion something in the way of unauthorised cooking was in progress and the Headmaster got wind of it. As he came along to investigate, all the culprits escaped, except one who retired to a cupboard, from which Joseph proceeded to extract him. This was Tom.

In speech he 'gobbled like a turkey,' Johnson (that refined elocutionist) tells us. And the authors of the *Probationary Odes* give us a glimpse of his appearance: 'a little, thick, squat, red-faced man . . . in a very odd dress' who unexpectedly confronts the King on the chapel stairs. He is about to be thrown out when 'by a certain hasty spasmodic mumbling, together with two or three prompt quotations from Virgil, the person was discovered to be none other than the Rev. Mr. *Thomas Warton* himself. . . .' Needless to say, the chapel concerned was not the Rev. Mr. Warton's. Although he held a couple of livings he seldom ventured anywhere near them.

Warton died on May 21st, 1790, as the result of a stroke. He was sincerely mourned by the whole university, and at their own request the Vice-Chancellor, the Heads of Houses, and the Proctors attended the funeral. More thoughtful than some of his predecessors, the late laureate left his Birthday Ode all ready for use on June 4th. Ironically enough, it is all about the blessings of good health.

10

Henry James Pye

ONCE more George III was left without a Laureate, and once
more the appointment went to a poet of whom posterity hardly
approves; but whereas Warton was a considerable man of letters,
Henry James Pye was strictly speaking an amateur, though a
voluminous one.

'Cowper was alive!' it has since been objected, but it must again be
emphasised that the Laureate tradition did not call for the appointment
of 'the best living poet.' Originally, the Laureate had been the political/
poetical defender of his royal master; then gradually he became rather
a panegyrist, a paid flatterer; and now, in 1790, what was wanted was
a safe, unambitious writer who could be relied upon to say the right
thing twice a year. A character in one of Hilaire Belloc's novels is
promoted 'for not having done anything silly' and Pye received the
laurel for very similar reasons. After all, in 1790 nobody could be
expected to foresee that there would be such victories as Trafalgar, in
the celebration of which a Pye would be taxed beyond his resources.

As for Cowper, he had his chance, for Southey[1] thinks the office
would have been readily secured for him, if he had allowed his cousin
Lady Hesketh to seek it. But knowing his uncertain temper in these
affairs, she prudently sounded him before going forward with the idea,
and received a firm refusal to entertain it:

> Heaven guard my brows from the wreath you mention, whatever wreath
> beside may hereafter adorn them! It would be a leaden extinguisher,
> clapped on all the fire of my genius, and I should never more produce a
> line worth reading. To speak seriously, it would make me miserable, and
> therefore I am sure that thou, of all my friends, would least wish me to
> wear it.

To another friend he said in conversation, 'I could neither go to court,
nor could I kiss hands, were it for a much more valuable consideration.'
All the same, he was much amused and possibly flattered a few days

---

[1] *Life of Cowper*, prefixed to Southey's edition of the *Works* (1836) which is still the
most attractive set to possess, and fortunately is not uncommon.

later to receive a letter asking his aid in the same matter; and he passed
the application on to Lady Hesketh:

> I have been applied to within these few days by a Welshman, with a wife
> and many children, to get him made Poet-laureate as fast as possible. If thou
> wouldst wish to make the world merry twice a year, thou canst not do
> better than procure the office for him.

He accordingly retires from the contest, taking with him the poetical
Welshman (of whom no more is heard in this connection) and we
cannot regret it. Cowper would have brought to the task the
genius, and the inadequacy that would have been brought by Gray.
They were both poets whose very strength lay in their limitations.

In 1790 there was, indeed, no bright particular star whose appointment would have seemed inevitable, then or now. Mason—the thing
was becoming a habit—was again passed over. Rogers had not yet
made his name (and his turn was to come in fifty years or so). The
idea of offering it to Burns would have occurred to no one, although
the praise of a German king in broad Scots might have afforded some
interesting verses—and Burns, incidentally, did write something very
like a Laureate Ode in *A Dream* 'on reading, in the public papers, the
Laureat's Ode, with the other parade of June 4th, 1786. . . .' The
verses are not calculated to predispose any monarch in favour of their
author.

The Laureateship did not come at once to Pye, for he was Pitt's
second choice. The first offer went to the celebrated William Hayley.

We owe a good deal to Hayley, for he preserved in his *Life* of
Cowper a great many of the poet's best letters, which otherwise might
have been lost; and in addition he was a friend to Blake when Blake
was in great need of a friend. These things were in the future, however.
Hayley's celebrity in 1790 was based on more immediate achievements.
He was the author of a very popular poem, *The Triumphs of Temper*.
An interesting essay, incidentally, could be written on poems now
forgotten, which in their day circulated in their thousands and were
read and admired by all, even by good judges. Who now reads *The
Choice*, or *The Grave*, or *The Pleasures of Memory*, or *The Course of
Time*? Or Hayley's *The Triumphs of Temper*?

This was published in 1781 and was a great popular success, perhaps
because it treats of marriage, women, and other matters of universal
interest. It was 'intended to promote the cultivation of good humour'
and does so in couplets owing everything to Pope except their feeble-
ness. This work, however, was not Hayley's sole claim to attention.

By 1785 he had written poems and plays enough to fill six volumes of a collected edition. He was therefore a respectable figure in letters, and a reasonable choice for Laureate. But he didn't happen to want to be Laureate (rather surprisingly) and when the offer was made he refused it, politely and in verse. So Pitt had to try again, and he transferred his attentions to Pye, who accepted, though whether in verse or plain prose is not stated.

'Pye . . . was eminently respectable in everything but his poetry,' says Byron in a famous note to *The Vision of Judgement,* and on the whole that has been the general opinion for a hundred and fifty years.

His early biographers agree that Pye came of an 'ancient and respectable family,' without giving too many tedious details. The one significant link in his ancestry is with one Sir Robert Pye, James First's Auditor of the Exchequer, to whom Jonson had addressed pathetic verses calling for payment of his pension.

Henry James Pye was born in London in 1745 and was educated under a private tutor until he was 17, when he became a Gentleman Commoner at Magdalen College, Oxford, where in due course he took the honorary degree of M.A. (1766) and in 1772 at the installation of Lord North was made LL.D. No doubt these distinctions were deserved; for we are told that from his earliest days he was devoted to reading, and moreover he read highly commendable books. At ten years old 'his father put Pope's Homer into his hand; the rapture which he received from this exquisite paraphrase of the Grecian Bard was never to be forgotten, and it completely fixed him a *Rhymer for Life,* as he pleasantly expressed it.' There were, however, more earnest things in life than rhyming, as he presently learned.

In 1766, just as Henry James was completing his university career, his father died, leaving him the family seat, Faringdon Hall, Berkshire, and debts which are said to have totalled £50,000. These in due time the younger Pye discharged, but not without some difficulty. In his time the practice of showing the family mansion for half-a-crown per head was hardly heard of, but in any case before Pye could have retrenched in this manner Faringdon Hall was burned down. Indeed— the M.A. apart—the only pleasant thing in this year for him was his marriage to Miss Mary Hook, who made him happy for thirty years and died in 1796, having produced two daughters and a farce called *The Capricious Lady* which was performed at Drury Lane.

For some years Pye lived as a country gentleman, attending to his estate—and rebuilding the house—hunting and shooting, and

performing conscientiously the duties of a local magistrate. In 1784, at
great cost, he contrived to be elected to Parliament, thus once more
crippling the estate, which (it is said) this time had to be sold. It
seems a large price to pay for the privilege of making only three speeches
in the House—if tradition be correct. The most eloquent was to
inform Parliament that his constituents had not enjoyed a good harvest.
Six years later he failed in the elections and left Parliament for ever.

Pye was 'fixed a rhymer' at ten, and he gave evidence of the fact in
1762 with his *Ode on The Birth of the Prince of Wales*; this was part of
the poetical bread which in 1790 the waters brought back to support
his pretentions to the Laureateship, though if George III had happened
to look it over, and reflect upon how that Prince had grown up, he
might have hesitated. However, the blame certainly did not rest with
Pye if King and Prince were not now on friendly terms.

Between 1762 and 1790 Pye added a round dozen works to his list,
including a bunch of *Elegies, Beauty, a Poetical Essay in Three Parts*
(one would have been sufficient), *The Progress of Refinement* (also in
three parts), a poem on *Shooting*, and *Faringdon Hill*, a poem in two
books. *Faringdon Hill* is very much in the topographical tradition
without adding anything original to it. Over a hundred years had
passed since Sir John Denham had started a fashion with *Cooper's Hill*
(1642) and by 1774 when Pye entered the lists there were literally
dozens of bits of local scenery (hills were the favourites, but Pope
chose *Windsor Forest*) embedded (mostly) in heroic couplets for the
inspection of the curious. Some, like Dyer's *Grongar Hill*, represented
a real and permanent contribution to our poetry; others were more
like *Faringdon Hill*, of which the reader may think the following
specimen enough:

> *Now the meridian sun with sultry ray*
> *Pours on our heads intolerable day,*
> *Amidst the effulgence of the blue serene,*
> *No fleecy cloud, or vapory mist is seen;*
> *The panting flocks, and herds, at ease reclined,*
> *Catch the faint eddies of the flitting wind;*
> *To silence hush'd is every rural sound,*
> *And noontide spreads a solemn stillness round:*
> *Alike our fainting limbs would now forsake*
> *The open meadow and the tangled brake;*
> *Here SOL intensely glows, and there the trees*
> *Exclude the cool refreshment of the breeze.—*

> *Come let us quit these scenes, and climb yon brow,*
> *Yon airy summit where the ZEPHYRS blow,*
> *While waving o'er our heads the welcome shade,*
> *Shuts out the sunbeams from the upland glade:*
> *No steep ascent we scale with feverish toil,*
> *No rock alarms us, and no mountains soil;*
> *But as we gently tread the rising green,*
> *Large, and more large extends the spacious scene;*
> *Till on the verdant top our labor crown'd;*
> *The wide Horizon is our only bound.*

As these are the opening lines of book one, the reader who cares to do so may go on from there. He is at the summit of Faringdon Hill. Other readers, perhaps, will find the work more intolerable than effulgent, and may prefer to descend.

It seems that Pitt must have thought something ought to be done for Pye, in view of the lamentable fact that the voters had failed to send him back to parliament; so he made him Poet Laureate.[1] At all events, I cannot learn of any other reason for the appointment, which was greeted with some surprise by the world. With surprise, and naturally with disapproval, for no Laureate yet had escaped that; but with comparatively little written satire. Pye has received his hardest knocks from posterity and the only considerable attack[2] upon him in 1790 was the anonymous *An Epistle to the Poet Laureate* which is very dull and ineffective. The writer takes the view I have suggested, that Pitt was doing a political job in appointing Pye, whom he thus addresses:

> *Thou, who of poetry or Pitt*
> *The merits canst rehearse,*
> *Prepared alike to show thy wit*
> *By venal vote or verse.*

[1] One action of Pye's has never been fully explained: he 'wretchedly commuted' the butt of sack for £27 in lieu; and this sum has been part of the salary ever since, leaving the Laureate richer and dryer. Today, alas, the £27 would not buy a butt of any drinkable wine.

[2] There were a few obvious jokes upon his unpoetical name—trifles about when the Pye was opened, and so on. Pye shares with Thomas Flatman, Stephen Duck, James Six and Jeremy Feeble the distinction of carrying the least inviting name in English poetry. Flatman was a delightful poet; Duck at least is readable at his best; with James Six—young Six, of course, not the father—it was presumably half a dozen of the other so far as the Muses were concerned; and Jeremy Feeble makes as yet no great figure. My friend Mr. Jonathan Routh has not yet completed his researches into the life and work of the footman poet, but it seems at least possible that this squib was aimed at Cibber some time after he took the Laureateship—especially as Feeble's tragedy was making no favourable impression on the actor-manager:

> 'I am Unworthy,' (Windbag *when appointed*)—
> *Within Six Months he Apes the Lord's anointed:*
> Windbag (*like many* Clowns) *is Double-Jointed.*

This weak stuff could hurt nobody (and, incidentally, there existed magnificent models for an attack on Pitt in the *Political Miscellanies* by the authors of *The Rolliad*). Peter Pindar was the most effective of Pye's attackers, but even he did it without rancour:

> 'Sir,' (he says) 'I allow your virtues; I allow your literary talents: but I will not subscribe to your *indolence*; one little solitary annual Ode is not sufficient for a *great* King. Whatever things are *done*, whatever things are *said*, nay, whatever things are conceived, by mighty Potentates, are *treasure* for the page of History. Blush, my friend, that a *volunteer* Bard should run off with the merit of recording the wonderful actions and sapient sayings of Royalty. . . .'

That from the 'Solemn and Reprimanding Epistle to the Laureat' which is prefixed to *The Royal Tour, and Weymouth Amusements*; this, one of several such passages, from *The Remonstrance*:

> As for Court Virtues, wheresoe'er they lie,
> I leave them all to Mister Laureat Pye,
> The fashionable Bard whom Courts revere;
>   Who trotteth, with a grave and goodly pace,
> Deep-laden with his Sovereign, twice a year,
>   Around Parnassus's old famous base:
> Not only proving *his great King* alive,
> But that like Docks the Royal Virtues thrive.

Elsewhere Pindar remarks concisely that it is 'better to err with Pope, than shine with Pye.' At that time it was certainly more usual.

Pye thought highly of Thomas Warton, and seems to have considered the task of matching his predecessor's annual odes an exacting one; he wrote them (however unimpressive the result) with conscientious care and promptitude, and in verse of this kind:

> The hour of vengeance comes—by Gades' tow'rs,
>   By high Trafalgar's ever-trophied shore,
> The godlike warrier on the adverse Pow'rs
>   Leads his resistless fleet with daring prore.[1]
> Terrific as th' electric bolt that flies
> With fatal shock athwart the thund'ring skies,
>   By the mysterious will of Heaven
>   On man's presuming offspring driven,
> Full on the scattered foe he hurls his fires,
> Performs the dread behest, and in the flash expires.

---

[1] This engaging word, now "*poet.* and rare" according to my dictionary, may be thought to have been employed to furnish the rhyme. But to give Pye his due, it *does* mean the front end of a ship.

Pye's great standby was his loyalty, which never faltered, and year by year he affirmed with real sincerity that there never was a king like George; but confronted with such an occasion as Trafalgar he was able to reach no uncommon heights, and the few other martial episodes he notices during his twenty active years of office receive the same rather perfunctory treatment. This is particularly surprising because Pye was by way of being a military man and was for many years a member of the Berkshire Militia; even the comparatively novel subject of naval warfare had engaged his attention long before Trafalgar, for in 1798 he issued a handsome quarto dedicated to the King, containing *Naucratia—or Naval Dominion*, an elaborate poem discussing war at sea since the earliest times—together with passing remarks on storms and other hazards—and coming right up to date with observations on the several Admirals whom George was fortunate enough to have on his establishment. These few lines on Millbrook[1] will surprise readers who know that unattractive suburb of Southampton today, and serve at the same time to show that Pye's talents had reached no final perfection in the forty-odd years of his practice.

> *O Millbrook! shall my devious feet no more*
> *Pace the smooth margin of thy pebbly shore?*
> *No more my eyes, when even the zephyrs sleep,*
> *View the broad mirror of thy glassy deep,*
> *Where the reflected spire and bordering shade,*
> *Inverted shine, by softer tint portray'd?*

Pye's other exercises in military verse include a translation of *The Art of War*, by the King of Prussia, written and published in 1778 'at his leisure hours during the encampment at Coxheath.' But most celebrated of all was his translation of the War Elegies of Tyrtaeus, which Mathias gives us an engaging glimpse of in a note to the 1796 edition of *The Pursuits of Literature*:

> Mr. Pye, the present poet laureat, with the best intentions at this momentous period, if not with the very best poetry, translated the verses of Tyrtaeus the Spartan. They were designed to produce animation throughout the kingdom, and among the militia in particular. Several of the *Reviewing* Generals (I do not mean the Monthly or Critical) were much impressed with their *weight* and importance, and at a board of General Officers, an experiment was agreed upon, which unfortunately failed. They were read aloud

[1] To Millbrook in the course of time came Robert Pollok to be buried; although one of the most phenomenally successful poets of his day, he is now almost completely forgotten—especially, it seems, by the citizens of Southampton, who have not thought it worth while to pluck the weeds from his grave.

at Warley Common and at Barham Downs, by the adjutants, at the head of
five different regiments, at each camp, and much was expected. But before
they were half finished, all the front ranks, and as many of the others as
were within hearing or verse-shot, dropped their arms suddenly, and were
all found fast asleep! Marquis Townshend, who never approved of the scheme,
said, with his usual pleasantry, that the first of all poets observed, 'that sleep
is the brother of death.'

'Mr. Pye is a man of learning, and of some little fancy; but I wish his
poetry had more force,' Mathias adds.

From time to time the advice has been given, 'write about what
you know,' and few writers have taken it more to heart than Pye.
From the encampment at Coxheath he was in a strong position to
discuss (with the aid of Frederick the Great) the art of war; from the
marge at Millbrook he was able to command a view of the great
ocean (and be it noted, Southampton has four high tides a day, no
common phenomenon); and now we come to a third subject about
which he wrote from practical experience. This was the life of a
country gentleman.

There are two principal expressions of this subject; *Shooting*, (1784)
a poem, and *The Sportsman's Dictionary* which was 'improved and
enlarged' by Pye in 1807. I suppose this edition to be Pye's first
connection with the *Dictionary*.

Shooting has an occasional tang of the open air, together with not
a few lines which might well have been left unwritten. The short
passage I quote seems to be a favourite with commentators, since it
was chosen by Austin and Ralph for their *Lives of the Laureates*, and
again by Mr. John Gawsworth in his note on Pye in *Backwaters* (1932).
No-one, I am sure, will be so uncharitable as to suppose that Mr.
Gawsworth and I have borrowed this passage from Austin and Ralph
in order to avoid the tedium of reading the original for ourselves.

> *When the last sun of August's fiery reign*
> *Now bathes his radiant forehead in the main,*
> *The panoply by sportive heroes worn*
> *Is rang'd in order for the ensuing morn;*
> *Forth from the summer guard of bolt and lock*
> *Comes the thick guetre, and the fustian frock.*
> *With curious skill, the deathful tube is made,*
> *Clean as the firelock of the spruce parade:*
> *Yet let no polish of the sportsman's gun*
> *Flash like the soldier's weapon to the sun,*

> *Or the bright steel's refulgent glare presume,*
> *To penetrate the peaceful forest's gloom;*
> *But let it take the brown's more sober hue,*
> *Or the dark lustre of the enamell'd blue.*
> *Let the close pouch the wadded tow contain,*
> *The leaden pellets, and the nitrous grain;*
> *And wisely cautious, with preventive care,*
> *Be the spare flint and ready turnscrew there;*
> *While the slung net is open to receive*
> *Each prize the labours of the day shall give.*[1]

The Sportsman's Dictionary is a thick quarto and has a comprehensive title which leaves the prospective reader in no doubt what to expect if he turns the following pages. *The Sportsman's Dictionary* (it runs) *containing Instructions for Various Methods to be Observed in Riding, Hunting, Fowling, Setting, Fishing, Racing, Farriery, Hawking, Breeding and Feeding Horses for the Road and Turf; the management of Dogs, Game and Dunghill-Cocks, Turkeys, Geese, Ducks, Doves, Singing-Birds, etc; and the manner of curing their various diseases and accidents.* As a work of this kind is seldom undertaken, and perhaps even less frequently completed, and as I think no other Laureate was ever concerned in anything so practical, I will give several specimens of useful information from it:

> ENTREPAS, is a broken pace, or going, and indeed properly a broken amble, that is neither a walk nor trot, but somewhat of an amble. This is the pace or gait of such horses as have no reins or back, but go upon their shoulders, or of such as are spoiled in their limbs.

[1] In fairness to Pye it must be admitted that his is not the worst poem on the subject of shooting, for in 1841 Alexander Webber published a poem of the same name, from which I extract the following:

> . . . *First, then, the Gun, on which so much depends,*
> *Polite remembrance for your worthy friends;*
> *I name no maker, be it understood,*
> *'Twould needless be, as all turn out some good,*
> *And oft a name unknown will kill as far*
> *As Manton, Golding, Moore, or Mortimer;*
> *But wheresoe'er you purchase, mind you try*
> *This sporting 'ne plus ultra,' 'fore you buy,*
> *And be it where it may, now mark this well,*
> *Be sure that bears his name, he you may sell,*
> *Then will his reputation be at stake,*
> *While one you use, he own of his best make;*
> *And if you pay a price, 'tis two to one*
> *He places in your hands a first-rate gun.*
> *Nor with a double ever shall I quarrel,*
> *Fourteen the guage, and two feet six the barrel* . . .

On this comparison, it will be seen that Pye was the more accomplished versifier; but perhaps Webber was the better shot.

HEAD, pain in, of goats, often happens through excessive heats or colds; also from wet or unwholesome feedings.

Take a handful of rosemary tops, an ounce of turmeric beaten into powder, and the like quantity of mithridate; boil them in water, and put a little vinegar to it, and so let him drink half a pint each morning: put vinegar, wherein hyssop has been seethed, into his nostrils, and hold up his head, that he turn it not out, for six minutes, or thereabout.

(Perhaps a future Laureate, happening to revise this work, will also explain how the goat makes it understood where the pain is, in the first place.) Finally, for those who like puzzles, there is this one:

CAPERON, of a BITT MOUTH, is a word only used for scratch mouths, and all others that are not cannon-mouths, signifying the end of the bitt that joins to the branch, just by the nanquet.

In scratch-mouths the chaperon is round, but in others it is oval; and the same part that in scratched, and other mouths, is called chaperon, is in cannon-mouths called froncean.

In 1792 Pye was appointed a Police Magistrate for Westminster. He had served as a magistrate in Berkshire, and no doubt entered upon his new duties light-heartedly; but perhaps in a great city the justices have a more exacting task. At all events there is reason to think Pye found it so, judging by a story told by Leigh Hunt in his autobiography:

I saw (Pye) once in a state of scornful indignation at being interrupted in the perusal of a manuscript by the monitions of his police-officers, who were obliged to remind him over and over again that he was a magistrate, and that the criminal multitude were in waiting. . . .

Hunt implies that the manuscript may have been the poems of Horace [and Pye did, indeed, re-edit the translation by Philip Francis], but I think it would be more charitable to suppose he was engaged upon his *Summary of the Duties of a Justice of the Peace out of Sessions* which appeared in 1808 and is said to have been of great service to his fellow magistrates.

Pye, as we have seen, was master of a curious prose style as well as of a style in verse which for want of an exacter word we may call 'interesting;' and in 1796 he put forth, anonymously, a little two volume tale called *The Democrat* which owes something to Johnson's *Rasselas*, and something possibly to Goldsmith's *A Citizen of the World*. It is the story of a young Frenchman, part idealist, part rogue, who comes to England full of democratic principles (the word had been somewhat less abused in 1796 than it has since) and observes how far life in this country measures up to his ideals. He puts his point of view somewhat less eloquently than Imlac does in *Rasselas*, but in a manner which may have influenced Marryat when he gave Mr. Midshipman Easy certain opinions on the rights of man.

Another celebrated character who is somewhat anticipated in *The Democrat* is Mr. Nupkins, the majestic magistrate of Ipswich, who makes a great figure in Chapters 24 and 25 of *Pickwick*. Pye's magistrate behaves in a manner uncommonly like that of Mr. Nupkins—and has to be kept within the law he administers by a clerk somewhat like the unfortunate who served Mr. Nupkins. As for Pye's hero, le Noir, he is a kind of Alfred Jingle.

The Democrat had a modest success and was followed in 1799 by *The Aristocrat*, which I have not examined. Pye's other excursions in prose include a book of essays, *Sketches on Various Subjects, Moral Literary and Political, by the Author of The Democrat* (1796). The subjects include 'The Antiquity of the Round Robin,' 'Some Thoughts on Gardening,' 'Old Age,' and 'The Effect of Music on Animals.' And here is an example of how to say in fifty-five words what might frugally have been said in ten:

> It is a proverbial observation, that, in this country, persons, for want of other topics of conversation, are very apt to introduce the weather, and so to inform the company, as if it were a discovery they had just made, and with which everyone else was unacquainted, that it is a fine or a bad day.
> —'On the Weather.'

In 1799 Pye sent forth his *Carmen Seculare for the Year* 1800 with a long preface in which he argues (with a table of figures to back him up) that 1800 and not 1801 is the first year of the new century; he calls on Dryden and Prior to support him. Something of the same problem cropped up in 1950 when various people thought we had reached the half-way mark in our own enlightened and unhappy century; and certain others thought we hadn't. *The Gentleman's Magazine* reviewed Pye's work respectfully, but refused to swallow his arguments; having summarised them, it continues, 'The worthy Laureate has certainly got into a scrape; and we wish him well out of it; but we have stated his arguments fairly: tho' not convinced by an iota of the statement that 99 can make 100.'

Getting into scrapes was another of Pye's customs—'scrapes' is just the word, for none of his quarrels and controversies amounted to much. In 1807 he published his *Comments on the Commentators of Shakespeare*. We have already seen the fun Mathias had with Warton and the Gibbe-cat. Pye approaches the matter in exactly the same

way, working through the plays and pointing out the absurdity of
learned men producing involved speculations to explain points which
are entirely clear to the ordinary reader; and there was some justification for the little book, for it must be agreed that many of the
eighteenth century critics of Shakespeare got hopelessly tangled up in
their erudition and were apt to overlook the plain merit of the man.
For, as Roscommon had remarked a century earlier,

> *He only proves he understands a text*
> *Whose exposition leaves it unperplex'd.*

and an anonymous praiser of Dryden's Virgil made a similar point:

> *. . . through the mazes of their comments led,*
> *We learn not what he writes but what they read.*

Pye, in a book full of good sense and odd information, does something
to undermine the pedants—and adds his own quota of mystification
here and there. Speaking for all those attacked, living and dead,
Francis Douce wrote a long letter to the *Gentleman's Magazine* setting
Shakespearian scholarship firmly back on its feet and putting Pye in
his place.

One other of the Laureate's many works claims a word here, and
that is *Alfred, an epic poem in six books* (1806). Alfred has fared rather
badly in English literature, for there are no important poems about
him in our earlier literature, and although the nineteenth century
produced several none of them has established its own fame or worthily
celebrated his. Even so early as 1806 Pye was not the first in the field,
for Joseph Cottle's *Alfred, an Heroic Poem, in twenty-four books* had been
available for six years, although the public seemed unaware of this.

It was noted above on Pye's behalf that his poem on *Shooting* is not
the worst on this subject in the language. It will be friendly now to his
memory to vindicate his *Alfred* in the same way, especially as neither
his poem nor Cottle's is to be found on every bookshelf.

Here, in book two of Pye's epic, we find Alfred at the most widely
known of his enterprises—burning the cakes:

> *. . . Sad o'er the hearth the pensive hero hung,*
> *Fix'd his unweening eye, and mute his tongue,*
> *Deeply intent on scenes of present woe,*
> *Or planning future vengeance on the foe,*
> *The objects round him, like the viewless air,*
> *Pass o'er his mind, nor leave an image there;*

> Hence oft with flippant tongue the busy dame
> The reckless stranger's apathy would blame,
> Who, careless let the flame those viands waste,
> His ready hunger ne'er refused to taste.
> Ah! little deeming that her pensive guest,
> High majesty and higher worth possess'd,
> Or that her voice presumptuous dared to chide
> Alfred, her country's sovereign and its pride.

From this it appears that the King made a habit of burning cakes, and didn't merely err on an isolated occasion. Cottle, as befits a poet having twenty-four books to his poem, takes time to turn round and tells the same story in much greater detail, with dialogue, too: (Acca, a neatherd's wife, has taken in the disguised Alfred and now explains his presence to Ceolric, her returning husband)

> . . . 'It is a friendless man
> Who sought our dwelling, and petition'd hard,
> For food and service in thy absence. I,
> Too readily by pity borne away!
> (Fault of my easy nature) stood and heard
> His mournful tale, who having promised fair
> To do the servant's part, him I received;
> But never came beneath a door, a man
> More thoughtless, or perversely bent on dreams
> Bewildering. Many an hour he sits and hums
> About one Caedman, and then stops and frowns
> At something in the air; then rises up,
> And walks with stately mien, then sits again,
> And shaves his bow, or with more furious eye,
> Gazes in vacancy. In truth I think
> The man half mad, for not an hour ago,
> The household cakes that yonder lie, half burnt,
> And smoking on the hearth, I to him gave,
> And with strict charge, and caution often told,
> Warn'd him to turn, and with due care preserve
> From scorching heat; then to the fields I sped
> To tend the kine; and now again return'd;
> When, as the door I opened and look'd round;
> Unmindful, on his chair he sat, his eyes
> Fix'd on the floor, his knife beside, while near
> Lay many a half-form'd bow. But, sad to tell!
> My cakes, for thy return, prepared to show
> A wife's affection, lay involv'd in smoke;

Now nothing worth; and this strange loon at hand,
Regardless. Dost thou hear?' she cried,
And stamp'd her foot, and with indignant ire,
Vow'd oft and bitterly, no other food
Should he receive, till he had eaten all
The black-burnt cakes.
                              Ceolric thus replied:
'Heed not the cakes. It was a small mishap . . .'

Ceolric was apparently a man of few words, which is more than could be said for Joseph Cottle.

Before leaving Alfred I cannot forbear to add that to the heroic poem of 1800 and the epic of 1806, Sir Coutts Lindsay, Bart., in 1845 added *Alfred, a Drama* in which the cake episode is unaccountably allowed to give place to the antics of several characters called Ulf, Ubbo, etc., most of whom stab themselves or each other; and in 1858 there was 'printed, not published' *Alfred, a Patriotic Play in five acts*, by Martin F. Tupper. Although, being 'not published' this work is nearly as unknown as those that were, we have a reference to it in Tupper's *Autobiography*. It was produced in Manchester and—'not thinking of what was expected of me in the way of thanks for the ovation their concluding cheers assailed me with, I got out of the theatre as quick as I could, and was half way to my hotel when two or three excited supers rushed after me with a "Good God, Mr. Tupper, come back, come back, or the place will be torn down!"' No such success attended Pye's efforts.

Here is Tupper on the cakes episode:

Alfred.   *But no, no, no!*
            My people, England—etc. (half a page omitted)
            (Enter Egga from behind)

Egga.   *How now?—What, a-mouthing again! How's the manchets?—*
            Whew! they're cinders!—why, thou poor harlotry play-actor, be
            this thy way o' winning bread?—to burn the manchets, and all
            for a spell o' speech-making?—Out on thee, thriftless! (She
            offers to strike him.)

            (Enter Ethelnoth, and Hereward with the neatherd.)

Wulf.   *Here, this way, mighty captains, here's our archer.*
Ethelnoth. *O king, O blessed hour!*
Hereward.   *England's darling!*

And finally—Tupper in the meantime having added a translation of Alfred's poems to the shelf—in 1896 another Laureate, Alfred Austin, published *England's Darling*, which also is a drama. In his preface Austin remarks that 'the greatest of Englishmen has never been celebrated by an English poet,' and (lest this point be not fully established) he adds 'No Englishman has sung Alfred the Great.' 'He is forgotten by Chaucer,' Austin writes, 'all but ignored by Spenser, unnamed by Shakespeare.' He is determined to remedy this, after affirming yet again that 'Alfred hitherto has been glorified in no English poem.' In Austin's drama the cake-burning is mentioned in passing:

> EDGIVA, entering, finds her mother upbraiding
> ALFRED for allowing the cakes to scorch.

EDGIVA

Nay, mother, but you must not flout him thus.
Heed his gray hairs, look on his furrowed brow,
And that strange something which nor you, nor I,
Nor any of the level breed of folk,
Have in their seeming. 'Tis a scholar's face,
With far-off gaze, away in other lands,
Whither we may nor fare nor follow him.
Look on his inkhorn. Nay, be quieted:
I'll rasp the cakes; they're but a trifle singed,
And we shall sup in plenty.

> DANEWULF'S wife, still muttering her laments,
> leaves ALFRED and EDGIVA alone.

Generally speaking, I think the nineteenth century did not say the last word on England's Darling.[1]

In 1810 Pye's last works appeared—a translation of Homer's *Iliad* and his *Epigrams*, and a translation of Pindar in which Pye revised the work of Gilbert West and Edward Burnaby Greene. In 1811 the King became insane and the Laureate Odes again ceased to be called for. Pye —never a prominent figure—disappears from the scene into a villa at Pinner, and there dies on August 11th, 1813, leaving his second wife and a son—with his daughters by the poetic Mary—to mourn him.

---

[1] In 1910 G. K. Chesterton's *Ballad of the White Horse* appeared. This is certainly the most vigorous and readable poem on Alfred I have yet come upon; but as we have seen, it is faced with little effective competition.

11

Robert Southey

NOW for the third time George III lacked a Laureate; but the appointment in 1813 was the concern of the Regent, for George was in no state of health to know or care about the promotion of poets. The appointment of Robert Southey is more fully documented than most, but before describing it a sketch of his life—it can hardly be more—may find a place. The reader who would know everything should consult the life by Professor Simmons,[1] which is among the best biographies of recent years, and at last does credit to one of the most neglected of our great writers.

Robert Southey was a Bristol man by birth, the son of a struggling draper; in or around Bristol he spent his first fifteen years, living much of the time with his formidable Aunt Tyler. He was then (1788) sent to Westminster School and in due course (1792) expelled again owing to a difference of opinion with the Headmaster on the subject of flogging. Southey had taken part in founding a school magazine called *The Flagellant*, to the fifth number of which he contributed his famous paper on flogging; it is clever nonsense which a sensible master would have attended to by redoubled efforts on the other side. But William Vincent took a much more serious view of the offence, perhaps, (Professor Simmons suggests) because it was a public rather than a domestic matter: the paper was produced by a well known printer and was on sale to all. Southey's nom-de-plume 'Gualbertus' was quickly penetrated and (after some angry exchanges) he was expelled; more than this, Vincent warned the Christ Church authorities at Oxford against him. In due course, Southey went to Balliol instead.

As he grew older Southey transferred his reforming zeal from flogging to graver matters; he watched the progress of the French Revolution with sympathy, even after England and France were at war. These harmless youthful enthusiasms were to get him into trouble

[1] *Southey* by Jack Simmons, 1945.

in later years, especially as he wrote some of them down. Meanwhile, he enjoyed Oxford, made new friends, and prepared first to take orders (against his inclination) and next to study medicine. After this he thought that perhaps he was more suited to the civil service. Like a great many clever young men, he couldn't really determine how to employ his life, and like most of us in the end he drifted into the way that served him best.

At Oxford he first met Coleridge—(who was only visiting the city, for he was a Cambridge man himself). They quickly became friends and in a very short time, with the help of one or two kindred spirits, had hatched the famous project for a joint emigration and settlement in America. A dozen young men, with their wives, were to found an agricultural community under 'Pantisocracy'—'the equal government of all.' Coleridge departed after three weeks full of the plan, and Southey was left at Oxford reflecting more soberly upon it. He thought it would work and he decided that his own first move must be to leave the university, which he did without taking a degree. The history of Pantisocracy from its enthusiastic inception to its miserable end cannot be told in detail here: 'America! Southey! Miss Fricker!' Coleridge exclaimed in that first enthusiasm, and a bare year later he and Southey could cut one another in the street. Indeed all they got from the scheme was a wife each.

One of the Pantisocrats, Robert Lovell, had married a Bristol girl called Mary Fricker, and Southey was keeping company with her sister Edith; it seemed a fine idea for Coleridge to have the third sister, Sara. Coleridge had no objection, but he was a bit vague in these matters as in others and he went off to London and began thinking how nice it would be to marry someone else. However, eventually he married Sara. In the meantime Southey had married Edith (on November 14th, 1795) and departed for Portugal, leaving his wife to wear her wedding ring round her neck in secret, for several rather complicated reasons.

Southey had now put out one or two books and had plans for writing more. He, Coleridge and Lovell had agreed to write a play, one act each; Coleridge had written his act, and Southey with characteristic energy had written his own and Lovell's. *The Fall of Robespierre* was published in 1794, not so very long after Robespierre's actual fall. In the same year Southey and Lovell shared in a volume of *Poems*, published at Bath. Now Joseph Cottle of Bristol, a clever and active young bookseller, had undertaken to publish a collection of *Letters* written from Portugal, and while these were being assembled gave Southey fifty guineas for his first long poem, *Joan of Arc*.

Although the trip to Portugal with his uncle, the Rev. Herbert Hill, (who held a chaplaincy at Oporto) was designed to bring Southey under a good influence for a time and knock silly ideas like Pantisocracy out of his head—his uncle, who had paid for his education, still hoped he would take orders—it seemed clear that Southey's career lay in letters. Whatever he said, he must himself have begun to think so.

Southey returned from Portugal in the early summer of 1796 still determined not to take orders, but ready to give the law a trial. His schooldays friend C. W. W. Wynn, with a generosity not sufficiently common in rich mens' dealing with poets, had promised to make him an annuity of £160 from his twenty-first birthday, and upon this Southey and his wife now based their economy. *Joan of Arc* had appeared, and had made a modest success; Southey's name was getting known, and he was able to obtain journalistic work. His *Letters Written during a Short Residence in Spain and Portugal* appeared in the spring of 1797, when he had taken up his studies at Gray's Inn, and at the same time Cottle put out a new volume of his poems. The early, short poems, incidentally, contain some of his most delightful work; and also the work which first exposed him to the attentions of the satirists. Here is a charming passage of the first sort; it is the dedicatory sonnet of the 1797 volume:

> With way-worn feet, a traveller woe-begone,
>   Life's upward road I journey'd many a day,
>   And framing many a sad yet soothing lay,
>   Beguiled the solitary hours with song.
> Lonely my heart and rugged was the way,
>   Yet often pluck'd I, as I past along,
>   The wild and simple flowers of poesy;
>   And sometimes, unreflecting as a child,
> Entwined the weeds which pleased a random eye.
> Take thou the wreath, BELOVED! it is wild
> And rudely garlanded; yet scorn not thou
> The humble offering, where dark rosemary weaves
> Amid gay flowers its melancholy leaves,
> And myrtle gathered to adorn thy brow.

Southey's love for Edith remained unchanging until her death in 1837.

The satirists who now took notice of the young poet were the authors of *The Anti-Jacobin*, and like the *Rolliad* authors before them, they were a mixed and somewhat numerous company.

In the autumn of 1797 Canning, assisted by Gifford, Ellis, Frere, and other young Tory men of letters, started *The Anti-Jacobin or Weekly Examiner* in support of Pitt. The paper ran for just over seven months and attained its greatest celebrity for the political and satirical verse which formed a large part of its contents. A number of poets were parodied and ridiculed, notably Erasmus Darwin, whose strange poem *The Loves of the Plants* inspired that masterpiece of satirical humour, 'The Loves of the Triangles.' Southey came in for notice by his experiments in metre, 'The Widow' (in Sapphics) and 'The Soldier's Wife' (in Dactylics). Southey's poems were not so very bad, although these metres do not adapt themselves readily to English verse.[1] I give 'The Widow,' in order to have the pleasure of transcribing the parody of it, which is perhaps the first great example of that entertaining art in the language.

THE WIDOW

Cold was the night wind; drifting fast the snows fell;
Wide were the downs, and shelterless and naked;
When a poor wanderer struggled on her journey,
    Weary and way-sore.

Drear were the down, more dreary her reflections;
Cold was the night wind, colder was her bosom:
She had no home, the world was all before her,
    She had no shelter.

Fast o'er the heath a chariot rattled by her:
'Pity me!' feebly cried the poor night wanderer.
'Pity me, strangers! lest with cold and hunger
    Here I should perish.

'Once I had friends—but they have all forsook me!
Once I had parents—they are now in heaven!
I had a home once—I had once a husband—
    Pity me, strangers!

'I had a home once—I had once a husband—
I am a widow, poor and broken-hearted!'
Loud blew the wind, unheard was her complaining;
    On drove the chariot.

[1] Tennyson and Bridges were the other Laureates with a special interest in classical metres.

Then on the snow she laid her down to rest her;
She heard a horseman: 'Pity me!' she groaned out.
Loud was the wind, unheard was her complaining;
　　On went the horseman.

Worn out with anguish, toil, and cold and hunger,
Down sunk the wanderer; sleep had seized her senses:
There did the traveller find her in the morning—
　　God had released her.

This was a sad tale, but it afforded excellent material for parody. As
the *Anti-Jacobin* authors rightly remarked, 'the pathos of the matter
is not a little relieved by the absurdity of the metre.' They then proceed
with their imitation:

SAPPHICS

THE FRIEND OF HUMANITY AND THE KNIFE GRINDER

Friend of Humanity

'Needy Knife-grinder! whither are you going?
Rough is the road, your wheel is out of order—
Bleak blows the blast; your hat has got a hole in't,
　　So have your breeches!

'Weary Knife-grinder! little think the proud ones,
Who in their coaches roll along the turnpike-
-road, what hard work 'tis crying all day, "Knives and
　　Scissars to grind O!"

'Tell me, Knife-grinder, how you came to grind knives?
Did some rich man tyrannically use you?
Was it the squire? or parson of the parish?
　　Or the attorney?

'Was it the squire, for killing of his game, or
Covetous parson, for his tithes distraining?
Or roguish lawyer, made you lose your little
　　All in a law-suit?

'(Have you not read the Rights of Man by Tom Paine?)
Drops of compassion tremble on my eyelids,
Ready to fall, as soon as you have told your
　　Pitiful story.'

Knife-grinder

'Story! God bless you! I have none to tell, sir,
Only last night, a-drinking at the Chequers,
This poor old hat and breeches, as you see, were
Torn in a scuffle.

'Constables came up, for to take me into
Custody; they took me before the justice;
Justice Oldmixon put me in the parish-
stocks for a vagrant.

'I should be glad to drink your Honour's health in
A pot of beer, if you will give me sixpence;
But for my part, I never love to meddle
With politics, sir.'

Friend of Humanity

'I give thee sixpence! I will see thee damned first—
Wretch! whom no sense of wrongs can rouse to vengeance—
Sordid, unfeeling, reprobate, degraded,
Spiritless outcast!'

(Kicks the Knife-grinder, overturns his wheel, and exit in a transport of Republican enthusiasm and universal philanthropy.)

This and other attacks in the same quarter seem to have troubled Southey little, although ten years later he wrote in a letter to John Rickman 'I have seen tonight what I never expected to see—a book of mine advertised with a recommendation from the Anti-Jacobins!' He went quietly on with his writing, doing more and more journalism and working at a long poem, *Thalaba*, the first of his epics (if we leave the not wholly successful *Joan of Arc* out of the reckoning.)

Gradually, as his writing commitments increased, and as they modestly prospered, too, he withdrew from the law. At last, in 1803, he and Edith moved up to Keswick to join the Coleridges at Greta Hall. Southey had found his home for forty years.

Greta Hall is not the least celebrated literary home in English literature. It was visited by many of the greatest men of the early nineteenth century, and from it issued a number of formidable books. Here, in half the house, lived Coleridge with his wife and three children—Hartley, Derwent, and Sara. The Southeys made two more, for their first child, Margaret, had just died; and the second, Edith May, was to be born a year or so later. With them came also Mary Lovell, the third Fricker sister. Coleridge was away when these additions to his household arrived and soon after his return from the tour of Scotland he had been taking with the Wordsworths his health made it needful for him to set forth again, this time for the Mediterranean. Southey settled down to care for the large and miscellaneous company of survivors,[1] a task which he performed, more or less, until the end of Coleridge's life, for that somewhat unsatisfactory husband and father found it difficult enough to manage his own affairs, without giving attention to those of his dependents.

Southey was perhaps the most indefatigable and tireless worker in our literature; no-one has ever computed how much he wrote, for his many books represent only a fraction of his output. He wrote extensively in magazines and reviews for forty years, and in 1804, with Coleridge gone, had settled at Greta Hall to this tremendous task. By 1813, when the Laureateship became vacant, he had published nearly a dozen books of verse, a number of large translations from French, Spanish and Portugese, and several prose works including the first volume of his great *History of Brazil*. He had also edited the works and written the lives of Chatterton and Kirke White, and had compiled various anthologies.

The day after Pye died was Southey's thirty-ninth birthday. He was at Greta Hall, but soon afterwards he found it necessary to make a trip to London on literary business, and so he found himself suddenly in the middle of the arrangements for the succession. It was not altogether a surprise. He was, after all, an established man of letters with a score of books to his name. His long poems—*Thalaba the Destroyer*, *Madoc* and *The Curse of Kehama*—were all respected, and better still, read—at least all had gone into two or more editions.[2] As historian, critic, translator, his name stood well before the world. He was, moreover, rather hard up, so that the income from the appointment would be useful. All these considerations, added to personal

---

[1] One result of this is noted by N. P. Willis in *Pencillings by the Way* (1830), where he thus quotes Christopher North: 'Walter Scott said of Southey, that he lived too much with women. He is secluded in the country, and surrounded by a circle of admiring friends, who glorify every literary project he undertakes, and persuade him, in spite of his natural modesty, that he can do nothing wrong or imperfectly. He has great genius, and is a most estimable man.'

[2] But without notably establishing the writer's finances. Anna Seward says, '[Southey] excites my concern and indignation by saying, that the profits on a year's sale of that glorious poem [Madoc] amounted to £3/17/1; a deep disgrace to the national sensibility and judgment.' (Letter to Scott, August 24, 1807).

friendship, prompted Walter Scott to put forward the name of Southey when refusing the appointment for himself.

It seemed natural for the Prince Regent to turn first to Scott. For some years the long narrative poems of Scott had made him the most widely read of contemporary poets, and the decline in his poetical reputation which began (as we can now see) with the publication of the first books of Byron's *Childe Harold* was hardly perceptible. No one— not even Scott himself—foresaw that he was soon to give up poetry for the composition of prose romances. He was still the Walter Scott of the *Last Minstrel, Marmion,* and the rest.

The offer of the vacancy to Scott, and its subsequent transferrence to Southey reflects credit on both parties, which isn't surprising for they were both admirable fellows and good friends.

In August, 1813, Scott was in the middle of the financial troubles which resulted from his complicated excursions into printing and publishing. Accordingly, his first reaction must have been one of relief when he received this letter from the Prince Regent's librarian:

> Pavilion, Brighton,
> August 18, 1813.
>
> My dear Sir,
>
> Though I have never had the honour of being introduced to you, you have frequently been pleased to convey to me very kind and flattering messages, and I trust, therefore, you will allow me, without any further ceremony, to say, — That I took an early opportunity this morning of seeing the Prince Regent, who arrived here late yesterday; and I then delivered to his Royal Highness my earnest wish and anxious desire that the vacant situation of poet laureate might be conferred on you. The Prince replied, 'that you had already been written to, and that if you wished it everything would be settled as I could desire.'
>
> I hope, therefore, I may be allowed to congratulate you on this event. You are the man to whom it ought first to have been offered, and it gave me sincere pleasure to find that those sentiments of high approbation which my Royal Master had so often expressed towards you in private, were now so openly and honourably displayed in public. Have the goodness, dear sir, to receive this intrusive letter with your accustomed courtesy, and believe me, yours very sincerely,
>
> J. S. Clarke,[1]
> Librarian to H.R.H. the Prince Regent.

[1] The Rev. James Stanier Clarke, F.R.S., Historiographer Royal and author of various forgotten works, mostly with a maritime flavour, including a two-volume life of Nelson, written in collaboration with John McArthur. Southey said of him on his appointment as Historiographer, 'he is a painstaking man, and so far fit for it, but a most extraordinary blockhead, and so far unfit.' Southey was an unsuccessful candidate for the same appointment.

This offer—when officially made—would be worth, Scott supposed, three or four hundred pounds a year, a most welcome thought. Meanwhile, the Regent's phrase, 'already written to' was not strictly true. Lord Hertford, the Lord Chamberlain, had perhaps more letters to write than Mr. Clarke. It was not until the 31st that he wrote to Scott:

> Ragley, 31st August, 1813.
>
> Sir,
>
> I thought it my duty to his Royal Highness the Prince Regent, to express to him my humble opinion that I could not make so creditable a choice as in your person for the office, now vacant, of poet laureate. I am now authorised to offer it to you, which I would have taken an earlier opportunity of doing but that, till this morning, I have had no occasion of seeing his Royal Highness since Mr. Pye's death. I have the honour to be, sir, your most obedient humble servant,
>
> Ingram Hertford.

Scott, with Clarke's letter before him, was already considering the offer and indeed had probably already decided to refuse it, for he had asked advice of the Duke of Buccleuch, who looked upon the idea with disfavour; and Scott was not the man lightly to ignore the opinion of the head of his clan. Buccleuch wrote unequivocally:

> . . . As to the offer of His Royal Highness to appoint you laureate, I shall frankly say that I should be mortified to see you hold a situation which, by the general concurrence of the world, is stamped ridiculous. There is no good reason why this should be so; but so it is. *Walter Scott, Poet Laureate*, ceases to be Walter Scott of the Lay, Marmion, &c. Any future poem of yours would not come forward with the same probability of a successful reception. The poet laureate would stick to you and your productions like a piece of *court plaster*. . . . I would write frankly to His Royal Highness, but with respectful gratitude, for he *has* paid you a compliment. . . . Only think of being chaunted and recitatived by a parcel of hoarse and squeaking choristers on a birthday, for the edification of the bishops, pages, maids of honour, and gentlemen-pensioners! Oh, horrible, thrice horrible!

This letter also included the Duke's acquiescence in a loan of £4,000 requested by Scott, and doubtless this made his advice extra palatable. Scott wrote at once to decline, officially to Lord Hertford and un-officially, at greater length, to Clarke. And, ever mindful of his friends, he whispered the name of Southey into Croker's ear; for John Wilson Croker, Secretary to the Admiralty, had influence over men as well as ships.

I have said it seemed natural for the Regent to turn first to Scott, the most prominent poet of the day; but in fact the Regent had done nothing of the kind. Within a few days of Pye's death Croker, after consulting with Gifford and with Southey himself when he reached London, had suggested to the Prince Regent that Southey was the right man; and the Prince agreed. Croker then learned that Lord Liverpool, the Prime Minister, and Lord Hertford, had decided to offer the post to Scott. Everybody was vexed, especially the Prince, but it was decided to wait and see what Scott said in reply. These events found a reflection in Clarke's letter to Scott: 'You are the man to whom it ought first to have been offered. . . .' but Scott was never fully informed of the secret history of the offer, which successfully adjusted itself when he declined.

Southey's position at this time was not so precarious as Scott's, but he was struggling, as he struggled all his life, to find enough money for all his many commitments, and he accepted at once when formally offered the appointment. A letter to his friend Charles Wynn puts his point of view:

> . . . Pye's death was announced a day or two before my departure from Keswick, and at the time I thought it so probable that the not-very-desirable succession might be offered to me, as to bestow a little serious thought upon the subject, as well as a jest or two. On my arrival in town Bedford came to my brother's to meet me at breakfast; told me that Croker had spoken with him about it, and he with Gifford; that they supposed the onus of the office would be dropt, or if it were not, that I might so execute it as to give it a new character; and that as *detur dignioi* was the maxim upon which the thing was likely to be bestowed, they thought it would become me to accept it. My business, however, whatever might be my determination, was to call without delay at the Admiralty, thank C. for what was actually intended well, and learn how the matter stood.
>
> Accordingly I called on Croker. He had spoken to the Prince; and the Prince observing that I had written 'some good things in favour of the Spaniards,' said the office should be given to me. You will admire the reason; and infer from it that I ought to have been made historiographer because I had written Madoc. Presently Croker meets Lord Liverpool, and tells him what had passed; Lord Liverpool expressed his sorrow that he had not known it a day sooner, for he and the Marquis of Hertford had consulted together upon whom the vacant honour could most properly be bestowed. Scott was the greatest poet of the day, and to Scott therefore they had written to offer it. The Prince was displeased at this; though he said he ought to have been consulted, it was his pleasure that I should have it, and have it I should. Upon this Croker represented that he was Scott's friend as well as mine, that Scott and I were upon friendly terms; and for the sake of all three he requested that the business might rest where it was.
>
> Thus it stood when I made my first call at the Admiralty. I more than half suspected that Scott would decline the offer, and my own mind was

made up before this suspicion was verified. The manner in which Scott declined it was the handsomest possible; nothing could be more friendly to me, or more honourable to himself.

Everybody in this affair was now writing letters back and forth and to transcribe them all would almost fill a book; but Scott's 'handsome' manner of declining must be given. He wrote to Southey at the same time as he wrote to Lord Hertford, but Southey didn't receive the letter at once, for it was addressed to Keswick and he was in London. When he did receive it he at once transcribed it for the benefit of his wife, who was still at home:

One of the letters which you forwarded . . . was from Scott. It will be easier to transcribe it than to give its contents; and it does him so much honour that you ought to see it without delay. 'My dear Southey,—On my return home I found, to my no small surprise, a letter tendering me the laurel vacant by the death of the poetical Pye. I have declined the appointment as being incompetent to the task of annual commemoration; but chiefly as being provided for in my professional department, and unwilling to incur the censure of engrossing the emolument attached to one of the few appointments which seems proper to be filled by a man of literature who has no other views in life. Will you forgive me, my dear friend, if I own I had you in my recollection? I have given Croker the hint, and otherwise endeavoured to throw the office into your *choice*[1] (this is not Scott's word, but I cannot decypher the right one). I am uncertain if you will like it, for the laurel has certainly been tarnished by some of its wearers, and, as at present managed, its duties are inconvenient and somewhat liable to ridicule. But the latter matter might be amended, and I should think the Regent's good sense would lead him to lay aside those biennial commemorations; and as to the former point, it has been worn by Dryden of old, and by Warton in modern days. If you quote my own refusal against me, I reply, 1st, I have been luckier than you in holding two offices not usually conjoined. 2dly, I did not refuse it from any foolish prejudice against the situation, otherwise how durst I mention it to you my elder brother in the muse? but from a sort of internal hope that they would give it to you, upon whom it would be so much more worthily conferred. For I am not such an ass as not to know that you are my better in poetry, though I have had (probably but for a time) the tide of popularity in my favour. I have not time to add ten thousand other reasons, but I only wished to tell you how the matter was, and to beg you to think before you reject the offer which I flatter myself will be made to you. If I had not been, like Dogberry, a fellow with two gowns already, I should have jumped at it like a cock at a gooseberry. Ever yours most truly, W.S.

. . . as soon as this letter reached me I wrote a note to Croker to this effect, — that I would not write odes as boys write exercises, at stated times

---

[1] Lockhart gives the word as 'option.' His text of this letter (*Life of Scott*, Vol. IV, pages 86–87) differs here and there in a word or two from Southey's and is probably the more strictly accurate, but the differences are unimportant.

and upon stated subjects; but that if it were understood that upon great public events I might either write or be silent as the spirit moved, I should now accept the office as an honourable distinction, which under those circumstances it would become. Tomorrow I shall see him. The salary is but a nominal £120; and, as you see, I shall either reject it, or make the title honourable by accepting it upon my own terms.

Southey's 'terms' were very properly rebuked by Croker with the observation 'it is not for us to make terms with the Prince Regent,'[1] but despite this Southey accepted. He seems to have been led to suppose the letter of the duties would not be insisted upon, though in fact he was called upon for an official poem almost at once.

Before this, however, the appointment had to be officially made, which seems a simple matter after all the preliminaries had been disposed of. But Southey's account is not simple.

On November 5th, Southey writes to Scott:

If you have not guessed at the reason why your letter has lain ten weeks unanswered, you must have thought me a very thankless and graceless fellow, and very undeserving of such a letter.[2] I waited from day to day that I might tell you all was completed, and my patience was nearly exhausted in the process. Let me tell you the whole history in due order, before I express my feelings towards you upon the occasion. Upon receiving yours I wrote to Croker, saying that the time was passed when I could write verses upon demand, but that if it were understood that, instead of the old formalities, I might be at liberty to write upon great public events or to be silent, as the spirit moved, — in that case the office would become a mark of honourable distinction, and I should be proud of accepting it. How this was to be managed he best knew; for of course, it was not for me to propose terms to the Prince. When next I saw him he told me that, after the appointment was completed, he or some other person in the Prince's confidence, would suggest to him the fitness of making this reform, in an office which requires some reform to rescue it from the contempt into which it had fallen. I thought all was settled, and expected every day to receive some official communication, but week after week past on. My headquarters at this time were at Streatham. Going one day into town to my brothers, I found that Lord William Gordon, with whom I had left a card on my first arrival, had called three times on me in as many days, and had that morning requested that I would call on him at eleven, twelve, one, or two o'clock. I went accordingly, never dreaming of what this business could be, and wondering at it. He told me that the Marquis of Hertford was his brother-in-law, and

---

[1] The same phrase occurs also in one of Southey's letters, as though original. I cannot determine whether Southey borrowed it from Croker or hit upon it unassisted. Throughout his years of office Southey, if he did not 'make terms' at least interpreted his obligations in his own way—nor was his performance the worse for that.

[2] Scott's letter before quoted in which he told Southey of his move to secure the place for him.

had written to him, as being my neighbour in the country,— placing, in fact, the appointment at his (Lord William's) disposal, wherefore he wished to see me to know if I wished to have it. The meaning of all this was easily seen; I was very willing to thank one person more, and especially a good-natured man, to whom I am indebted for many neighbourly civilities. He assured me that I should now soon hear from the Chamberlain's office and I departed accordingly, in full expectation that two or three days more would settle the affair. But neither days nor weeks brought any further intelligence; and if plenty of employments and avocations had not filled up my mind as well as my time, I should perhaps have taken dudgeon, and returned to my family and pursuits, from which I had so long been absent.

At length, after sundry ineffectual attempts, owing sometimes to his absence, and once or twice to public business, I saw Croker once more, and he discovered for me that the delay originated in a desire of Lord Hertford's that Lord Liverpool should write to him, and ask the office for me. This calling in the Prime Minister about the disposal of an office, the net emoluments of which are about £90 a-year, reminded me of the old proverb about shearing pigs. Lord Liverpool, however, was informed of this by Croker; the letter was written, and in the course of another week Lord Hertford wrote to Croker that he would give orders for making out the appointment. A letter soon followed to say that the order was given, and that I might be sworn in whenever I pleased. My pleasure, however, was the last thing to be consulted. After due inquiry on my part, and some additional delays, I received a note to say that if I would attend at the Chamberlain's office at one o'clock on Thursday, November 4, a gentleman-usher would be there to administer the oath. Now it so happened that I was engaged to go to Woburn on the Tuesday, meaning to return on Thursday to dinner, or remain a day longer, as I might feel disposed. Down I went to the office, and solicited a change in the day; but this was in vain, the gentleman-usher had been spoken to, and a Poet-Laureate is a creature of a lower description. I obtained, however, two hours' grace; and yesterday, by rising by candlelight and hurrying the postboys, reached the office to the minute. I swore to be a faithful servant to the King, to reveal all treasons which might come to my knowledge, to discharge the duties of my office, and to obey the Lord Chamberlain in all matters of the King's service, and in his stead the Vice-Chamberlain. Having taken this upon my soul, I was thereby inducted into all the rights, privileges, and benefits which Henry James Pye, Esq., did enjoy, or ought to have enjoyed.

The original salary of the office was 100 marks. It was raised for Ben Jonson to £100 and a tierce of Spanish canary wine, now wickedly commuted for £26; which said sum, unlike the canary, is subject to income-tax, land-tax, and heaven knows what taxes besides. The whole net income is little more or less than £90. It comes to me as a Godsend, and I have vested it in a life policy: by making it up to £120 it covers an insurance for £3000 upon my own life. I have never felt any painful anxiety as to providing for my family,—my mind is too buoyant, my animal spirits too good, for this care ever to have affected my happiness; and I may add that a not unbecoming trust in Providence has ever supported my confidence in myself.

But it is with the deepest feeling of thanksgiving that I have secured this legacy for my wife and children, and it is to you that I am primarily and chiefly indebted.

To the manner of your letter I am quite unable to reply. We shall both be remembered hereafter, and ill betide him who shall institute a comparison between us. There has been no race; we have both got to the top of the hill by different paths, and meet there not as rivals but as friends, each rejoicing in the success of the other. . . .

As a footnote to this admirable letter these verses sent to Mrs. Southey at the same time may be added: 'I composed them,' Southey says, 'in St. James's Park yesterday, on my way from the Chamberlain's office, where a good old gentleman-usher, a worthy sort of fat old man in a wig and bag and a snuff coloured full dress suit with cut steel buttons and a sword, administered an oath. . . .'

> *I have something to tell you, which you will not be sorry at,*
> *'Tis that I am sworn in to the office of Laureat.*
> *The oath that I took there could be nothing wrong in,*
> *'Twas to do all the duties to the dignity belonging.*
> *Keep this, I pray you, as a precious gem,*
> *For this is the Laureat's first poem.*

All too soon, however, the Laureate's second poem was required: and it needed more care than the little composition made in St. James's Park.

For the half-promise that the official Odes would not be insisted on came to nothing, as such things usually do; and Southey had barely begun to enjoy Pye's 'rights, privileges and benefits' when he received the request for his first New Year Ode. 'Go you,' he reports Croker as saying, 'and write your Ode for the New Year. You can never have a better subject than the present state of the war affords you.' This advice was speedily followed by a note from Sir William Parsons, 'Musician in Ordinary to His Majesty,' who pointed out that Mr. Pye had always furnished his Ode six weeks in advance, to allow time for setting it to music, and it would be very convenient of Mr. Southey would do the same.[1]

[1] Writing to Grosvenor Bedford a few years later Southey remarked, 'If I give the composer more trouble than poor Pye did, I am sorry for it; but I can no more write like Mr. Pye, than Mr. Pye could write like me. The Pye crust and mine were not made of the same materials. But I suppose there can be no more difficulty in fitting my rhythm to the fiddle, than there is setting an anthem.' Sir William Parsons had now departed to a better world and the King's music was in the hands of William Shield; somewhat livelier, no doubt, than his settings for the Laureate Odes, and certainly more familiar, is his song 'The Arethusa,' which was still being sung with fine effect, though somewhat out of tune, when I was a schoolboy.

Mr. Southey set to work; but like a prudent man attempting a new and important duty for the first time, he didn't rely entirely upon his own judgement. He sent the completed poem to his friend John Rickman for comment. Rickman advised some deletions: after all, he argued in effect, it's well enough to say rude things about Napoleon now, but if peace comes we may be friends with Napoleon and it would never do for your official words to be on record against him!

Southey thought this a sorry argument (as indeed it was) but acquiesced by removing a long passage in which he said what he really thought of Napoleon. Croker on consultation advised further modifications and finally the poem appeared as *Carmen Triumphale, for the Commencement of the Year* 1814.[1] It is a vigorous and on the whole successful piece, although it met with a rather mixed reception— since then, as sometimes now, not merit but faction dictated the comments. As for Napoleon, the frugal Southey inserted his rejected verses into 'The Courier' anonymously, and in due course in to his Collected Poems as 'Ode Written During the Negotiations with Bonaparte in January, 1814."

From the first Southey took his office seriously. His desire not to be obliged to furnish, willy-nilly, the annual Odes, did not spring from indolence. It was simply that he conceived a Laureate's duties to lie in something a little more dignified: 'I am disposed to do all that is in my power to render the óffice honourable,' he wrote to Neville White (Kirke White's brother) and his plans to this end included 'a series of inscriptions, recording the achievements of our army in the Peninsula —triumphal for the battles won and fortresses taken, and monumental for some of the more distinguished persons who have fallen.'

It would be a laborious business chiselling some of the resultant verses into a stone slab, yet they have a certain appropriateness which had formerly been lacking from most Laureate work; and they have the added merit of not springing from a commanded impulse, but from one both spontaneous and genuine:

AT CORUNA

When from these shores the British army first
Boldly advanced into the heart of Spain,

[1] No Laureate, it seems, but has his attendant 'volunteer.' Southey's *Carmen Triumphale* had, however, 'no connection with the opposition next door'—*Carmen Triumphale for the Year* 1814, by J. Sansom, author of *Greenwich, a poem; Tributary Stanzas to The Memory of Lord Nelson; Mr. Pitt; The Lion and the Pumpkin*, etc. Alas, Sansom's fame has not survived him.

> The admiring people who beheld its march
> Call'd it 'the Beautiful.' And surely well
> Its proud array, its perfect discipline,
> Its ample furniture of war compleat,
> Its powerful horse, its men of British mould,
> All high in heart and hope, all of themselves
> Assured, and in their leaders confident,
> Deserved the title. Few short weeks elapsed
> Ere hither that disastrous host return'd,
> A fourth of all its gallant force consumed
> In hasty and precipitate retreat,
> Stores treasure and artillery, in the wreck
> Left to the fierce pursuer, horse and man
> Founder'd, and stiffening on the mountain snows.
> But when exulting enemy approached
> Boasting that he would drive into the sea
> The remnants of the wretched fugitives,
> Here ere they reach'd their ships, they turn'd at bay.
> Then was the proof of British courage seen;
> Against a foe far overnumbering them,
> An insolent foe, rejoicing in pursuit,
> Sure of the fruit of victory, whatsoe'er
> Might be the fate of battle, here they stood
> And their safe embarkation, . . . all they sought,
> Won manfully. That mournful day avenged
> Their sufferings, and redeem'd their country's name;
> And thus Coruna, which in this retreat
> Had seen the else indelible reproach
> Of England, saw the stain effaced in blood.[1]

Now this does not stir the blood as does such a poem as Drayton's
'Agincourt,'—or as the war songs of Campbell stir it—but I cannot
feel that this is a reproach. For *an inscription* it has the proper grave
dignity required; and the writing of such poems, if his bent lies that
way, is a more suitable employment for a Laureate than the composition of birthday flatteries. Oddly enough, despite his announced
intention, Southey did little further in this line beyond the set of

[1] The battle of Corunna was fought on January 16th, 1809, but if Southey was nearly
five years late with his 'inscription' he was not alone, for Charles Wolfe's famous poem,
'The Burial of Sir John Moore' had yet to be written—and, incidentally, it was written as
a direct result of reading Southey's prose account of Moore's death in the *Edinburgh Annual
Register*. Southey knew something of Corunna: he had landed there in December, 1795,
on his first visit to Portugal.

Peninsular war inscriptions of which I have quoted one, although the forty years of his tenure of office provided battles and to spare.

The New Year Odes—but not their Birthday counterparts—Southey composed, it seems, every year promptly and punctiliously until 1820. The music for them was written also, but they were never performed, and the Laureate carefully excluded them from his published works.[1] For this reason the body of work in his collected poems springing directly from his laureateship is not unimpressive, for it fulfils his original principle that the Laureate should write, or remain silent, as the spirit moved him. The principle is somewhat elaborated in the letter to Bedford quoted in a note on page 137 above:

> . . . for the fitness of expressing [in the Ode] political opinions which are perfectly in unison with those of the Prince and his Ministers, as pronounced by him in his speech, and by them in the measures which they are now adopting, I can have no doubt. My opinion is, that a New Year's ode should always relate to public circumstances; and a Birth Day one to the person or family of the Prince to whom it is addressed. When the latter comes upon me, I shall lower the tone to the subject. As long as I can help it, I will never suffer any of these compositions to get abroad. This is, as far as I can, lessening the folly of the custom, and preparing the way for its abolition; for you may be sure, it is generally supposed that I am not called upon to write, as my predecessors were.

The last sentence is interesting; what was then apparently the received opinion has, generally speaking, been maintained. But this letter (written in 1819) and other evidence, proves the opinion to be mistaken. Southey furnished a good many Odes up till the time the death of George III and possibly some later; but he managed to prevent them 'getting abroad.'

At the accession of George IV the Laureate was in some apprehension that the Birthday Ode would now be called for—since George IV, whatever his other failings, at least was not insane; but in fact both Birthday and New Year Odes were allowed to lapse and Southey obtained his own, and all later Laureates' release from this six-monthly tyranny. But the custom died not with a whimper, but a bang.

Southey conceived the unfortunate idea of commemorating the

---

[1] 'His official Odes indeed, among which the Vision of Judgement must be classed, are, for the most part, worse than Pye's and as bad as Cibber's' says Macaulay. This is one more example of 'Tom's snip-snap' and like many of them, it is simply untrue and I should say deliberately so; Macaulay was too intelligent seriously to think such a thing, but it suited him to say it; accordingly, he discredits himself rather than Southey. Elsewhere in the same essay—the review of Southey's *Colloquies*—he says some shrewd and true things about the Laureate.

death of George III by a poem describing that monarch's arrival in Heaven, and in 1821 appeared *A Vision of Judgment*. It is a longish poem —some five or six hundred lines—and it is furnished with a longish preface in which Southey discusses the hexameters in which his poem is written. He also by implication attacks Lord Byron in a passage which didn't commend itself any more to the noble Lord for being essentially true.

Southey had a lively sense of humour, but it was apt to desert him when he was composing verse, and it never entered into such self-criticism as he applied to the verse when written. So he missed the absurdity of his theme, and the weakness of the 'English hexameters" in which he clothed it:

> *O'er the adamantine gates an Angel stood at the summit.*
> *Ho! He exclaim'd, King George of England commeth to judgment!*
> *Hear Heaven! Ye Angels hear! Souls of the Good and the Wicked*
> *Whom it concerns, attend! Thou, Hell, bring forth his accusers!*

But it has beauties too, for those who do not ask every poem to be an impeccable masterpiece. There is a dignity in the opening lines which gives a hint of Robert Bridges:

> *'Twas at that sober hour when the light of day is receding,*
> *And from surrounding things the hues wherewith day has adorned them*
> *Fade, like the hopes of youth, till the beauty of earth is departed:*
> *Pensive, though not in thought, I stood at the window, beholding*
> *Mountain and lake and vale; the valley disrobed of its verdure;*
> *Derwent retaining yet from eve a glassy reflection*
> *Where his expanded breast, then still and smooth as a mirror,*
> *Under the woods reposed: the hills that, calm and majestic,*
> *Lifted their heads in the silent sky, from far Glaramar,*
> *Bleacrag, and Maidenmawr, to Grizedal and westermost Withop.*
> *Dark and distinct they rose. The clouds had gather'd above them*
> *High in the middle air, huge, purple, pillowy masses,*
> *While in the west beyond was the last pale tint of the twilight . . .*

At their first meeting Byron and Southey had made a good impression upon one another, although Byron was never an admirer of Southey's work. He admired Southey's appearance: 'To have that

---

[1] 'He has raised the more than German obstinacy of the pig-headed George III to the honours of an absolute canonisation,' remarks that acute and uncompromising historian, Thomas B. Shaw, in his *Outlines of English Literature* (St. Petersburg, 1847). 'Southey's laureate odes' (Shaw says) 'exhibit a fierce passionate controversial hatred of his former liberal opinions, which gives interest even to the ambitious monotony, the convulsive mediocrity, of his official lyrics.'

poet's head and shoulders, I would almost have written his Sapphics,'
he wrote to Thomas Moore.[1] But that was in 1813. The first Canto of
Don Juan was now before the public, with its unfriendly 'dedication'
to Southey and—which, to do Southey justice, he disliked far more—
its loose morality and tone.

Discussing 'the Satanic School' of younger poets, as he called it, in the
Preface to *A Vision of Judgement*, with Shelley and Byron particularly
in view, Southey remarked that 'their productions breathe the spirit
of Belial in their lascivious parts, and the spirit of Moloch in those
loathsome images of atrocities and horrors which they delight to
represent. . . .' There is a good deal in this vein to which Byron at
once replied, in the new canto of Don Juan (the third) then about to
be published; and with a number of other references elsewhere. But
this was mere skirmishing; within a very few months *The Vision of
Judgement* appeared[2]—if not one of the greatest, certainly one of the
most effective satires in the language. Satire is almost always unfair,
for only the supreme satirists understand the art of strengthening their
case by judicious praise of the victim. Byron's portrait of Southey is
brilliant and perverse; it carries that particular vein of satire as far as it
could go, and with the unthinking reader the destruction of Southey
is complete; but it stops there, for no reasonable person would
acquiesce in so one-sided a portrait, however brilliant. That Southey
was a great writer, and in certain ways a greater than Byron, remains
true; and so does the fact that Byron's satire is gloriously funny. So
posterity is in the happy position of having it both ways.

> *He said—(I only give the heads)—he said*
>   *He meant no harm in scribbling; 'twas his way*
> *Upon all topics; 'twas, besides, his bread,*
>   *Of which he butter'd both sides; 'twould delay*
> *Too long the assembly (he was pleased to dread),*
>   *And take up rather more time than a day,*
>   *To name his works—he would but cite a few—*
>   'Wat Tyler'—'Rhymes on Blenheim'—'Waterloo.'*

---

[1] 'I had a letter from Southey today . . . he says there was an insidious softness in
Byron's manner which made him compare it at the time to a tiger patting something
which had not angered him with his paw, the talons being all sheathed; "and the prevailing
expression on his fine countenance was something which distrusted you, and which it
never could have been possible for you or me to trust".' This comment of Southey's on
his first meeting with Byron is recorded by Sir Henry Taylor, *Correspondence* (1888).

[2] It was first published in Leigh Hunt's journal *The Liberal* in 1822—Hunt called it 'the
most masterly satire since the time of Pope,' and I'm inclined to agree with him, although
some less 'masterly' ones were equally amusing.

> He had written praises of a regicide;
>   He had written praises of all kings whatever;
> He had written for republics far and wide,
>   And then against them bitterer than ever;
> For pantisocracy he once had cried
>   Aloud, a scheme less moral than 'twas clever;
> Then grew a hearty anti-jacobin—
> Had turn'd his coat—and would have turn'd his skin.
>
> He had sung against all battles, and again
>   In their high praise and glory; he had call'd
> Reviewing 'the ungentle craft,' and then
>   Became as base a critic as e'er crawl'd—
> Fed, paid, and pamper'd by the very men
>   By whom his muse and morals had been maul'd:
> He had written much blank verse, and blanker prose,
> And more of both than any body knows.

This was the most effective satirical portrait since Pope's Atticus a century earlier. Somewhat less effective was Byron's challenge to a duel which he sent to a friend to forward to Southey; it was never forwarded and accordingly the duel was never fought. Southey went on with his own affairs and seemed not greatly upset by Byron's attacks; and Byron within a short time was caught up in the greater quarrels attending the struggle for Greek independence.

When George IV came to the throne Southey's working days as a poet were almost over, although nearly twenty years of authorship lay ahead of him; only one long poem, *A Tale of Paraguay* (1825) and a few minor verses were to come (and, in 1837-8, the careful ten-volume edition revised and edited by Southey, with its interesting prefaces and notes: a book still fairly easy to come by, and well worth having.) But because Southey had forsaken the practice of poetry, he did not take his Laureateship lightly, nor did he consider the place a sinecure. He wrote much and often on national questions; he undertook large and important prose works in support of Church and State; and—as throughout his career—he gave encouragement and assistance to poets and poetry. Such employment as the editing of Chatterton, Cowper, Kirke White and others was a real service to letters, and a more valuable one than the writing of Birthday Odes. For this he has never had adequate recognition, although in his time he perhaps thought he had received too much. At all events, we find him writing in the introductory essay to the *Attempts in Verse, by John Jones, an old servant*

(1831), 'Before I conclude, I must, however, in my own behalf, give notice to all whom it may concern, that I, Robert Southey, Poet Laureate, being somewhat advanced in years, and having business enough of my own fully to occupy as much time as can be devoted to it, consistently with a due regard to health, do hereby decline perusing or inspecting any manuscript from any person whatsoever, and desire that no application on that score may be made to me from this time forth. . . .'

It has been Southey's misfortune that—as Byron pointed out—he wrote more prose and verse than anybody knows. He is generally remembered only for the *Life of Nelson*, and a few short pieces, such as 'The Inchcape Rock' and 'The Battle of Blenheim.' His admirable biography of John Wesley is almost wholly forgotten, his great histories are almost wholly ignored, and the very solid merits of his poems fail to secure them readers.[1] I know of no great writer who is so sparingly read and yet *The Doctor* is the best bedside book in the language.

Southey's last years were saddened by the death of his devoted wife in 1837 and towards the end his mind failed. Those last years, too, were saddened by family dissensions occasioned by his marriage in 1838 to the poetess Caroline Bowles, whom he had known for twenty years. The end came on March 21st, 1843, and two days later the Laureate was buried at Crosthwaite. On his memorial are the lines written by Wordsworth[2]—Wordsworth, the last survivor now of the brilliant band, Coleridge, Southey, Lamb, friends of nearly fifty years before, when 'to be young was very heaven.'

---

[1] 'If there were a tradition that Southey had got tipsy, and had tried to kiss Miss Maria Edgeworth, or that he had pledged the "Curse of Kehama" at the pawnbroker's, perhaps people would think a good deal more of the "Curse of Kehama".' Frederick Locker, *Patchwork* (1879).

[2] See page 258 below.

12

William Wordsworth

GEORGE III had outlived three Laureates; Southey, his fourth, outlived three kings, the last of whom, William IV, was never faced with the task of finding a Laureate—for which no doubt, if he ever thought about it, he was very thankful.[1] It was now Victoria's turn.

In 1843 the young Queen had yet to become an author, and her interest in contemporary literature was not extensive. She 'entirely approved of the nomination' of William Wordsworth. After all, he was the greatest living·poet, and the Laureateship was beginning to be thought a mark of distinction rather than the title for a paid rhymer.

Ten days after Southey died Wordsworth received the Lord Chamberlain's letter offering him the vacant office. The old poet was within sight of his seventy-third birthday, and he probably felt that Southey's death had severed his last link with the old days; he was a man of few friendships, and many of the best of these had been taken from him now. Moreover it was well over twenty years since he had published a new work of any importance. As T. F. Powys remarked on a similar occasion, he 'was not in business now.' He was too old for honours, and he hastened to tell the Lord Chamberlain so:

To the Right Hon. Earl De La Warr, Lord Chamberlain.
Rydale Mount, Ambleside, April 1, 1843.
My Lord,

The recommendation made by your Lordship to the Queen, and graciously approved by her Majesty, that the vacant office of Poet Laureate should be offered to me, affords me high gratification. Sincerely am I sensible of this honour; and let me be permitted to add, that the being deemed worthy to succeed my lamented and revered friend, Mr. Southey, enhances the pleasure I receive on this occasion.

[1] William IV also had a volunteer Laureate in the person of Charles Doyne Sillery, Esq., 'late of the Hon. East India Company's Sea Service' and author of *Vallery; or The Citadel of the Lake, Eldred of Erin*, etc. Sillery's *The Royal Mariner, etc., etc.* (1834) is a two-canto celebration of the sailor king's exploits prefixed with a portrait of his majesty holding a telescope.

The appointment, I feel, however, imposes duties which, far advanced in life as I am, I cannot venture to undertake, and therefore must beg leave to decline the acceptance of an offer that I shall always remember with no unbecoming pride.

Her Majesty will not, I trust, disapprove of a determination forced upon me by reflections which it is impossible for me to set aside.

Deeply feeling the distinction conferred upon me, and grateful for the terms in which your Lordship has made the communication,

I have the honour to be,

My Lord,

Your Lordship's most obedient humble servant,
William Wordsworth.

To his friend Lady F. Bentinck (Christopher Wordsworth tells us) he wrote that had he been several years younger 'I should have accepted the office with pride and pleasure. . . . For though, as you are aware, the formal task-work of New Year and Birthday Odes was abolished when the appointment was given to Mr. Southey,[1] he still considered himself obliged in conscience to produce, and did produce, verses, some of very great merit, upon important public occasions. He failed to do so upon the Queen's Coronation, and I know that this omission caused him no little uneasiness. The same might happen to myself upon some important occasion, and I should be uneasy under the possibility. . . .'

The Lord Chamberlain was perhaps unwilling, or too busy with other matters, to go looking in the highways and hedges for a Laureate; having chosen his man, he meant to have him. He wrote back that the 'duties of Laureate had not recently extended beyond the Annual Ode' and might in Wordsworth's case be considered merely nominal, and would not in any way interfere with his repose and retirement.

Nor was this all. The Earl called upon Peel, the Prime Minister, for reinforcement, and Peel ('I write this in haste, from my place in the House of Commons') lost no time in coming with assistance:

'I hope you may be induced to reconsider your decision with regard to the appointment of Poet Laureate. The offer was made to you by the Lord Chamberlain, with my entire concurrence, not for the purpose of imposing on you any onerous or disagreeable duties, but in order to pay you that tribute of respect which is justly due to the first of living poets. The Queen entirely approved of the nomination, and there is

---

[1] As we have seen, this was not strictly so; but at that time Wordsworth would not have possessed all the facts.

one unanimous feeling on the part of all who have heard of the proposal (and it is pretty generally known), that there could not be a question about the selection. Do not be deterred by the fear of any obligations which the appointment may be supposed to imply. I will undertake that you shall have nothing required from you. But as the Queen can select for this honourable appointment no one whose claims for respect and honour, on account of eminence as a poet, can be placed in competition with yours, I trust you will no longer hesitate to accept it.'

To this renewed invitation Wordsworth yielded. Crabb Robinson doubted the wisdom of his action: 'April 5th. I had a letter from Wordsworth this morning informing me that he had declined the laureateship, and on going out I found that it was announced in the papers that he had done so, alleging . . . advanced age (he becomes 73 on the 7th instant.) This I approved of and rejoiced in; but I have now heard (the 6th) that he has yielded on a second application, which I am sorry for, as I am sure his motives will be misconstrued.' Wordsworth's change of mind brought no severe censure on him; the party factions were beginning to leave the laureateship alone, and henceforth the satire the office or its holders provoked was to be literary and personal.

The best examples on this occasion are to be found in the once-famous *Bon Gaultier Ballads* of Aytoun and Martin, in which are parodies of Macaulay, Moore, Tennyson, Lytton and others, some-what on the lines of the *Probationary Odes*.[1] 'This and the five following poems,' writes 'Bon Gaultier,' 'were among those forwarded to the Home Secretary, by the unsuccessful competitors for the Laureate-ship. . . . The result of the contest could never have been doubtful least of all [to] the great poet who then succeeded to the bays. His own sonnet on the subject is full of the serene consciousness of superiority, which does not even admit the idea of rivalry, far less of defeat.'

Then follows this parody, which has sometimes since been thought a genuine production by Wordsworth:

> *Bays! which in former days have graced the brow*
> *Of some, who lived and loved, and sung and died;*
> *Leaves, that were gathered on the pleasant side*
> *Of old Parnassus from Apollo's bough;*

[1] But more probably inspired by the *Rejected Addresses* of 1812—the most brilliant book of comic parodies (as Hogg's *Poetic Mirror* is the most brilliant of serious parodies) in the language.

> *With palpitating heart I take ye now,*
>   *Since worthier minstrel there is none beside,*
>   *And with a thrill of song half deified,*
> *I bind them proudly on my locks of snow,*
> *There shall they bide till he who follows next,*
>   *Of whom I cannot even guess the name,*
> *Shall by Court favour, or some vain pretext*
>   *Of fancied merit, desecrate the same—*
> *And think, perchance, he wears them quite as well*
> *As the sole bard who sang of Peter Bell!*

As for the Macaulay parody, it contains these stirring lines:

Then up and spake young Tennyson—'Who's here that fears for death?
'T were better one of us should die, than England lose the wreath!

'Let's cast the lots among us now, which two shall fight tomorrow;—
For armour bright we'll club our mite, and horses we can borrow.
'T were shame that bards of France should sneer, and German Dichters too,
If none of British song might dare a deed of derring-do!'

'The lists of love are mine,' said Moore, 'and not the lists of Mars;'
Said Hunt, 'I seek the jars of wine, but shun the combat's jars!'
'I'm old,' quoth Samuel Rogers.—'Faith,' says Campbell, 'so am I!'
'And I'm in holy orders, sir!' quoth Tom of Ingoldsby.

—They all draw lots and the champions are then seen to be Wordsworth and one Ned Fitzball; the latter makes a terrible figure in
armour, and Wordsworth ambles on to the jousting field on a weak
little steed, so that Lord Brougham lays two to one against him. But
it works out otherwise, the noble Lord loses his bet and Fitzball comes
by a shrewd blow from which he never recovers.

They led our Wordsworth to the Queen—she crowned him with the bays,
And wished him many happy years, and many quarter-days,—
And if you'd have the story told by abler lips than mine,
You've but to call at Rydal Mount, and taste the Laureate's wine!

Well, as we know, there was in fact no wine; and it is doubtful if
the bard ever knew the sport that was made of him; for the jests that
made much noise in London, in the remote and austere fastnesses of
Mr. Wordsworth's mountains were diminished to an impertinent
whisper, or were not heard at all.

Nobody seriously attacked Wordsworth for accepting what he
called a 'distinction sanctioned by her Majesty, and one which expresses

upon authority entitled to the highest respect, a sense of the national importance of Poetic Literature.' That sense was to come to its highest suffrage in the term of Tennyson's office, beginning seven years later: for Tennyson was to be the first poet recognised in his lifetime by the ordinary man in the street as the greatest living representative of a living branch of letters.

No poems were required of Wordsworth, but within a few weeks he was summoned to London to attend the Queen. Something more than this however was needed to move the Sage of Rydal from his native heath, and the Queen had to manage without him. The tale is best told by his son-in-law, Edward Quillinan, in a letter to Crabb Robinson, dated July 23rd: '. . . Mr. Wordsworth ought to have been at Buckingham Palace, at the Queen's Ball, for which he received a formal invitation: "The Lord Chamberlain presents his compliments. He is commanded by Her Majesty to invite Mr. William Wordsworth to a ball at Buckingham Palace, on Monday, the 24th July—ten o'clock. Full dress." To which he pleaded, as an apology for non-attendance, the non-arrival of the invitation (query command?) in time. He dated his answer from this place, "The Island, Windermere," and that would explain the impossibility; for the notice was the shortest possible, even if it had been received by first post. But a man in his seventy-fourth year would, I suppose, be excused by Royalty for not travelling 300 miles to attend a dance, even if a longer notice had been given—though probably Mr. Wordsworth would have gone had he had a fortnight to think of it, because the Laureate *must* pay his personal respects to the Queen sooner or later; and the sooner the better, he thinks.'

The letter continues with some interesting observations which suggest that Wordsworth might, perhaps, have written some official poems, although in fact he never did:

'I have been lately reading many of the old New Year and Birthday Odes, and nothing struck me so disagreeably as their *idolatry*. The Royal personage is not panegyrised but idolised: the monarch is not a king, but a god. It has occurred to me that Mr. Wordsworth may, in his own grand way, compose a hymn to or on the King of kings, in rhymed verse, or blank, invoking a blessing on the Queen and country, or giving thanks for blessings vouchsafed and perils averted. This would be a new mode of dealing with the office of Laureate, and would come with dignity and propriety, I think, from a seer of Wordsworth's age and character. I told him so; and he made no observation. I therefore think it likely that he may consider the suggestion. . . .'

Although Wordsworth desired to pay his respects and 'the sooner
the better' it was two years after his appointment that he came to
London to attend a levee. The question of 'Full dress' once more
cropped up: it was a form of raiment not worn at Rydal Mount, but
Samuel Rogers came to the rescue. Unfortunately the Banker poet was
small in size as well as in genius: and Wordsworth was large. The
occasion, before and while in progress, was an anxious one, and made
quite a ripple in various lives, judging by the references in the memoirs
of the time—Haydon, Crabb Robinson, Henry Taylor and several
others speak of it. Haydon says:

> 16th (of July). Dined with my dear friend Serjeant Talfourd. He said
> Wordsworth went to Court in Rogers's clothes, buckles and stockings, and
> wore Davy's sword.[1] Moxon had hard work to make the dress fit. It was a
> tight squeeze, but by pulling and hauling they got him in. Fancy the high
> priest of mountain and of flood on his knees in a court, the quizz of courtiers,
> in a dress that did not belong to him, with a sword that was not his own, and
> a coat which he borrowed.

Wordsworth's own account of the affair, in a letter to the American
professor, Henry Reed, is somewhat self-consciously solemn, but
makes no mention of tightness under the arms:

> The reception given me by the Queen at her ball was most gracious.
> Mrs. Everett, the wife of your minister, among many others, was a witness
> to it, without knowing who I was. It moved her to the shedding of tears.
> This effect was in part produced, I suppose, by American habits of feeling,
> as pertaining to a republican government. To see a gray-haired man of
> seventy-five years of age kneeling down in a large assembly to kiss the hand
> of a young woman is a sight for which Institutions essentially democratic do
> not prepare a spectator of either sex, and must naturally place the opinions
> upon which a Republic is founded, and the sentiments which support is, in
> strong contrast with a government based and upheld as ours is. . . .

But Wordsworth's biographer, Professor Harper, believes Mrs.
Everett was moved chiefly by the elderly poet's curious appearance.[2]

There are but two poems of these years that may be considered the
product of Wordsworth's office. The first is the famous *Ode On the
Installation of His Royal Highness Prince Albert as Chancellor of The
University of Cambridge*, in July 1847. It is 'famous' not for its merit,

---

[1] Elsewhere in his journals Haydon exclaims: 'What would Hazlitt say now? The poet
of the lakes and mountains in bag-wig, sword and ruffles!'

[2] Aubrey de Vere, however, records Wordsworth's own opinion that 'Mr. Rogers's
court dress . . . fits him so well, that, with the help of Sir Humphrey Davy's sword
"science and art being thus fraternally united" he will have no trouble about his apparel.'
(Quoted in Una Taylor's *Guests and Memories* (1924).)

but because although it appears in Wordsworth's complete poetical works, it was apparently mainly the work of Edward Quillinan. The other poem was inscribed in a copy of his poems sent to the Queen in 1846. The book was intended for the Royal Library at Windsor, and in so far as the poet inscribed in it a seven-stanza poem, was a Laureate offering; but the poem itself was careful to point out that no more need be expected: 'Deign, Sovereign Mistress! to accept a lay, No Laureate offering of elaborate art. . . .'

For her part the Queen—unable to offer anything in the sonnet line—sent to Rydal Mount an 'engraving of the Royal Children' which was hung in the hall beside portraits of Chaucer, Spenser, Shakespeare, Ben Jonson, and Milton.

The *Installation Ode* Wordsworth undertook, but found himself unable to write it because of the increasingly grave illness of his daughter, Dora (Mrs. Quillinan). She died, in fact, on July 9th, 1847; the Prince Consort was installed as Chancellor of the University of Cambridge in mid-July. Greville reports in his *Diary* that 'the installation went off with prodigious *éclat*, and the Queen was enchanted at the enthusiastic reception she met with. . . .' He makes no mention of the reception met with by the Laureate's Ode, although it ends with a fine burst of capital letters:

> . . . that Presence fair and bright,
> Ever blest wherever seen,
> Who deigns to grace our festal rite,
> The Pride of the Islands, VICTORIA THE QUEEN!

But, 'Not here, O Apollo, are haunts meet for thee. . . .' and the measure of what Wordsworth might have done as Laureate is to be seen in the great patriotic sonnets, and in certain early poems. No previous poet, perhaps, had been so well equipped to make a great Laureate; but the office came to him forty years too late.

Once or twice in those last years Wordsworth met Tennyson and the younger man shyly paid homage to the poet whose place he was so soon to fill; so the poet who might have been a great Laureate was linked, briefly, with the poet who in his turn became one. For Tennyson was 'the perfect Laureate.' Of his merit as a poet Wordsworth was in no doubt.

I saw Tennyson, when I was in London, several times [he wrote to Professor Reed]. He is decidedly the first of our living poets, and I hope will live to give the world still better things [he was writing in 1845, when

Tennyson's principal work was in the two-volume *Poems* of 1842]. You will be pleased to hear that he expressed in the strongest terms his gratitude to my writings. To this I was far from indifferent though persuaded that he is not much in sympathy with what I should myself most value in my attempts, viz., the spirituality with which I have endeavoured to invest the material universe, and the moral relations under which I have wished to exhibit its most ordinary appearances.

'I shall never forget my deep emotion the first time I had speech with him,' Tennyson said later, of Wordsworth. He thought the old Laureate the greatest poet since Milton, and that poet's equal—a judgment which echoed an opinion expressed by Southey so long ago as 1817. It is a judgment with which catholic modern criticism will not quarrel.

Wordsworth was content to wear the laurel on the terms with which it was awarded, and he lived his last years quietly in the Lake District until he died there on April 23rd, 1850.

In this short chapter I have not given a sketch of Wordsworth's life; he was Laureate for seven only out of his eighty years, and his activities during that term were almost nil. To record a life in which the Laureateship played so small a part—especially as Wordsworth's life is readily accessible, and is generally well known, would be to invite the old comment: 'Who has tied my son to this sword?'

13

Alfred, Lord Tennyson

SEVERAL poets have refused the Laureateship at various times. Gray was firm in his intention from the first, Scott hesitated and then declined, Wordsworth declined at once and was afterwards persuaded to have second thoughts. In 1850 the comedy was played with another actor in the leading role: this was the ancient Samuel Rogers.

Wordsworth when appointed at seventy-three had done little in active authorship[1] for a quarter of a century—nothing bulky since the publication of *The Waggoner* in 1819. Samuel Rogers was in a similar position, 'only more so.' Rogers, at the age of eighty-seven, had long (and mainly malicious) memories going back to the time of Dr. Johnson. It was however nearly thirty years since he had published a new book, and nearly twenty since the definitive collection of his poetical works. He was moreover a poet having nothing in common with the spirit of 1850; his roots were nourished in the soil of a hundred years earlier. But it was with flattering promptness that the offer was made to him on May 8th, a couple of weeks after Wordsworth's death—and in Prince Albert's own hand:

> My dear Mr. Rogers,
>
> The death of the lamented Mr. Wordsworth has vacated the office of Poet Laureate. Although the spirit of the times has put an end to the practice (at all times objectionable) of exacting laudatory Odes from the holder of that office, the Queen attaches importance to its maintenance from its historical antiquity and the means it affords to the Sovereign of a more personal connection with the Poets of the country through one of their chiefs. I am authorised, accordingly, to offer to you this honorary post, and can tell you that it will give Her Majesty great pleasure if it were accepted

---

[1] Unless, indeed, the extensive revisions to which in later years he subjected his poems be considered 'active authorship.' As Byron remarked (though I can't say I wholly agree with him) 'Second thoughts in everything are best, but in rhyme third and fourth don't come amiss.' Certainly Wordsworth was never idle in the sense of being indolent and the fact that some readers prefer the 1805 to the 1850 text of *The Prelude* is neither here nor there.

by one whom she has known so long, and who would so much adorn it; but that she would not have thought of offering it to you at your advanced age if any duties or trouble were attached to it.

This was the clearest statement ever made by a Sovereign of what the office was taken to imply; and, like everything initiated by Victoria and carried out by Albert, sensible, direct, and uncomplicated. Rogers—says his biographer Claydon—'was sorely tempted to accept it, but his shrewd common-sense, which never failed him all through life, suggested that the honour was in the offer, and that as he was approaching the close of his eighty-seventh year, it was his duty not to accept it.' So Rogers refused; but he was not yet quite done with the Laureateship, for—like Scott before him—he now found himself giving advice upon the succession. Prince Albert retires from the correspondence—baffled, no doubt—and Lord John Russell appears. (He was Prime Minister. It is curious in these affairs to see how many parties interest themselves: a specially good example is that of Southey's appointment. The office today is finally and completely in the hands of the Prime Minister—but who can ever tell what goes on behind the scenes?)

My dear Rogers (Lord John writes),
As you would not wear the laurel yourself, I have mentioned to the Queen those whom I thought most worthy of the honour. H.M. is inclined to bestow it on Mr. Tennyson; but I should wish, before the offer is made, to know something of his character, as well as of his literary merits. . . . I should be glad if you could let me know something of his character and position. . . .

Wordsworth had died in April; Russell was writing in October; and all through the summer the vacancy had been in the public mind. *The Times*, two days after Wordsworth died, suggested that the moment had come for the office to be abolished; several journals suggested a woman for the place, perhaps in compliment to the Throne, but the greatest woman poet then living, Elizabeth Barrett Browning, was already domiciled in Italy and unlikely to return to make a permanent home in England. Mrs. Browning's own choice was Leigh Hunt, who was Leigh Hunt's choice, too. In the *Autobiography* which he published at this time he mentions 'verses . . . on occasions connected with the happiness of the Queen, such as the celebration of her Majesty's birthday, the births of the royal children, etc.' and goes on to remark upon the excellence of his own private character. Why not? Hunt was

certainly one of the most distinguished writers then living, if not one
of the most distinguished poets; and if he had formerly suffered at the
hands of Royalty—anyhow, by proxy—he might now hope to benefit
from them.

After it was all over he wrote with characteristic generosity: 'if the
Office in future is really to be bestowed on the highest degree of
poetical merit, and on that only, then Mr. Alfred Tennyson is entitled
to it above any other man in the Kingdom.'

On the whole, despite some disappointments, people agreed with
Hunt that—once again—'the Laurel was bestowed on Merit.'

Alfred Tennyson was forty-one. He was the son of a Lincolnshire
parson, in whose rectory at Somersby he was born—the fourth of
twelve children—on August 6th, 1809. He was educated at the
Grammar School, Louth, and subsequently at home under his father's
tuition; he went on to Trinity College Cambridge with his brother
Charles in 1828 and there joined their elder brother, Frederick. These
three had shared in the publication of *Poems by Two Brothers* at Louth
in 1827 (it appeared, Tennyson notes, late in 1826). At Cambridge,
Tennyson won the Chancellor's Medal in 1829 with 'Timbuctoo,' a
somewhat better work than Christopher Wordsworth's 'The Invasion
of Russia' which was successful the previous year and a considerably
better work than W. C. Kinglake's 'Byzantium' which took the
medal the following year. But, generally speaking, prize poems are
sad affairs.

Tennyson made rather a stir at Cambridge: 'Six feet high, broad-
chested, strong-limbed, his face Shakespearian, with deep eye-lids, his
forehead ample, crowned with dark wavy hair, his head finely poised,
his hand the admiration of sculptors, long fingers with square tips, soft
as a child's but of great size and strength. . . .' From the first he looked
like a great poet, and as the years advanced the magnificence of his
presence increased. In that century of impressive figures Tennyson
stood out like a king.

In 1830 Tennyson put out his *Poems, Chiefly Lyrical* and drew from
Coleridge the remarks that although they had a good deal of beauty
'he has begun to write verses without very well understanding what
metre is.' To this criticism Tennyson appears to have given no hasty
consideration, for his reply was made sixty years later. 'Coleridge did
not know much about my poems,' he said in 1890, 'for he confounded
Charles and me.' This is rather hard on Charles, whose sonnets keep
excellent metre.

It was the 1830 collection which launched Tennyson as a poet to be reckoned with, and at the same time exposed him to the big guns of contemporary criticism. John Wilson's review in *Blackwood's* extends to more than forty pages as reprinted in his *Works*, and—much perverse bias apart—contains some shrewd comments. He quotes the 'English War-Song' and remarks, 'miserable indeed." He quotes 'We are Free' and says 'That is drivel.'[1] But—Wilson goes on—in the 'Ode to Memory' there is fine music; in 'The Deserted House,' 'every word tells;' in 'Mariana' there is 'profound pathos;' and at the close he says with fine modesty, 'our critique is near its conclusion; and in correcting it for the press, we see that its whole merit, which is great, consists in the extracts. . . .' 'Alfred Tennyson is a poet!'[2] This is more than *Maga* had been willing to concede to John Keats.

At Cambridge the young poet had made many friends, of whom the closest was Arthur Henry Hallam. How much this friendship meant to him can be discerned in the darkest passages of *In Memoriam*, which he began to write shortly after Hallam's untimely death in 1833, but did not publish until 1850

In 1833 (so dated; but copies were circulated late in 1832) Tennyson's second considerable collection, *Poems*, was published; it, too, met with both praise and criticism, and again both were justified. A long silence —broken only by a few 'anthology appearances'—followed. Tennyson was for some time greatly affected by Hallam's death; he was also a good deal disturbed by the criticisms of his work, although he recognised their justice. He published little, but he did not cease to write, and in 1842 his *Poems* appeared in two volumes, the early work much revised, and some admirable later things added. The book established him in contemporary eyes as an important poet, and extended his reputation to America and to the Continent. The two small volumes contained poems which became familiar to generations of readers—'Morte D'Arthur,' 'Sir Galahad,' 'Lady Clare,' 'Break, Break, Break' and a dozen more.

---

[1] Well, the 1830 version is not impressive; the first two lines read (as Wilson quotes them—for I have no copy of the very rare original):

> *The winds, as at their hour of birth,*
> *Leaning upon the rigid sea . . .*

In the greatly revised 1842 volumes the poem does not appear, but in the latest collected edition issued by Tennyson at the end of his life the word 'rigid' has become 'ridged'— quite a different thing, as Wilson would have agreed, although the sea-scapes in his own poem *The Isle of Palms* are entirely commonplace.

[2] Tennyson thought this review 'somewhat too skittish and petulant, tho' it was re- deemed to me by a vein of boisterous and picturesque humour such as I love.'

The following year, as we have seen, Tennyson had reputation enough to be named as a possible successor to Southey; and incidentally the parody of his 'The Merman' in *Bon Gaultier Ballads* is not at all bad.[1] But the Laureateship was not yet to be his. He went quietly on, doing nothing hastily, but writing enduring things. In 1847 he published 'the exquisite Medley,' as Saintsbury calls it, of *The Princess*. Here again were unforgettable lyrics—'Sweet and Low,' 'The splendour falls,' 'Tears, idle tears,' 'Now sleeps the crimson petal, now the white,' and others. Finally, in 1850 after working intermittently at it for some seventeen years, he published *In Memoriam*.

The anonymous *In Memoriam* (the authorship was an open secret) represented to perfection the Victorian temper; with Coventry Patmore's *The Angel in the House* which began to be published four years later it shares the distinction of being, (in the best sense) the most completely 'Victorian' long poem that we have. And 'Victorian' is no longer a term of reproach.

The Prince Consort was one of the earliest admirers of *In Memoriam* and very soon after he had read it the question of the Laureateship was solved: Albert was content to let Sam Rogers go, and settle for this new splendid singer.

During the summer since Wordsworth's death it had never seemed to Tennyson that the offer might come to him, but when at length he did receive the invitation he was not entirely unprepared. The night

---

[1] So, Tennyson:

> Who would be
> A merman bold
> Sitting alone,
> Singing alone
> Under the sea,
> With a crown of gold,
> On a throne?
> I would be a merman bold;
> I would sit and sing the whole of the day . . .

And thus, *Bon Gaultier*:

> Who would not be
> The Laureate bold
> With his butt of sherry
> To keep him merry,
> And nothing to do but to pocket his gold?
> 'Tis I would be the Laureate bold! . . .
> Oh, would not that be a merry life,
> Apart from care, and apart from strife,
> With the Laureate's wine, and the Laureate's pay,
> And no deductions at quarter day?

We must not expect pedantic accuracy in parody: but apart from the fact that there was now no wine it must also be objected that the pay was not free of tax!

before 'he dreamt that Prince Albert came and kissed him on the cheek, and that he said in his dream, "Very kind, but very German".'

Windsor Castle, Nov. 5th, 1850.

By the death of the late lamented Wm. Wordsworth the Office of Poet Laureate to the Queen became at Her Majesty's disposal.

The ancient duties of this Office, which consisted in laudatory Odes to the Sovereign, have been long, as you are probably aware, in abeyance, and have never been called for during the Reign of Her present Majesty. The Queen however has been anxious that the Office should be maintained; first on account of its antiquity, and secondly because it establishes a connection, through Her Household, between Her Majesty and the poets of this country as a body.

To make however the continuance of this Office in harmony with public opinion, the Queen feels that it is necessary that it should be limited to a name bearing such distinction in the literary world as to do credit to the appointment, and it was under this feeling, that Her Majesty in the first instance offered the appointment to Mr. Rogers, who stated to Her Majesty in his reply, that the only reason which compelled him gratefully to decline Her Majesty's gracious intention, was, that his great age rendered him unfit to receive any new office.

It is under the same desire that the name of the poet appointed should adorn the Office, that I have received the commands of the Queen to offer this post to you, as a mark of Her Majesty's appreciation of your literary distinction.

I have the honour to be, Sir,
Your obedient humble servant,
C. B. Phipps.

Hallam Tennyson, who prints this letter in his *Life* of his father, throws an interesting light on Tennyson's character in his account of what followed. Tennyson wrote two letters, 'one accepting, one refusing' and left the thing open until dinner, when he talked it over with his family and guests. 'In the end I accepted the honour,' he used to say afterwards, 'because during dinner Venables told me, that, if I became Poet Laureate, I should always when I dined out be offered the liver-wing of a fowl.'

To T. H. Rawnsley he wrote:

I thank you for your congratulations touching the Laureateship. I was advised by my friends not to decline it. . . . I have no passion for courts, but a great love of privacy. It is, I believe, scarce £100 a year, and my friend R. M. Milnes tells me that the price of the patent and court dress will swallow up all the first year's income. . . .

The question of the court suit was solved once more by the civil assistance of Rogers. Sir Henry Taylor records a dinner at Rogers's house when 'the question arose whether Samuel's suit was spacious enough for Alfred.' Perhaps the larger presence in it once of Wordsworth had stretched it a little here and there; at all events, it served the new laureate as it had served his predecessor. No doubt some time in the next forty years Tennyson acquired one of his own—though if he did I cannot learn that it was ever lent to Alfred Austin!

Almost at once Tennyson began to experience the cares and drawbacks of high office. The Victorians, more than any other English generation, were a race of would-be poets. Those who didn't paint in water colour or practice poker-work, wrote poetry—some did all three. 'I get such shoals of poems that I am almost crazed with them; two hundred million poets of Great Britain deluge me daily with poems: truly the Laureateship is no sinecure. If any good soul would just by way of a diversion send me a good tome of prose!' So the new Laureate wrote soon after his appointment. The years brought no relief, for in 1858 he is still protesting:

> Sir,
>
>   Thanks for your clever little book. I have such reams of verses to acknowledge that I cannot even get through the work of thanking the Authors for them. A furious letter of insult from one whom I had neglected has so alarmed me just now that I dared not put off acknowledging your book any longer—but I *read* your book[1] otherwise I should not have called it clever. Now, there are twenty more to answer.
>
> Farewell
Yours
A. Tennyson
(in the 8th year of my persecution).

Tennyson had not long assumed his office when the Duke of Wellington died. This was a true opportunity for the Laureate, for Wellington had been a tremendous figure in English life for half a century, and the victory of Waterloo had been the peak, but not the climax of his career. He had had his triumphs and his reverses, but his

---

[1] The book was Frederick Locker's *London Lyrics* (1857), a volume the first edition of which is now very rare. Locker had the amiable habit of re-issuing his book every now and then, omitting some poems and adding others; so that a bibliography of this one book (he published no other of original poems) makes an extensive document. Fourteen years later Tennyson writes: 'Your *London Lyrics* are very good and skilful. They are even better than I thought.' He was presumably then acknowledging a copy of the edition of 1872. As to the book's merit, he was perfectly right.

death removed from the contemporary scene a figure that had seemed immortal. He was as much a part of the nation's life as St. Paul's or the Houses of Parliament. On the fourteenth of September, 1852, he died.

Tennyson's great *Ode*, published on the morning of the funeral (November 17th) was not well received in general, although plenty of good judges recognised its merit. Tennyson was no lover of adverse criticism, a characteristic he shared with most of the rest of us, and in his twenty-odd years before the public he had met with his share of it; but whereas the criticism of his early poems was largely justified (as he himself implicitly acknowledged by extensive revision) it is difficult to see why this noble poem failed to impress the reading public. Incidentally, it was in keeping with the Laureate's character that he at once write to Moxon, the publisher: 'If you lose by the *Ode*, I will not consent to accept the whole sum of £200 which you offered me. I consider it quite a sufficient loss if you do not gain by it.'[1]

Although Tennyson's hold on the public increased steadily right up till the time of his death his success was not without its setbacks— *Maud*, for example, was a great disappointment to many uncritical admirers of his work. Generally speaking, he was successful with all his official poems, the initial dislike of the Wellington *Ode* apart— and that was never wholly without admirers. Sir Henry Taylor said, 'It has a greatness worthy of its theme and an absolute simplicity and truth. . . .' W. J. Cory said 'I read the Ode aloud again and again in those days, never without high emotion and lumps in the throat. . . . I read it in 1888 to my son, with more thrill and throb than ever.'[2]

The early years of Tennyson's Laureateship were politically un-settled, with wars and rumours of war. The 'National Songs for Englishmen' of 1852 were examples of work directly resulting from his official position, although the impulse that inspired them was

---

[1] Tennyson made a fortune by his poetry, but not at the expense of his publishers. This question is carefully examined by Sir Charles Tennyson in his admirable *Life* of the Laureate. Although at the end Tennyson's was probably the greatest fortune among his poet-contemporaries, he was not alone. In 1861 he chanced to meet Sir Henry Taylor at Brockenhurst Junction—Tennyson going to the Isle of Wight, and Taylor on his way to Bournemouth. 'Discoursing over tea and bread and butter and ale,'—the ale being for the Laureate—'Alfred Tennyson spoke of the disparity of poets' merits and their rewards. "I find he is receiving about two thousand a year from his publisher",'—Sir Henry Taylor is writing to his wife—' "But alas, Longfellow, he says, receives three thousand, and he has no doubt that Martin Tupper receives five thousand".' (Una Taylor's *Guests and Memories*.)

[2] From Cory's privately printed *Letters and Journals* (1897). I must add a story from Michael Field's *Works and Days* (1933): '. . . at a certain house he was asked to read from his works: in a memorable monotone he gave the *Ode on the Death of the Duke of Wellington*. He ended—there was a silence, a pause I suppose of English sheepishness: at last a voice was heard—his own—in strong commendation, "It's a fine rolling anthem".'

genuine and not assumed for the occasion. Such poems as 'Britons, guard your own' were a new expression of the office of Laureate, and they had a wide currency.

> . . . *If you be fearful, then must we be bold* (he told the Peers)
>   *Our Britain cannot salve a tyrant o'er.*
> *Better the waste Atlantic rolled*
>   *On her and us and ours for evermore.*
> *What! have we fought for freedom from our prime,*
> *At last to dodge and palter with a public crime?*

('*The Third of February*, 1852')

This met with a good response; the nation had seldom been so directly spoken to by a poet before, and never in this strain by a Laureate.

Tennyson never took quite literally the lack of obligation now attaching to his office. He felt a moral obligation to write, from time to time, poems on national occasions; but, more than this, such poems were usually produced by his own inward convictions chiming with the mood or need of the moment. That is why they are usually good poems within their terms of reference. 'The Charge of the Light Brigade' is something finer than a mere school anthology set-piece, and the poems written for the Queen on various domestic occasions (for example, the moving dedicatory lines to the complete *Idylls of the King*: 'These to His Memory—since he held them dear') have dignity, simplicity and sincerity. They are not the work of a man obliged by his salary to put pen to paper.

Accordingly, as these poems were not obligatory, so they were spontaneous; and they were not necessarily 'topical.' It is reasonable to believe that Tennyson chose some of his subjects because they seemed appropriate to the Poet Laureate of England: scenes in English history, or evocations of her countryside and manners. The great Arthurian cycle is an obvious example, and such poems as 'The Revenge,' 'Boadicea' and some of the English Idylls.[1] Of 'official' poems there are a good many, some like 'The Defence of Lucknow,' well known, and others like 'The Third of February, 1852' less familiar. It is worth noting, too, that his plays were mainly concerned with English history.

Allowing for natural differences in temperament it is true to say that Tennyson dedicated himself to being a poet as deliberately and as consistently as did Milton and Wordsworth before him; these three,

---

[1] These last owe their inspiration, perhaps, to the *English Eclogues* of Southey.

indeed, are the three great English poets who most formally and consciously took up their chosen profession and never faltered from it. And Tennyson's success within his personal limits was not less complete than theirs. He approached the Laureateship in the same spirit, and he succeeded in being the first 'complete Laureate'—the pattern, that is, of what 'the chief of living poets' ought to be. He was a public figure because he was a national figure, but not because of occasional activities. He maintained that shyness and mystery that ought to attach to poetry; he was retiring, and accordingly, when he moved from his retirement to speak, he was heard with respect and honour. He was, and he behaved as if he was, an Elder in the people's councils: and so they heard him. Such poems as 'Riflemen, Form!' had influence out of all proportion to their length or weight. That poem,[1] incidentally, was published anonymously; but this doesn't affect my argument.

One other aspect of Tennyson's Laureateship set him apart from his predecessors. He became a personal friend—no other term will suit—of the sovereign he served. The Queen, in his later years, sought guidance and comfort from him, a fact which Sir Max Beerbohm's enchanting cartoon cannot obscure. The story of their friendship is unique in English letters, a rather touching story but not a sentimental one. And, incidentally, it didn't interfere with what the Queen thought suitable to dignity and the thing that is right. Her reaction to Tennyson's little jaunt to Scandinavia with Mr. Gladstone was comically characteristic. Tennyson had thrice refused a baronetcy—with the curious provision that he would like it to be conferred on his eldest son instead, which two successive Prime Ministers found too far outside precedent to countenance—and at last, in 1883 he accepted a peerage. The offer was made, discussed, pondered anxiously upon, and finally accepted while Tennyson was cruising with Gladstone on the liner 'Pembroke Castle,' and on the same occasion, finding themselves near Copenhagen, the party ventured to land.

Now the Prime Minister of these islands is not supposed to leave them and go off to foreign parts without mentioning the matter to the

---

[1] 'Riflemen, Form!' appeared in *The Times* on May 9th, 1859, under the title, 'The War,' with the letter T as sole signature. Trouble in Europe had brought home to Britain her own unpreparedness, and the need for a Volunteer movement was again being freely canvassed. These anonymous verses were widely discussed—and generally attributed to that other popular 'laureate' of the Victorians, Martin F. Tupper, who had been active in that department. Although he could not claim these particular verses, Tupper had others which soon appeared on the stalls; and for good measure he designed a uniform for the bold volunteers, in which, however, no army (not even a volunteer one) has ever yet advanced to do battle.

Sovereign, and this Gladstone had failed to do. Moreover, at Copenhagen there happened to be assembled a score or so of kings and queens, with some of whom—notably the Tzar—it was not then convenient for the Prime Minister to hob-nob. Queen Victoria's wrath was large and all-embracing—at least it embraced Mr. Tennyson, although he was an innocent member of the party. Sharp letters flowed from the Queen and conciliatory ones from Mr. Gladstone, and when the smoke of battle thinned a little this curious sentence emerged: 'The Queen quite understands how Mr. Gladstone was led on to visit Copenhagen and how the Poet Laureate wished to visit that country. She will gladly sanction a barony being conferred on him, but thinks it would be well to delay it till the beginning of next year.' And so, 'next year,' in the Spring of 1884, Mr. Tennyson became a Lord.

He was now, of course, the most famous poet in the world; thirty-three years of Laureateship lay behind him, and a dozen new volumes had been added to his list. *Idylls of The King* (1859), *Enoch Arden* (1864) and several 'collected' editions had carried his lyric fame to the ends of the earth; the Arthur poems had been added to over the years by *The Holy Grail* (1869), *Gareth and Lynette* (1872) and others. And now, with *Queen Mary* (1875), *Harold* (1876), and other dramas he was looking for a new medium and finding success in it—though *Becket*, with Sir Henry Irving, was still to come.

Satire of the old sort—even satire of a Laureate—was a thing principally of the past. To some extent parody had taken its place, and parodies of Tennyson abound, some of great merit, others commonplace: for, as Tennyson himself remarked, 'All can raise the flower now, for all have got the seed.' In 1877 'a Newdigate Prizeman'[1] supplied a recipe for using the seed in the kitchen:

How to make an Epic Poem like Mr. T*NN*S*N.

(The following, apart from its intrinsic utility, forms in itself a great literary curiosity, being the original directions from which the Poet Laureate composed the Arthurian Idylls.)

To compose an epic, some writers instruct us first to catch our hero. As, however, Mr. Carlyle is the only person on record who has ever performed this feat, it will be best for the rest of mankind to be content with the nearest approach to a hero available, namely a prig. These animals are very

---

[1] *Every Man His Own Poet, or The Inspired Singer's Recipe Book*, by A Newdigate Prizeman (1877, 'Third edition, enlarged') is by W. H. Mallock. It is capital fun, but very rare; which makes me regret that Matthew Arnold was never Poet Laureate, so that I might extract the Prizeman's recipe for a poem by M.A.: 'Take one soulful of involuntary unbelief . . .', etc. What a deal of fine things are lost to us for want of reprinting!

plentiful, and easy to catch, as they delight in being run after. There are however many different kinds, not all equally fit for the present purpose, and amongst which it is very necessary to select the right one. Thus, for instance, there is the scientific and atheistical prig, who may be frequently observed eluding notice between the covers of the *Westminster Review*; the Anglican prig, who is often caught exposing himself in the *Guardian*; the Ultramontane prig, who abounds in the *Dublin Review*; the scholarly prig, who twitters among the leaves of the *Academy*; and the Evangelical prig, who converts the heathen, and drinks port wine. None of these, and least of all the last, will serve for the central figure, in the present class of poem. The only one entirely suitable is the blameless variety. Take, then, one blameless prig. Set him upright in the middle of a round table, and place beside him a beautiful wife, who cannot abide prigs. Add to these one marred goodly man; and tie the three together in a bundle with a link or two of Destiny. Proceed, next, to surround this group with a large number of men and women of the nineteenth century, in fancy-ball costume, flavoured with a great many very possible vices, and a few impossible virtues. Stir these briskly for about two volumes, to the great annoyance of the blameless prig, who is, however, to be kept carefully below swearing-point, for the whole time. If he once boils over into any natural action or exclamation, he is forthwith worthless, and you must get another. Next break the wife's reputation into small pieces; and dust them well over the blameless prig. Then take a few vials of tribulation and wrath, and empty these generally over the whole ingredients of your poem: and, taking the sword of the heathen, cut into small pieces the greater part of your minor characters. Then wound slightly the head of the blameless prig; remove him suddenly from the table, and keep in a cool barge for future use.

Tennyson was a man of great intellectual vigour, which the years failed to diminish; indeed his latest poems contain some of his best work and the range of his interests was always widening: politics, science, religion, world affairs, all the tangled, exciting and eager wealth of nineteenth century thought—he embraced them all and 'followed The Gleam.' He was—as we now again see, after the customary few decades of neglect—a giant; but more than this, he was a man it is possible now, 'sixty years after' to know and to love; he comes alive in a hundred books, allusions, stories. Here is a glimpse of him in 1845, calling unexpectedly on Carlyle and finding the Sage from home and only Mrs. Carlyle to entertain him:

. . . I heard a carriage drive up, and men's voices asking questions, and then the carriage was sent away! and the men proved to be Alfred Tennyson of all people and his friend Mr. Moxon—Alfred lives in the country, and only comes to London rarely and for a few days so that I was overwhelmed with the sense of Carlyle's misfortune in having missed the man he likes best. . . . Alfred is dreadfully embarrassed with women alone—for he entertains at one and the same moment a feeling of almost adoration for them and an ineffable contempt! adoration I suppose for what they *might be* —contempt for what they *are*! The only chance of my getting any right good of him was to make him forget my womanness—so I did just as Carlyle would have done, had he been there; got out *pipes* and *tobacco* and *brandy and water*—with a deluge of *tea* over and above. The effect of these accessories was miraculous—he *professed* to be *ashamed* of polluting my room, 'felt' he said 'as if he were stealing cups and sacred vessels in the Temple'— but he smoked on all the same—for *three* mortal hours!—talking like an angel—only exactly as if he were talking with a clever man—which—being a thing I am not used to—men always *adapting* their conversation to what they take *to be a* woman's taste—strained me to a terrible pitch of intellectuality.

When Carlyle came home at twelve and found me all *alone* in an atmosphere of tobacco so thick that you might have cut it with a knife, his astonishment was considerable! . . .[1]

Anne Thackeray Ritchie gives us another very different vignette:

. . . perhaps the best compliment that Tennyson ever received was one day walking in Covent Garden, when he was suddenly stopped by a rough looking man, who held out his hand, and said 'You're Mr. Tennyson. Look here, sir, here am I. I've been drunk for six days out of the seven, but if you will shake me by the hand, I'm d——d if I ever get drunk again!'

This second quotation effectively demonstrates how, in the later years of the century, Tennyson had become a national figure—perhaps the last English poet (perhaps also the first) to occupy such a position. This ability to walk with kings, nor lose the common touch, made Tennyson the ideal Laureate, and the barony was a fitting recognition of his supreme success in the office. When, on October 6th, 1892, the old poet died, the whole nation mourned. There was an impressive service at Westminster Abbey on the 12th in the presence of a great congregation, of whom before it began 'many were seen reading *In Memoriam*.'[3]

[1] From *Jane Welsh Carlyle: a new selection of her letters,* arranged by Trudy Bliss (Gollancz, 1949).
[2] From *Tennyson, Ruskin and Browning,* by Anne Thackeray Ritchie (1892).
[3] *Alfred, Lord Tennyson* by his son (1897).

14

Alfred Austin

THE most interesting thing about the vacancy left by the death of Tennyson is that it took four years to fill. England was full of poets, good and bad, but nothing happened. The interval gives me time to repeat an engaging little story.

At Tennyson's death, 'the whole nation mourned'—but some people didn't allow this to interfere with business, as W. H. Mallock notes in his *Memoirs of Life and Literature*:

> The scene was not in London but at (Lady Marian Alford's) house in the country, where a few guests were staying with her for the inside of a week. Two of these guests were poets; we may call them Sir E. and Sir L. The visit co-incided with the time of Tennyson's last illness, the reports of which were daily more alarming. The two poets evinced much becoming anxiety, though this did not interfere with the zeal with which one day at luncheon they consumed a memorable plum tart. Next morning neither of them appeared at breakfast; and when both of them remained in their bedrooms for the larger part of the day I came to the prosaic conclusion that the plum tart had been too much for them. Next morning came the news of Tennyson's death. The two bards remained in their cells till noon, after which they both reappeared like men who had got rid of a burden. The true secret of their retirement revealed itself the morning after, when each of two great newspapers, with which they were severally connected, was found to contain long columns of elegy on the irreparable loss which the country had just suffered—compositions implying a suggestion on the part of each of the elegists that a poet existed who was not unfit to repair it.

The rival bards departed the same day, Mallock records, 'waving independent adieux, one from a first, the other from a third class carriage.' I don't pretend to identify the two poets, but it cannot be a coincidence that Sir Lewis Morris has a poem called 'October 6th, 1892;' or that Sir Edwin Arnold in his last portraits looks so exactly like a man who would have been Laureate if invited. Indeed, when at length the appointment was made, he admitted as much in a generous telegram to the successful poet:

> Accept my heartiest congratulations with which no grudge mingles, although I myself expected the appointment. I rejoice at continuance of this appointment, which will be worthily and patriotically borne by you.

Immediately after Tennyson's death there was, of course, the customary newspaper discussion of the Laureateship, and a number of names were put forward, notably that of Swinburne; and certainly Swinburne's mastery of noble and moving verse fitted him for the office. No conceivable Laureate occasion could find him at a loss for rhymes; but Gladstone perhaps wondered if his potential Laureate would always be on the Queen's side. It was to be doubted if a handful of silver would stop him from being a Republican. He might not be acceptable to the Church, either—that powerful force. 'I am told that Mr. Swinburne is the best poet in my dominions,' the Queen is reported to have remarked; but she was not heard to quote 'Dolores.'[1]

For eighteen months Gladstone did nothing positive,[2] although he kept the vacancy in mind. Then he went out of office and Lord Rosebery became Prime Minister. But the new Prime Minister had many things to think about, and before he was able to give his attention to all of them his government had fallen too. It was Lord Salisbury's turn.

In the appointments of Wordsworth and Tennyson the Queen had taken an active interest, and had appeared then to establish the principle that the Laureate should be one of 'the Chiefs' among living poets. But perhaps now her interest was less active; or perhaps she didn't read the works of the newer Chiefs. She was content to leave the thing to the Prime Minister.

And Lord Salisbury—that wily Cecil,[3] sprung from a long line of royal right-hand-men, preferred a poet who would support the

---

[1] 'May I die a Poet Laureate!' Swinburne was apt to exclaim in moments of stress—rather as the rest of us might say, 'God forbid!' After the appointment H. C. Beeching remarked that it came to Austin, he thought, because of a confusion in Lord Salisbury's mind between Swinford and Swinburne. Swinford was Austin's manor house, already famous through *The Garden that I Love*.

[2] J. W. Mackail in his *Life of William Morris* (1899) says the office was actually offered to Morris; but the offer seems to have been tentative and "off the record": '. . . Morris was sounded by a member of the Cabinet, with Mr. Gladstone's knowledge and approval, to ascertain whether he would accept the office in the event of its being offered to him. His answer was unhesitating. He was frankly pleased that he had been thought of, and did not undervalue the implied honour; but it was one which his principles and his tastes alike made it impossible for him to accept. . . . In private conversation Morris always held that the proper function of a Poet Laureate was that of a ceremonial writer of official verse. . . .' Morris survived Tennyson by barely four years.

[3] This illustrious family has something to answer for: their patronage has given us two of the least admirable of our laureates—Pye and Austin.

Government to one who expressed dubious opinions in magnificent verse. So he chose Alfred Austin.

Few have been found to say a good word for this poet, but as George Herbert points out, 'Good words are worth much, and cost little.' In the work of Alfred Austin the candid inquirer can find at least something to commend.

Austin, like Pye, was rather an amateur of letters—of poetry, anyway. He had many interests, and to some he gave more attention than to book-writing. All the same, in 1896 he could point to a respectable list of successful publications—enough, certainly, to carry those that had been less successful, in which we must include his first excursion into authorship, *Randolph, a Tale of Polish Grief*,[1] the publication of which was subsidised in 1854 by the poet's uncle. Of this work seventeen copies were sold.

This future Laureate was born at Headingley, Leeds, on May 30th, 1835; his father was a prosperous merchant in the wool trade. After a spell at the village school, young Alfred was sent to St. Edward's, the Roman Catholic school at Everton, and later to Stonyhurst, where his career terminated almost as abruptly as did that of Southey at Westminster. After three years there 'my Father received a letter from the Rector saying that he had come to the conclusion that my character was calculated to create insubordination, and that he would rather, therefore, I did not return.' Exactly what lay behind this, Austin never knew; but it didn't worry him unduly, nor did it upset his father very much.

Off went Austin to Oscott to finish his schooling, after which he began to read Law in the Inner Temple, and in 1857 he was called to the Bar. But his interest lay rather in literature—despite the unhappy circulation of *Randolph*—and in 1861 he published *The Season, a Satire*, which—he tells us—more than one critic hailed as the best satire since Byron's *English Bards and Scotch Reviewers*. Well, of course, between 1809 and 1861 there had been not so very much competition; satire is a branch of letters somewhat neglected now, and perhaps Bryon was the last to practice it in the regular 18th century way. Here's a passage from *The Season*:[2]

> *Look! as we turn, most loved of all her Line,*
> *If not by Right, by deeds at least divine,*

---

[1] So Austin calls it in his autobiography; but in fact it was called *Randolph* and has nothing to do with Poland. He was confusing this title with that of a later work, *Leszko the Bastard, a Tale of Polish Grief*.

[2] It and its successor attracted attention enough to be the subject of a rejoinder, *Seasoning of a Seasoner* by one Stevens. It is a mean performance.

By Nature's self equipped for kind command,
Onward she comes, the Lady of the Land!
Long may each zone its wealth profusely pour
Upon her laplike, peace-protected shore!
Long may the strain come swelling from the ships,
Which keeps Victoria on a Nation's lips!
Long, long in thousand eyes that smile be seen
Which thinks her woman, though it hails her Queen:
Queen, wife, or mother, perfect in each part,
And throned securely in a People's heart!

This, we may hope, was not intended as part of the satire. The poem went into a second edition quite quickly, and a few years later into a third, which was much revised. Meanwhile, very shortly after its first publication the author came out with *My Satire and Its Censors* (1861) in which he carries on the good work and lashes about him with great vigour, although it must be confessed that 'nobody seemed one penny the worse.' The young writer was certainly very few pennies the better, but in those days a little money went a long way. He threw up the law, took a cottage in the country (having promised to build another to accomodate its existing tenants) and set off for Rome. Really, it makes one wish to have lived a hundred years ago!

He tells in his *Autobiography* a rather charming and touching little story about this visit to Rome. He visited Shelley's grave and found it much neglected; so he wrote an indignant letter, anonymously, to an English newspaper and he also wrote a poem; more effectively, he paid the cemetery keeper to look after the grave, and himself planted there pansies and violets. All this, years later, came to the notice of Lady Shelley, and occasioned an exchange of letters, poems, visits, etc. which gave the poet great pleasure, and doubtless pleased Lady Shelley too.

Two idle years abroad were followed by two equally idle in England and then two more in Italy, after which Austin felt qualified to stand for Parliament; but the borough of Taunton preferred to elect someone else. Mr. Austin returned therefore, not to Westminster but to Italy. His writings by now (he tells us) included a novel *An Artist's Proof*, published in 1864, and another (unpublished) which Chapman and Hall refused because 'they had been much disappointed in the number of copies they had sold' of the first.[1] Austin, however (just married),

[1] Austin's *Autobiography* is not to be relied upon for accurate detail. Writing over fifty years later, his memory was at fault. His three novels were: *Five Years of It* (J. F. Hope, 1858); *An Artist's Proof* (Tinsley Bros., 1864) and *Won by a Head* (Chapman & Hall, 1866). They are unreadable today—they were probably unreadable then.

was not particularly cast down. He wrote to the Editor of the *Standard* offering to write leading articles (just like that!) and his offer was accepted (just like that!) 'Never, I suppose,' says Alfred Austin, 'did anyone have so easy an entrance into journalism.'

For the next thirty years he followed the profession he had thus so casually adopted, and he saw a good deal of international affairs by reporting various Councils, meetings, and the like. He also had a sort of ring-side seat at the Franco–German war and gives a long account of a talk with Bismarck. All round, he lived a busy life, dashing hither and yon on the Continent and in between writing epics (if that is the word for *The Human Tragedy*—1862,[1] and extended later editions). He had come to the aid of Shelley in the matter of the weed-choked grave. Now he lent his support to Byron in the controversy, still wearily dragging on, about the noble poet's relationship with his wife, which had been revived by Harriet Beecher Stowe. In 1872 he gathered most of his lyrics into a collection called *Interludes*. It was the year of *Gareth and Lynette*—if we note what his Laureate predecessor Tennyson was doing and if we glance at the activities of Austin's successor, we find Robert Bridges preparing to send his first poems to press. This is a fair example of Austin's muse in that year:

> *The flower, full blown, now bends the stalk, now breaks;*
> *The mellow fruit inclines the bough to earth;*
> *The brow which thought impregnates ofttimes aches;*
> *Death-stricken is the womb in giving birth.*
> *Cracked is the vase by heat which doth illume,*
> *The driest logs the swiftest burn to nought,*

---

[1] The original edition (dated 1861) is so completely different from the poem of 1862 as revised and reissued that it is in fact another work. It is rather fun in a Byronic way:

> *A very learned man, and very saintly,*
> *   One Alban Butler, now among the dead,*
> *Has written rather lengthily, but quaintly,*
> *   A book that you, I'll wager, never read:*
> *'Lives of the Saints.' I still can hear, though faintly,*
> *   Its pages echoing from my schooldays sped.*
> *'Twas always read aloud through Sunday dinners.*
> *Will no one write for us 'The Lives of Sinners?'*
>
> *Gods! how the book would sell! The first edition*
> *   Would, ere a week elapsed, be out of print.*
> *Of course, I'd take a copy; with permission*
> *   Would give its editor a useful hint:*
> *Which (underneath the rose) would be, 'Contrition*
> *   After long sinning, throw in without stint.'*
> *The British Public dearly loves a scoundrel,*
> *If, in the end, he weepeth like a drowned rill.*

> Sweet flowers are stifled by their own perfume,
> And bees when honey-clogged are easy caught.
> Snapped are true chords e'en by the note they give,
> The largest wave is broken by its weight,
> Choked by its sheer sufficiency the sieve,
> And blunted soon the shaft which flieth straight.
> And so the largest mind and richest soul
> Are always most amenable to dole.

Every year or so thereafter Austin published something—*The Tower of Babel*, a poetic drama in 1874, the revised *Human Tragedy* in 1876, *Leszko the Bastard, a Tale of Polish Grief* in 1877—the Poles have been, with cause, a sad race. *Leszko* is full-blooded, tumbling stuff:

> He loved me. Do you ask if I
> His love returned? Go, ask the sky
> If it in vain pours sun and shower
> On herb and leaf, on tree and flower.
> Go, ask of echo if it wakes
>   When voice in lonely places calls;
> Ask of the silence if it takes
>   The sound of splashing waterfalls:
> Ask the parched plains if they refuse
> The solace of descending dews;
> Ask the unrippled lake that lies
>   Under faint fleecy clouds that flit,
> If it reflects with tender eyes
>   The heavenly forms that gaze on it;
> But ask not me if I returned
> The love with which his being burned . . .

In 1885 *At the Gate of the Convent and other Poems* was well received, and in 1887 another drama, *Prince Lucifer*, appeared with a dedication to the Queen. These are but a few of the works Austin had to offer when, at the age of 56 he gathered his poems and dramas into the first volumes of a collected edition, which by 1896 and his appointment to the Laureateship, made seven respectable volumes.

The poet, then, could not be ignored even by those who thought Mr. Kipling (say) or Mr. Swinburne, or Mr. Coventry Patmore would have made a more suitable successor to Tennyson.

It happened also that in 1890 William Watson had made a selection from Austin's shorter pieces, and had prefixed to it an interesting and on the whole very temperate essay in which he made the claim that as a poet of England and of her countryside, Austin was Tennyson's legitimate successor—in these matters, not in the Laureateship. The claim might be questioned; there were, for example, the poems of Lord de Tabley very much in the same tradition, and there were delightful things in Christina Rossetti, Thomas Ashe, and others: still, the claim could be made and the volume in which it appeared circulated widely.

An even greater circulation attended *The Garden that I Love* (1894), in which Austin described, very pleasantly, the garden at Swinford Old Manor and his life there. Dean Hole's *A Book About Roses* had been before the public for twenty-five years, but no other gardening book had ever enjoyed the same success until Austin's appeared. He followed it with *In Veronica's Garden* (1896) and a similarly discursive volume about Italy, *Lamia's Winter Quarters* (1898). Finally, in 1902 *Haunts of Ancient Peace* completed a quartet of books which had a great success in their own day, and are by no means unreadable in ours. *The Poet's Diary* and a second series of *The Garden that I Love* were less successful.

Alfred Austin was a Tory, and an articulate one; and these facts would certainly weigh with Lord Salisbury. Moreover, Austin wrote the kind of poetry a busy Prime Minister might find time to appreciate:

> *The Spring-time, O the Spring-time!*
> *Who does not know it well?*
> *When the little birds begin to build,*
> *And the buds begin to swell.*

One of Mr. Austin's poems had a title Lord Salisbury could not but be pleased by: 'Why England is Conservative.' Besides, something ought to be done for so loyal a champion, whose support in the *Standard* had now for some years past been augmented by his vigorous editing of the *National Review*.[1] And had he not twice been unsuccessful in his attempts to get into the House?—for, taking their cue perhaps, from the electors of Taunton, the electors of Dewsbury in 1880 had given overwhelming support to his opponent.

There was no elaborate negotiation this time. Austin, in his *Autobiography*, simply prints a single note, and the thing was done:

30th December, 1895.

My dear Austin,

I have much pleasure in telling you that the Queen has approved your appointment to the post of Poet Laureate. It will be announced tomorrow.

Yours very truly,
Salisbury.

---

[1] 'This foolish Tory magazine,' Sidney Colvin called it, and would be 'really and seriously hurt' if Robert Louis Stevenson contributed.

The announcement, on the whole, was met with respectful dis-interest; it appeared among the New Year Honours and received the patronising faint praise of *The Times:*

> To the public in general the most interesting announcement of the day, next to that of Sir Frederic Leighton's peerage, will be that of Mr. Alfred Austin's appointment as Poet Laureate.[1] If the Laureateship was to be filled up at all—and we do not see why it should not be simply because there is no competitor to be compared with Tennyson—a better choice among those available could hardly be made than Mr. Austin. Among living poets he holds his own with the foremost, Mr. Swinburne alone excepted, and Mr. Swinburne has never seriously been regarded as an aspirant to the laurel. Mr. Austin's poetry is always scholarly and refined, often very graceful and touching, especially when he is inspired by the country life of which he has a real and appreciative love; and, when the subject demands it, his muse is capable of rising to a high level of patriotic and imperial spirit. We do not suppose that Mr. Austin will leave behind him works like those of Words-worth and Tennyson, but we have no fear that he will prove unworthy to take his place in the roll of Poets Laureate.

Swinburne was a great poet, but unpredictable; Kipling was a lively poet, but unpredictable; Patmore was a remarkable poet, but he had already had three wives . . . and so perhaps had the Prime Minister run through the list. Austin was dull and safe, as Salisbury probably thought. He would hardly put a foot wrong.

Alas, within a couple of weeks the new Laureate put wrong not merely a foot but the best part of a leg! For he rushed into print in *The Times* with verses celebrating the news of the Jameson Raid; and the Jameson Raid turned out to be an embarrassment to the Govern-ment, a source of annoyance to the Queen, a singular fiasco in its own right, and a contributory cause of one of England's less spectacularly successful wars.

All this may be seen to be true in retrospect; but the Laureate was fired by the newspaper reports—as Tennyson had been at the time of Balaclava—and he did no more than his predecessor had done. He sat down and dashed off a very creditable piece of ballad verse in the manner successfully employed on similar occasions by Kipling, Conan Doyle and Edgar Wallace:

---

[1] Meredith told Michael Field that he thought it would 'suit little Alfred to hymn the babies of the house of Hanover.' It would perhaps not have suited Meredith; but he could have brought to the task a largeness of spirit and a breadth of understanding quite outside Austin's scope. As to Alfred being 'little,' incidentally, Meredith's adjective was aptly chosen: a voter introduced to him at Dewsbury cried, 'Ee, but you're a very little un!'— 'You wait till you see my wife,' Austin answered.

' "*Wrong! Is it wrong? Well, may be:*
   But I'm going, boys, all the same.
Do they think me a Burgher's baby
   To be scared by a scolding name?
They may argue, and prate, and order,
   Go, tell them to save their breath:
Then over the Transvaal border
   And gallop for life or death!"

'*So we forded and galloped forward,*
   As hard as our beasts could pelt,
First eastward, then trending norward
   Right over the rolling veldt;
Till we came on the Burghers lying
   In a hollow with hills behind
And their bullets came hissing, flying,
   Like hail on an Arctic wind!

'*I suppose we were wrong, were madmen,*
   Still I think at the Judgment Day,
When God sifts the good from the bad men
   There'll be something more to say.
We were wrong, but we aren't half sorry
   And, as one of the baffled band,
I would rather have had that foray
   Than the crushings of all the Rand.'

Perhaps Lord Salisbury was looking obliquely at this poem when, in the course of praising another a year or two later, he remarked 'The Muse on this occasion has been an excellent diplomatist.'[1] It was the last two words the poet valued and took to heart; but perhaps the nub lay in the phrase 'on this occasion.' At all events, he never erred again and his Laureate verses—on the Jubilee, the Queen's death, the centenary of Trafalgar, the death of Edward VII, and others—were respectable and blameless. Alfred Austin took his position seriously, and it was his misfortune that his work did not carry the weight necessary to sustain the title. In his prefaces, and other incidental references to the Laureateship, he speaks in tones that would be suitable in a Wordsworth, but are pompous in the author of *The Garden that I Love.*

[1] Austin published some verses after Mafeking and someone asked the Prime Minister if he thought 'wrestle' a good rhyme to 'Cecil.' He replied (and we may see in his words a world of meaning) that 'he had thought it best not to read the poem of his Poet Laureate.'

In his *Autobiography* Austin says little directly about the Laureateship, but he gives us one rather charming glimpse of himself in the role of Laureate. Having sent his Diamond Jubilee verses to the papers, he had a copy specially printed for the Queen, and he decided to take it along to Windsor Castle himself, together with a few roses from his garden. The bunch of flowers was much appreciated (the verses, too, no doubt) and shortly afterwards the Queen (who had long since become an author herself) sent him copies of her two Highland books in which she had inscribed her own name and his.

The Laureate was not a man of wide literary friendships, and he makes no large figure in the memoirs of his time—indeed, he is most often encountered in the index of political rather than literary biographies. There are malicious references to him in *As We Were* which reflect more discredit on the author, E. F. Benson, than on Austin. I shall not trouble to repeat them. There are too, the curious peevish passages in Browning, who was much annoyed (not without justice) by Austin's essay on his work in *The Poetry of the Period* (1870). Tennyson and Swinburne were somewhat roughly handled in the same book, and indeed in 1873 Austin withdrew it. Years later when Tennyson met Austin he grumbled a bit and Austin replied nonchalantly, 'It was a long time ago!' and assumed that he was forgiven. As for Browning, he called Austin 'a filthy little snob' (among other things) which however, was not so neat as Austin's remark of Browning that 'He is the real M. Jourdain who has been writing prose all his life without knowing it.' Browning tells one amusing story about Austin, in a letter to Isabella Blagden:

> . . . I heard a good story, the other day, about this literary 'cad' and Thackeray—at all events, a story which is true to my knowledge. The little fool sent Thackeray, when editor of the Cornhill, an article for insertion, accompanied by a letter about his own genius, his wrongs, the result of a conspiracy, and so forth—sent them up stairs and waited below for an answer: Thackeray understood nothing but that there was a petition in the case from some broken down devil, and—as best remedy for his sorrows, and way to an immediate riddance of a bore—benevolently sent him down half-a-crown! . . .

It is pleasant to turn from this to a reminiscence by a friendlier critic Edmund Yates, who in his engaging *Recollections and Experiences* (1884) mentions a tour in Switzerland with Austin in 1861 during which Yates was taken seriously ill: 'Clear-headed Alfred Austin telegraphed at once, indicating the symptoms, to the English physician at Geneva, begging him to hurry to my aid; but many hours necessarily elapsed before he could arrive, during which I lay in fearful agony, becoming weaker and weaker, and desperately alarming the village medico, who was probably a farrier, who for all my convulsions proposed internally a tisane, and externally a cataplasm.' Despite these 'the devoted attention of my two companions turned the scale' and the author of *Nobody's Fortune* lived.

Alfred Austin passed a full and happy life; his *Autobiography* is a confused and rather unsatisfactory book, but at least it amply shows that the writer enjoyed all the things he saw and did; and the same spirit informs the other prose works of his maturity. His poems are full of the same eager appreciation of flowers, sunshine and 'the pleasure that there is in life itself.' It would have surprised him to know of the neglect and contempt that would come upon his name after his death. It is difficult to take him so seriously as he took himself, but that is no reason to under-rate him. Anyone who will open his volumes of verse with tolerance, and read them with patience, will be rewarded here and there with a respectable passage, and will come upon a handful of lyrics of real charm.

His tenure of the Laureateship was certainly less successful, all round, than Tennyson's. When appointed, he was sixty and he lived through the whole reign of Edward VII, whose death he marked with some stanzas in which he gave warning of the necessity for continuing the King's work for peace. He did not live to see its failure, for he died on June 2, 1913.

Generally speaking, poetry in England was marking time during the twenty years succeeding Tennyson's death. No very great poet was active in the way that Tennyson had been active—speaking to and for the whole nation and Empire, and making the people everywhere aware of poetry and interested in it. Poetry began to be the province and preserve of a minority. A lead from Austin—as Laureate—if he had been capable of giving it, might have kept the idea of poetry before the wider public that Tennyson had so easily commanded. But there was no lead, and not until 1914—when Austin was dead—did poetry again enter the general consciousness.

In his anonymous *Pages from a Private Diary* (1898) H. C. Beeching illustrates the point lightheartedly enough, without destroying its underlying truth:

> Said A.: 'I see that the Poet-Laureate is about to give up writing in the *Standard*, in order to devote more time to the Muses.' Said B.: 'Oh, who is

the Poet-Laureate?' A.: 'For shame, Sylvia; what ignorance! His name is Alfred Austin. . . . It is a rather poetical name, don't you think?' B.: 'Yes, dear. But we always take the *Standard* at home, and I have never seen any poetry in it.' A.: 'Oh no; that's just it. The Poet-Laureate has not had any time to write any poetry yet, because he has had to write the *Standard*. But now he's going to begin. You see, the Poet-laureate in these days has to be such a political person. My father said, when Mr. Austin was appointed, that it was a happy return to the sound Conservative principles that prevailed in Mr. Shadwell's time; and he hoped the Government, with their large majority, would have the courage to make the post a genuinely party one, so that Sir Lewis Morris might come in when Mr. Austin went out.' B.: 'Oh yes, I do so hope he will. I do so dote on his wallpapers. But who was Mr. Shadwell?'

Such a conversation, even an imaginary one, would have been impossible twenty years earlier.

Perhaps W. H. Mallock's words make Austin's best epitaph: 'Though his poetry has not commanded any very wide attention, he had more of true poetry in him than many people imagine. He had all the qualifications of a really great poet except a sustained faculty for writing really good poetry.'

15

Robert Bridges

The death of Mr. Alfred Austin which occurred on Monday cannot be said by any stretch of imagination to leave a gap in literature; but it does leave a gap in officialdom. It is a very curious fact that while the Laureateship has reached the Pye level, poetry has flourished outside, and is now flourishing as it has not done for years.

This, however, makes the choice of a successor more difficult. It would be a very graceful act if the Laureateship were conferred on Mr. Thomas Hardy, for his 'Dynasts' places him among the immortals. Failing him, why not Mrs. Meynell, even although a woman Laureate would be forming a precedent? Some of the other poets have made poetry and politics too interchangeable.

SO wrote *The Graphic* (in rather doubtful taste) a few days after Austin's death. Accompanying the notice were a picture of Austin in his study and pictures of 'possible successors'—Hardy, Laurence Binyon, Stephen Phillips, John Masefield, Kipling, Alice Meynell, Maurice Hewlett and William Watson.

Now—apart from others not mentioned—there was first class Laureate material here. Binyon (as events proved) could write solemn, moving and dignified verse, capable of impressing the whole nation; and 'For the Fallen' is not alone among his poems. Hewlett commanded a similar fitting gravity of tone when the occasion required it; Sir William Watson was a better poet than his later reputation suggests. Alice Meynell was, perhaps, too personal and restricted in her range, and Stephen Phillips was a spent force; to Kipling's vigorous style the Laureateship would have been a hindrance—he was better as an influential private voice. Hardy might have said some grand things—but, Laureate or not, he said them anyway and we have no cause for complaint at the quantity of his poems: perhaps, indeed, he too would have found the office restricting. John Masefield's turn was to come.

Besides the names noted in *The Graphic* there were others equally respectable, for the first decade of the new century had seen the making of several solid reputations—which the passing of forty more years has not essentially diminished, and has in some cases enhanced. Foremost among these was W. B. Yeats, and others were Sir Henry Newbolt, Alfred Noyes, Lascelles Abercrombie, and that sombre, powerful poet, Wilfrid Gibson. But—rightly, I think—Mr. Asquith was not looking for a younger man. His choice fell unexpectedly, but fittingly, on a poet with the achievement of forty years behind him: Robert Bridges.

Robert Seymour Bridges was born at Walmer, Kent, on October 23rd, 1844, and ten years later he went to Eton; in 1863 he went on to Corpus Christi College, Oxford, and in 1869 to St. Bartholomew's Hospital were he took his M.B. in 1874. He had—Edward Thompson tells us[1]—no intention of following this career all his life; he meant to retire at forty, for like Milton, Wordsworth, Tennyson, he was content to be a poet and only a poet. Like them, he would have thought it as high a calling as any; and when followed by such men as these, so it is.

At school he wrote his first poems, but did not neglect the other good things. Cricket and rowing were his sports: he recalls (in the *Memoir* of Dolben) reading Tennyson's *Enoch Arden* 'without all Digby's enthusiasm, in the hot sun on a treeless cricket-field waiting for my innings.' He tells us he was not wholly won to Tennyson: '. . . well as I loved some of Tennyson's early lyrics, and had them by heart, yet when I heard *The Idylls of the King* praised as if they were the final attainment of all poetry, then I drew into my shell, contented to think that I might be too stupid to understand, but that I could never expect as good a pleasure from following another's taste as I got from my own.' His great enthusiasm was for Shakespeare, Milton, and Keats (whose poems he carried about in his pocket). Even as a boy his critical eye at once detected the second-rate—Dolben admired one Faber, but Bridges was provoked to disgust by 'a maudlin hymn of his.' His own poems included ('the last I wrote at school') an imitation of Spenser; but he also 'put comic rhymes together.'

Bridges was doubtless a good doctor; he held the appointment of Assistant Physician at the Hospital for Sick Children, in Great Ormond Street, and he served on the staff of the Great Northern Hospital, Holloway. But an attack of pneumonia in 1881 brought his medical career to a close, for after a trip abroad for his health he married and settled at Yattendon, in Berkshire. He had sufficient means, and from 1882 until his death in 1930 poetry and the study of music and language were his only employment.

His first poems were published in 1873, a little book now, like

[1] *Robert Bridges, 1844–1930* (Oxford, 1944).

many good things, very rare. It contained perfect, imperishable lyrics such as 'Clear and gentle stream,' and 'I will not let thee go.' In 1876 —almost unnoticed—the anonymous first draft of *The Growth of Love* was printed, and in 1879 a second collection of lyrics among which were 'I have loved flowers that fade' and 'Whither, O splendid ship?' Bridges—like Wilfrid Blunt whose finest work was appearing about the same time—neither courted fame nor then attained it. Many of his books were privately printed; all had a limited circulation. Bridges was oddly reticent, too; Gerard Manley Hopkins had known Bridges ten years before he discovered—from a review—that he wrote poetry, yet the greater part of their intercourse concerned poetry. (John Cowper Powys records a similar reticence. He tells us that in 1902 he—Powys —arranged for the publication of Alfred de Kantzow's poems, without ever telling the old poet of his own two books of verse.)

Accordingly, Bridges made his way slowly, so that by 1890 when his *Shorter Poems* was first issued commercially he had published a body of magnificent lyrics of which hardly anyone had ever heard; the *Shorter Poems* were a revelation to poetry lovers. 'The most perfect book of verse ever written,' A. E. Housman afterwards called it; and perfection is a quality of which few had a better right to speak than the author of *A Shropshire Lad*.

In 1890 Bridges also published commercially (that is, with a commercial publisher, publishing books for profit in the usual way) *The Growth of Love*, one of the great sonnet-sequences of the nineteenth century. This, like some of its fellows—Rossetti's *The House of Life*, for example—was built over the years. It had originally twenty-four sonnets; it was left with sixty-nine. It tells autobiographically a love story about which elsewhere Bridges says little—but it really is not necessary every time to know names and dates and details.[1] Poetry such as this can be enjoyed supremely without speculation as to the lady's identity. The sequence makes a remarkable foil to Meredith's *Modern Love* and it is an interesting comment on the diversity of human nature that two such poems could have been in composition at roughly the same time.

To these works the reader in 1890 might have added, if they had come his way, the mask of *Demeter* (1883) and the long narrative poem *Eros and Psyche* (1885). During the seventeen years of Austin's Laureateship Bridges added a further group of lyrics and published some studies in classical prosody which were the forerunners of a whole

---

[1] 'That's telling secrets!' as Hopkins said to Patmore.

body of experiment and innovation. His work in the drama, begun in 1885 with *Nero*, he continued with *The Return of Ulysses* (1890) and others, but without receiving any wide recognition. The verse drama from Tennyson to Christopher Fry would make an interesting study; the first thing a researcher would notice would be its bulk; and the next, its general unsuitedness to the stage. Yet in the dramas of Bridges, Bottomley, Trevelyan, Michael Field—and a dozen others— there is buried, and virtually lost, a wealth of fine poetry. Even in plays once successfully staged and now ignored—those of Stephen Phillips are the obvious example—there is an excellence our fathers were not mistaken in praising.

In 1912 'E. M.' published the first volume of *Georgian Poetry*, with contributions by Abercrombie, Rupert Brooke, de la Mare, Drinkwater, Gibson, Flecker, and almost a dozen more. Well, forty years later most of these 'Georgians' come in for critical hard knocks from a generation satisfied that it can write better; but, all the same, they were persons of importance in their day, and they may be so again. They joined with the editor to dedicate their anthology to Robert Bridges.

'This is not merely a tribute to a consummate artist,' Walter de la Mare wrote in reviewing the new Laureate's life-work after the appointment, 'it implies the recognition also that Mr. Bridges's devotion to his art has been in the service of an unalloyed ideal with other, though not necessarily meaner, enthusiasms. His work is not only incontestably his own and no other man's, but its aim has always been essentially poetry, and only indirectly ethical, didactic, circumstantial. This probably accounts for the fact that his admirers until the other day were comparatively few, that his name was rather a touchstone and assurance to his fellow-craftsmen than a household word or a party battle-cry.'

'Until the other day'—for what had considerably increased the company of the new Laureate's admirers was the publication of his poems by the Oxford University Press in a handsome collected edition uniform with the works of the classic English poets, Milton, Arnold, and the rest. It was an unusual honour, paralleled I believe only once later by the issue during his lifetime of the collected poems of Lascelles Abercrombie. And as Bridges said later to Humphrey Milford (not then Sir Humphrey, and head of the great Press) 'Milford! You've made me Laureate!'

When the offer reached Bridges from Mr. Asquith, then Prime

Minister, the poet accepted, although he had no personal ambition for the appointment. 'He accepted it largely because he felt he owed it to his publishers, who had made his name widely known,' says Edward Thompson. But—Bridges insisted—'there must be no damned nonsense of Knighthoods or anything of that kind!' There was also, of course, 'no damned nonsense' in the way of obligations, but Bridges like Tennyson before him wrote certain poems which perhaps but for the Laureateship he would not have written, and in them he spoke magnificently for England.

His 'Laureate' poems properly so called are few: the first, 'Noel: Christmas Eve, 1913' was written for the King and sent as a personal tribute to mark the poet's becoming Laureate. The King sent it to *The Times* for publication 'by his Majesty's express desire.'

Thereafter Bridges from time to time, but rather infrequently, wrote poems by virtue of his office, or to which his office lent authority. They include 'Britannia Victrix' (1918), the moving little Epitaph on the Worcesters, October 31st, 1914—'Gheluvelt':

> *Askest thou of our graves? They'll tell thee, O Stranger, in England*
> *How we Worcesters lie where we redeem'd the battle.*

and the 'Ode on the Tercentenary Commemoration of Shakespeare, 1916'. In 1916 he published his anthology, *The Spirit of Man*, in which by a choice of prose and verse in English and French he affirmed for both allies the ideals for which they were fighting. 'The progress of mankind on the path of liberty and humanity has been suddenly arrested,' he wrote in the preface, 'and its promise discredited by the apostasy of a great people, who, casting off as a disguise their professions of Honour, now openly avow that the ultimate faith of their hearts is in material force. . . . From the consequent miseries, the insenate and interminable slaughter, the hate and filth, we can turn to seek comfort only in the quiet confidence of our souls; and we look instinctively to the seers and poets of mankind, whose sayings are the oracles and prophecies of loveliness and lovingkindness.' How many, reading this, have regretted that Bridges left so little in prose; it would have been such prose as we have hardly seen since Walton's *Life of Herbert*.

There is, indeed, a considerable body of prose in the collected essays of Bridges—ten small volumes; but this writing is almost all critical (the essay on Keats, originally contributed to the Muses' Library edition edited by G. Thorn Drury, is one of the finest pieces that poet's work ever inspired). We have from Bridges nothing comparable with (say) those delightful essays which complement the poetry of R. C. Trevelyan, or with the delicate and perceptive prose which accompanies that of Patmore. Even the three essays in biography, models though they are, impose upon him certain restraints, certain limitations, so that he is time and again recalled to his subject when he might have digressed into reminiscence and comment.

Inevitably, there was some criticism during the 1914–18 war of a Poet Laureate whose occasional poems were not patriotic exhortations to kill Germans; even the vigorous measure of Austin's 'Jameson's Ride' might now have come into its own; but—his anthology apart— Bridges held aloof. There were plenty of other poets writing upon the war for those who wanted to read about it in rhyme. But this didn't suit Mr. Horatio Bottomley, who (it was learned later) was himself a poet. He asked questions in Parliament about the indolence of the Laureate; and for a wider public he expressed his dissatisfaction in the pages of *John Bull*. Robert Bridges went on quietly taking no notice.

After the more or less definitive collection of his poems in 1912 —he was never a heavy reviser (as was Wordsworth, say) because he got his work 'right' before its initial publication—he published two comparatively small collections. *October, and Other Poems*, after a few of the poems had been printed privately in 1914 was published with additions in 1920; and *New Verse* appeared in 1925. The poet was then eighty—a commanding figure still, upright, bearded, as much the poet as Tennyson at eighty before him. His vigorous interest in the art he had served for fifty years was demonstrated by a pamphlet he wrote examining the work of a poet then not yet thirty—Mr. Edmund Blunden.

In 1913 Bridges was one of the founders of The Society for Pure English, a body which issued many tracts upon questions of language, and did much good work without receiving conspicuous support or thanks. He also, like Southey before him, edited the poems of others, though in the case of Bridges those poets were also his friends. In 1911 he published, with a long *Memoir*, the poems of Digby Mackworth Dolben, the Eton friend who was drowned soon after Bridges went up to Oxford; and in the memoir gives us several snatches of autobiography. His *Selected Poems of R. W. Dixon* (1909) contains another long introductory essay, somewhat less personal in tone, for Dixon was an older man and Bridges met him later in life. Finally, his most famous task of the kind, Bridges edited in 1918 *The Poems of Gerard Manley Hopkins*, whose work was virtually unknown, despite the presence of a handful of his poems (also sponsored by Bridges) in the last volume of *Poets and Poetry of the Nineteenth Century*, a comprehensive anthology edited in the late 'nineties by Alfred Miles.

This, then, was the sum of Robert Bridges's achievement in 1928 when he was admitted to the Order of Merit, the first, but it is pleasant to think, not the last Laureate to be so honoured.

And then on his eighty-fifth birthday he published *The Testament of Beauty* (1929). This is not a work of which to speak in a few paragraphs, neither is it a work to pronounce judgment upon after a single reading. It is perhaps the most astonishing single work ever put out by a poet in his ninth decade—and many poets have done remarkable things even so late in life as that: there are fine verses of undiminished force in the last works of Landor, for example, and more recently we have had the unforgettable grace and loveliness of Mr. de la Mare's *Winged Chariot* (but I am forgetting: Mr. de la Mare was then a mere seventy-eight!) *The Testament of Beauty* was written in something under four years—it has well over four thousand lines—but, like Whistler's paintings, it represented 'the experience of a life-time.'

The verse was the product of fifty years and more of deliberate and conscious seeking for perfection. The philosophy—that Beauty is a well-spring behind all life's good—is developed in four books, with the given titles, 'Introduction,' 'Selfhood,' 'Breed' and 'Ethick,' and the argument buds, flowers, and comes to fruition as the poem proceeds. It is a work that may be read with pleasure and excitement by one uncomprehending of the implications, for the rare music of the verse; and returned to, later, for the closer attention which will reveal a thinker directing the musician. For, as Charles Williams said, even Tennyson's music is no finer, and his philosophy is less fine, because less original. The success of this poem—my copy, the ninth impression, was printed less than a year after the first—gave Bridges great pleasure in the last months of his life. It was indeed the crown to a career given wholly to poetry; such a crown as could be attained only by such unaltering singleness of purpose.

Robert Bridges died at Chiswell, where he had lived for the last twenty-three years of his life, on April 21st, 1930. He wished no biography to be written, and he recalled as many of his own letters as he could, and destroyed them. It was his wish that by his work alone he should be remembered; and it is a monument that will not perish.

16

John Masefield

IN 1930 Britain had a Labour Government, and the task of appointing a Laureate fell to Mr. Ramsay MacDonald. It has jokingly been suggested that he appointed a poet likely to be understood by the working man—a poet in whose works are to be found the words the working man uses, 'bloody' and the like. But these days such words have a universal currency! It is true John Masefield uses them, and with good effect; but he uses plenty of others more conventionally 'poetic.' Whatever prompted the Prime Minister, he made a good choice from the very respectable group of poets available; a choice that could not have been easy. *The Times* welcomed the appointment and struck only one false note in mentioning Spenser as one of the previous holders of the office, a remark which can hardly be pardoned for it was made at a time when Professor Broadus's *Poets Laureate* (which has all the answers) was readily available.

John Edward Masefield was born at Ledbury, in Herefordshire, on June 1, 1878. His childhood would seem to have been disturbed and unhappy and at thirteen he joined the *Conway* training ship, proceeding thence to sea. After some years of mixed fortunes he began to write. He made steady progress in journalism and worked for *The Speaker* under J. L. Hammond, and was also for a time with *The Manchester Guardian*.

In 1902 he published *Salt Water Ballads* which contained several of the lyrics that have become so widely known as to be almost a part of that great body of anonymous poetry of which 'everyone' has a stock—such lyrics as 'Sea-Fever,' 'Tewkesbury Road,' and the dedicatory lines, 'A Consecration.' This was the first of a series of collections of shorter poems which is happily not yet completed.[1]

[1] One collection, *Midsummer Night* (1928) calls for separate mention. It is a collection of narrative pieces loosely linked, on King Arthur. Masefield's way is his own, and the reader of these graphic poems will nowhere be closely reminded of Tennyson. In our day three poets have written notably on King Arthur—Laurence Binyon, Charles Williams and

Next he turned to gathering his prose; some of those early essays from the literary weeklies appeared in *A Mainsail Haul* (1905) and *A Tarpaulin Muster* (1907). His first novel—and like almost all his novels, a good one—was *Captain Margaret* (1908). His first play was written, it is said, after someone had asked permission to dramatize one of his stories. His attention thus invited to the theatre, Masefield wrote *The Tragedy of Nan* (1909).

He was now settled as a man of letters; his work was appreciated by fit judges and was also making its way among the uncritical, those highly sensible people who know what they like and make up the bulk of readers, the public whom only writers of small talent and less wit will despise. He was sufficiently established by 1913 to be named as a possible successor to Alfred Austin. But as we know the appointment then went to Bridges.

Robert Bridges lived a life devoted wholly to poetry, like Tennyson and Wordsworth before him, but John Masefield is an all-round man of letters and his affinities are with Southey and Dryden.

It is interesting to pursue the parallel. Dryden was perhaps our first professional man of letters: the first, that is, to whom the completion of one work was the necessary signal for beginning another; a writer of books as another man might be a builder of boats or a mender of shoes. His work was of many kinds—verse, criticism, drama, translation, religious commentary and controversy, political commentary and controversy—anything for which a demand existed or could be created. For Dryden depended mainly on writing for his daily bread: 'It is laudable in a man to wish to live by his labours; but he should write so as he may *live* by them, not so as he may be knocked on the head.' So Johnson defines the matter. The considerable bulk of Dryden's work contains many characteristics, but the final impression is that he was by nature primarily a critic.

Southey was equally a man of letters, and a more voluminous one than Dryden or Masefield; he, too, wrote in several ways—biography,

---

John Masefield. The contrast in their purpose and in their achievement is marked. Binyon's *The Madness of Merlin* (1947) left unfinished at his death, is the beginning of a drama owing little to the conventional conception of its hero; his play, *Arthur* (produced at the Old Vic in 1923) is nearer to the legends as they are popularly understood. The strange and impressive poems of Charles Williams have a mystical content not readily followed, but that they are fragments of a work that would have been among the glories of twentieth century literature I think is undeniable; and as they stand they are head and shoulders above the bulk of the poetry of the past twenty years. Masefield, here as everywhere, is concerned to tell a story; as everywhere, he tells it superbly.

criticism, poetry, history . . but the final verdict pronounces him an historian, for whether in verse or prose it is history that inspires his finest work.

And Masefield, of course, is a teller of tales, though he, too, has done fine work in criticism,[1] and like Dryden and Southey before him, as an editor and commentator. In fifty years—1902 to 1952—Masefield has published nearly a hundred original books, and has edited or written introductions to many others. In mere bulk, he is with Southey the most voluminous of the Laureates; and of this solid body of writing the major part is narrative fiction—a score of plays, a score of novels, a dozen long narrative poems, and many short narrative poems and short stories. To these may be added such works as *Gallipoli* (1916) and *The Nine Days Wonder* (1941) which make history quite as exciting as any novel.

Poetry apart, these three great writers, the critic, the historian, and the story-teller had something in common: they all wrote memorable prose and this link between them they share with none of the rest of the Laureates—for Wordsworth's prose is too slight in bulk, and that of Bridges too specialised in appeal to stand with the great essays of Dryden, the solid achievement of Southey, or the present Laureate's long row of tales and romances.

Certain special interests stand out in the work of John Masefield, whether in prose or verse. First, his interest in the sea, dating from his days in the *Conway* training ship, and thereafter on the oceans of the world. His earliest books reflected this interest—*Salt Water Ballads*, and *Ballads* with their tales (both realistic and romantic) of business in great waters; and the early prose, *A Mainsail Haul*, *A Tarpaulin Muster* and others. Next comes Masefield's love for England, and England's countryside and country ways in particular; he spent his first years on a farm, and the landscape is an integral part of his work. Who could doubt it, reading *The Daffodil Fields* (1913) or *Reynard the Fox* (1919) or *Right Royal* (1920). Then there is Masefield's abounding pity for the under-dog:

> Not the ruler for me, but the ranker, the tramp of the road,
> The slave with the sack on his shoulders pricked on with the goad,
> The man with too weighty a burden, too heavy a load . . .

so he wrote in 'A Consecration' over fifty years ago; and so he

---

[1] Notably in *Shakespeare* (1911) the best short study of Shakespeare, and in his illuminating essay on *Chaucer* (1931).

practiced in his writings. There was *Dauber* (1913) the butt of the crew, who wanted to be an artist:

> *And paint great ships at sea before I'm dead;*
> *Ships under skysails running down the Trade—*
> *Ships and the sea; there's nothing finer made.*

For him the sea held in the end only suffering, persecution and death. There was *The Everlasting Mercy* (1911) with its background of farming and poaching against which is set the drama of a man who finds Christ's 'Everlasting Mercy.' There was *The Widow in the Bye Street* (1912) a sordid tragedy told with a restrained sense of pity even for the meanest of its characters; and *Reynard the Fox* (1919) that magnificent picture of the countryside in which the pity now is transferred to the fox—and by implication to all hunted things—and Masefield joins hands with that other master of pity, Ralph Hodgson:

> *He made his spurt for the Mourne End rocks.*
> *The air blew rank with the taint of fox;*
> *The yews gave way to a greener space*
> *Of great stones strewn in a grassy place.*
> *And there was his earth at the great grey shoulder,*
> *Sunk in the ground, of a granite boulder.*
> *A dry, deep burrow with rocky roof,*
> *Proof against crowbars, terrier proof,*
> *Life to the dying, rest for bones.*
>
> *The earth was stopped; it was filled with stones.*

With these poems Masefield was doing more than he had promised in 'A Consecration'—

> *Of these shall my songs be fashioned, my tales be told,*

though that promise he was splendidly fulfilling. He was also making an important contribution to English poetry in a *genre* at that time almost wholly his own, the long narrative.

Up till the mid-nineteenth century the long story in verse was not common in English poetry, except in the form of epic;[1] and epic is an exalted and heightened form of story, something quite different in scope and intention from such poems as *Right Royal*. Epic deals with Gods and Kings, the fall of angels, the clash of empires, the struggles of mankind against impossible odds. *Right Royal* tells of a horse race.

---

[1] There were, of course, many *short* verse stories, mainly in ballad form.

Epic properly so called has almost disappeared from our poetry.[1] In the nineteenth century R. H. Horne's *Orion* (the 'farthing epic') of 1843, and Lewis Morris's *An Epic of Hades* (1876) are two late examples (there are others) of a tradition which ceased to have any real force after Southey's *Roderick* (1814). Its place was taken by (on the one hand) vast overloaded novels like *The Ring and The Book* (1868) and *Aurora Leigh* (1857) and (on the other hand) by tales like *Enoch Arden* (1864) and the narratives of Arnold, Swinburne, William Morris, and others. These were well enough of their kind, but somewhat remote from the average reader's experience: Morris's burly heroes, Swinburne's robust adventurers, Arnold's sad lovers, all interesting, all clothed in excellent verse. None of them a bit like *Right Royal*.

What Masefield did, about 1910, was to take the old ballad tradition which told a fast-moving, action-filled story in a couple of hundred lines or less, and (using a slower-moving measure to modify the gallop of ballad into something nearer a canter for the longer form) expand those couple of hundred lines into something more like two thousand: the short story of the ballad became the long-short story—the *conte*—of the Masefield narratives. But it lost nothing in dramatic interest; it never dragged; it never digressed into side-plots, extended character studies, or long descriptive passages of the kind common in Scott. It never got lost in examinations of motive, in the way that (say) *The Angel in The House* does, so that the story becomes so thin and uninteresting that one almost forgets who the people are and what they are up to. It has, in fact, the verve of Davidson's *The Runnable Stag* with the length of Browning's *Sordello*.

The long narratives, then, were something more or less new, and the public responded to them as it had responded to no poetry since the later volumes of Tennyson. Masefield was the most talked-of poet of the years 1911–1914: talked of, not by the small circle of critics and writers, but by the general reader. He was known as a poet to people who normally cared nothing for poetry, just as briefly at the end of the century Kipling had been known; but Kipling's was a more diffused fame, springing at least as much from his tales as from his verses. Masefield neither then nor later ever quite attained to popular celebrity as a novelist, although many of his novels had a very respectable circulation. None was a best seller in the sense that *The Widow in the*

[1] Nothing ever wholly disappears, of course; even in the twentieth century epic survives, in the strange, impressive work of Doughty, and the bold rhymed tapestry of Alfred Noyes.

Bye Street and *The Everlasting Mercy* were best sellers—books read, argued over, talked about, known familiarly to a great circle of readers.

During the 1914–18 war Masefield served with the Red Cross and was present during the struggle at Gallipoli, which he described in his first considerable piece of narrative history, *Gallipoli* (1916). This is a book which had a wide circulation and is now (1954) very easily come by in the second-hand book shops; which suggests that a later generation is unaware of its excellence. A very similar military situation twenty-five years later produced Masefield's other major war-book, *The Nine Days Wonder* (1941). The Dunkirk epic makes a terse, unhysterical and restrained essay—it is hardly more—which must always rank high among the writings inspired by the late war. It was true 'Laureate' work, much better worth doing than mechanical birthday tributes and new year odes.

Masefield has broadened the Laureate tradition by such writings as *Gallipoli*, *The Nine Days Wonder*, his poem *Land Workers* (1942) and others arising directly out of the nation's affairs in crisis. In peace time he has similarly broadened the tradition by lending his name and authority to the work of such bodies as The National Book League, and by encouraging verse speaking, the 'uncommercial' production of verse drama—he built his own private theatre at Boars' Hill—and other similar activities calculated to bring literature into good report among the widest possible circle of the public, and so keep alive one of this country's greatest glories.

The Laureate's own contribution to literature was fittingly recognised in 1935 when he received the Order of Merit. It was the year of the Silver Jubilee, the occasion for one of his poems written as Laureate:

A PRAYER FOR THE KING'S MAJESTY

> *O God, whose mercy is our state,*
> *Whose realms are children in Thy hand,*
> *Who willed that, in the years of Fate,*
> *Thy servant George should rule this land*
> *We thank Thee, that the years of strife*
> *Have changed to peace, and for this thing*
> *That Thou hast given him length of life*
> *Under Thy Hand to be our King.*
> *O God vouchsafe him many years*
> *With all the world as England's friend*
> *And England bright among her peers*
> *With wisdom that can never end.*

This prayer the Poet Laureate broadcast on May 6th, 1935. In less than nine months he wrote again, on a sadder occasion, for George V died in January, 1936. His tributes to King George V, and again to King Goerge VI moved many to whom those kings were more than titular sovereigns, the hereditary holders of an outworn place. In the years of Masefield's Laureateship the throne and the monarchy have been closer to the people than ever before, and the uncomplicated expression of sorrow in these verses spoke for millions. On happier occasions—his charming lines at the commencement of the Princess Elizabeth's Commonwealth Tour, in 1952, for example—he has again struck a note in which all can share. His lines on the Coronation in 1953 were a timely reminder of the deeper issues that lie behind the outward pageantry of such ceremonies.

John Masefield's biography will be written, but the time is not yet, and we may hope will not be soon. In this brief appreciation I have not attempted to fill in gaps he has chosen to leave unfilled. He has written two chapters of his own life in *In the Mill* (1941) and *New Chum* (1944) and has told something of his literary development in *So Long to Learn* (1952). In his books, who can doubt that a hundred graphic incidents spring from personal experience? And in his poems, notably in 'Biography,' he gives us further hints. (Southey, incidentally gives us an autobiographical text of a similar sort in 'The Retrospect' an attractive and little-known poem.)

We must look for John Masefield in his writings. They reveal a gentle spirit, often in opposition to evil and terrible things; a spirit full of understanding and pity, aware of the ill chances that trouble men and women everywhere, and have troubled them through all history; but aware, too, of the beauty that underlies all man's days, and filled with a determination to help him find it.

❖

The process of reprinting by photo-litho necessitates leaving the chapter on John Masefield in the present tense, although he has since died. It is hoped that the reader will accept this as a minor blemish, no real hindrance in the reading.

17

C. Day Lewis

THIRTY-SEVEN years is a long time in a rapidly changing world, and the years of John Masefield's laureateship had been riven by a great war and marked by technological advances which almost seemed to make so old-fashioned an art as poetry irrelevant to every-day life—except that human nature is apt to come bobbing up like a cork from the most engulfing of maelstroms. When Masefield died on May 12, 1967, at the age of eighty-eight, many people thought that the office of Poet Laureate might well die with him. Said *The Observer*, 'The cultural consensus has broken down almost completely. For a great writer the Poet Laureateship is an inadequate honour. For a minor versifier it is an excessive one. So why not abolish it?'

Not for the first time, there is a confusion. Neither *The Observer*, nor any other commentator, public or private, is in a position to abolish the Laureateship, nor even to advocate its abolition. The Laureate is a member of the Sovereign's household, and only the Sovereign is to decide how many parlourmaids, and how many gardeners, and how many laureates to employ. So far as the Laureateship goes, it is customary for the Prime Minister of the day to make a recommendation when it is necessary to fill a vacancy, and no doubt before making this he in his turn seeks informed advice—and he is also exposed to a great deal of uninformed advice from other quarters. List of 'candidates' appear in the press and their pretentions are canvassed, and for a few weeks or months poets who chance to meet eye one another warily. Some forestall failure by announcing that they are not interested, others look wistful. To suggest that for a great poet the Laureateship is an inadequate honour is to discount the fact that no poet need feel ashamed to join a company which has included Dryden, Wordsworth, Tennyson and Bridges. There has not been for many years (except in the columns of the *Observer*) any suggestion that the appointment should be bestowed on a minor versifier. At the time when a vacancy occurs, certain poets who might seem suitable for the appointment may in fact privately decide that they would not wish to receive it, perhaps because of ill health, perhaps because of an aversion from public honours, perhaps because of advanced years—which was the reason given by Samuel Rogers when he asked to be excused. Reservations of this kind may appear as the Prime Minister makes his enquiries, but the general public can hardly expect to be taken into the confidence of those responsible for making the choice. However, it may express an opinion on the result.

When a vacancy occurs in the Laureateship it is unusual for any one poet to be the obvious and inevitable choice, for it is unusual for any one poet to be universally acclaimed as head and shoulders above all his fellows. Only two Laureates, Dryden and Wordsworth, were generally acknowledged at the time of their appointments to be the prime living poet. Accordingly, it follows that there will usually be a short list from which the final choice is made. The names which were on the short list in 1967 cannot be known, but it is clear that such poets are Richard Church, Robert Graves, Edmund Blunden and W. H. Auden must have passed in review. But three of these poets were in their seventies, and the fourth had taken American citizenship. These might have been among the reasons for making the selection else-where, but there were also excellent positive reasons why the choice should fall where it did, and when announced the name of C. Day Lewis was generally welcomed. This name was respected in literary circles, and known to the wider public which rarely opens a book of verse.

The new Laureate had been in the forefront of the literary renaissance of the nineteen-thirties, when the young poets brought poetry into affairs and politics, and the publicity of those turbulent times made his name widely known. His later critical work included commentaries and antholo-gies widely used in schools, so that his name was familiar to the young. His voice was well-known to radio listeners, and his face to television viewers, and he was one of the group of poets whose reading of poetry had done much to bring the appreciation of spoken verse into the general con-sciousness—something the previous Laureate, Masefield, had also worked for. And Day Lewis had a large following for his detective stories, written under the nom de plume Nicholas Blake. To have written crime fiction can hardly be a reason for receiving the Laureateship, but it can be a reason why the public at large may give a nod of friendly recognition to the recipient.

Cecil Day Lewis was born April 27, 1904, at Ballintubber, Queen's County, Ireland, where his father, the Rev. F. C. Day-Lewis, was curate. Day Lewis's mother was Kathleen Blake Squires, and through her the poet had Goldsmith blood; he may also through his Butler grandmother have had a kinship with W. B. Yeats, a fact which he reports with some satisfaction. In speaking of his family in his autobiography, *The Buried Day*, Day Lewis also explains why he did not use the hyphen in his name, although it occurs in writing the names of his family. The name was originally Day, the Lewis being 'tacked on' later; but the poet calls his scruples 'inverted snobbery' and remarks that the result is that many people think him Welsh. He was in fact squarely Anglo-Irish on both sides, and both England and Ireland influenced his childhood, for he spent long periods in each. The same influences went to produce that other engaging poet, his friend L. A. G. Strong.

Day Lewis was educated at Sherborne School and at Wadham College, Oxford (where, incidentally, Strong had preceded him), and as a young man he taught at Summer Fields,[1] Cheltenham College, and elsewhere, before taking up authorship full time in the 'thirties.

Those were years in which a new generation of poets was emerging, poets who had been too young to take part in the 1914-18 war and who were reaching manhood now determined to shape the world into something better. Indeed, their quarrel with the elder poets was that many of the more prominent of these did not concern themselves with reforming, but only with recording the world in which they found themselves. Such a poem as 'The Waste Land' seemed to these younger poets wholly negative. To the rhetorical question, *What are you going to do about it?* which Aldous Huxley used as a title for a pamphlet, Day Lewis replied with an answering pamphlet, *We're not going to do Nothing* and indeed the poets of the 'thirties took an active part in political controversy and public events. Many of them went off to fight in the Spanish Civil War—and some were killed. In a symposium on the subject Day Lewis wrote:

> The struggle in Spain is part of a conflict going on now all over the world. I look upon it quite simply as a battle between light and darkness, of which only a blind man could be unaware. Both as a writer and as a member of the Communist Party I am bound to help in the fight against Fascism, which means certain destruction or living death for humanity.

The majority of the younger intellectuals at that time were uncompro-

---

[1] It was L. A. G. Strong who helped Day Lewis to get a job at Summer Fields, and in another place an interesting essay might be written on his influence on Day Lewis during the thirty-odd years of their friendship, although perhaps this was personal rather than literary. How many mourn Leonard Strong, even now many years after his death!

misingly left wing; many of them modified their views later on not because they turned from the principles of communism, but because the Communists did so. 'My communism had a religious quality,' Day Lewis writes, and his adherence to the party did not survive the things afterwards done in communism's name.

These young poets had little in common with their elders, many of whom were working in the early post-war years to restore poetry to what it had been in the halcyon days of Edward the Seventh, 'before the troubles'. Such poets as Frances Cornford, Harold Monro, John Freeman, John Drinkwater, Sylvia Lynd, and W. H. Davies are not to be dismissed, but their viewpoint and their practice in poetry was entirely different from that of their juniors. Stephen Spender, Louis MacNeice, W. H. Auden, C. Day Lewis—and all the writers gathered in the famous anthology, *New Signatures*—these were speaking for the nineteen thirties, *and looking forward*. For them, 'Georgian Poetry' was as much an irrelevance, rooted in the past, as the poetry of the Spasmodics, or the Della Cruscans, or any other forgotten movement. For them, poetry was a living part of day-to-day living, not a diversion to enliven damp weekends.

Day Lewis began with two small books of verse, in 1925 and 1928, which he afterwards desired to forget—or desired to be forgotten. Perhaps the poems were youthful and derivative—mere 'prentice work. This doesn't matter: who would recognise a great poet, turning over the early poems of Shelley? With *Transitional Poem* (1929) the case is quite different. Suddenly the young poet writes with authority and confidence, reviewing the spiritual steps by which he has reached his present philosophical position in the search for 'the single mind', the 'transitions' being the shifts of emphasis by which each step is taken from the last. The poem is also 'transitional' because it concludes at a point from which the writer may be expected to make a new beginning, and advance further. This, and *From Feathers to Iron* (1931) at once established Day Lewis as a significant original poet, a man capable of adding a new dimension to poetry, and this is something few poets have the luck (or the equipment) to achieve. These poems, and two later works, *The Magnetic Mountain* (1933) and *An Italian Visit* (1953) are sustained meditation and commentary presented in a series of related lyrical poems of varying length and measure. The short pieces may be read separately, but each contributes to the development of the continuing argument, taking strength from it and adding strength to it. From most book-length poems it is possible to extract self-contained passages, but yet they must be displayed out of context. The triumph here is in making each poem a part of the larger design, and at once independent of it; so:

> With me, my lover makes
>   The clock assert its chime:
> But when she goes, she takes
>   The mainspring out of time.
>
> Yet this time-wrecking charm
>   Were better than love dead
> And its hollow alarum
>   Hammered out of lead.
>
> Why should I fear that Time
>   Will superannuate
> These workmen of my rhyme—
>   Love, despair and hate?
>
> Fleeing the herd, I came
>   To a graveyard on a hill,
> And felt its mould proclaim
>   The bone gregarious still.
>
> Boredoms and agonies
>   Work out the rhythm of bone:—
> No peace till creature his
>   Creator has outgrown.
>
> Passion dies from the heart
>   But to infect the marrow;
> Holds dream and act apart
>   Till the man discard his narrow
>
> Sapience and folly
>   Here, where the graves slumber
> In a green melancholy
>   Of overblown summer.

(*Transitional Poem*, number 27)

From Feathers to Iron is an extended soliloquy of a father's reflections on the birth of his child, his awareness of the mother's familiarity and strangeness, his consciousness of the coming new consciousness growing within her. Apprehension and anticipation move forward together, so that the poem is part epithalamion, part threnody, which at the happy outcome bubbles with irrepressible delight. It is the greatest celebration of marriage in English verse, an altogether deeper thing than Patmore's *The Angel in the House*, charming though that poem is, and only to be compared with Meredith's *Modern Love*, which shows so tragically the other side of the medal. See how verse such as this extends the convention of love poetry without any perverse effort at originality for its own sake—which was one of the characteristics of poetry written in the 'thirties, and is one of its characteristics still, forty years after:

> Beauty breaks ground, oh, in strange places.
> Seen after cloudburst down the bone-dry watercourses,
> In Texas a great gusher, a grain-
> Elevator in the Ukraine plain;
> To a new generation turns new faces.
>
> Here too fountains will soon be flowing.
> Empty the hills where love was lying late, was playing,
> Shall spring to life: we shall find there
> Milk and honey for love's heir,
> Shadow from sun also, deep ground for growing.
>
> My love is a good land. The stranger
> Entering here was sure he need prospect no further.
> Acres that were the eyes' delight
> Now feed another appetite.
> What formed her first for seed, for crop must change her.
>
> This is my land. I've overheard it
> Making a promise out of clay. All is recorded—
> Early green, drought, ripeness, rainfall,
> Our village fears and festivals,
> When the first tractor came and how we cheered it.
>
> And as the wind whose note will deepen
> In the upgrowing tree, who runs for miles to open
> His throat above the wood, my song
> With that increasing life grew strong,
> And will have there a finished form to sleep in.

Perhaps there are 'imprints' here, echoes and similarities reminding the reader of Hopkins and Blunden, but they are such echoes as all good poetry affords as demonstrating in the poet an awareness of and a respect for his forerunners; the originality in this poetry far outweighs its echoes, and at the same time the echoes enhance its music.

The next poem, *The Magnetic Mountain* (1933) continues Day Lewis's extension of the limits of verse autobiography: the autobiography, not of recorded events, but of 'the growth of a poet's mind'. These long early poems express the poet's beliefs, and suggest tentative answers to problems of his own and of the world around him. He is not a parson's son for nothing, he is prepared to preach. It is not necessary to be a Christian to respond to a sermon by Donne, and in the same way a reader standing far outside the preoccupations of the nineteen thirties may find in Day Lewis's work of that time an excitement and a satisfaction having nothing to do with the stresses from which the verses spring. These poems do not date, except superficially, for their content of poetry gives them the same timeless quality that carries over the centuries the poems of Skelton and Cowper and Clare. What they had to say was important to these poets, the manner in which they said it affords them readers long after the contemporary urgency is over. It is this quality that keeps a poet in memory; its lack that leads to oblivion. Who now reads Lewis Morris?

The two first small books apart—and he felt no regard for these in later years—Day Lewis was slow to issue collections of shorter poems and in the immediate pre-war years he turned to prose with the purpose, perhaps, of extending the range of his writing. He published the verse play, *Noah and The Waters* (1935), at a time when his immediate contemporaries were also experimenting with the drama—Auden and Isherwood's *The Ascent of F6* came a year later, in 1936, Spender's *The Trial of a Judge* in 1938 and, of course, there were others, encouraged it may be by the authority, and the success, of T. S. Eliot with *Murder in the Cathedral*; but Day Lewis did not follow this line further. In the same period he published several novels and his first volumes of criticism. From *Overtures to Death* (1938) the bulk of his poetry was in short pieces, mainly lyrical, and over the next thirty years he published an impressive body of varied work, very personal and expressed in an accent unmistakably his own. He also began a series of translations from Virgil which mirrored his own spirit without obscuring their original.

Day Lewis, then, was a working man of letters of many parts, like his predecessors Masefield, Southey and Dryden. A complete survey, even in little, of all his work would no more be appropriate here than a reference to every book of theirs, but something may be said of his writings in prose even though the consideration of a Laureate must of necessity be interested mainly in his verse.

The two major critical essays are *The Poetic Image* (1947) which consists of the Clark Lectures delivered at Cambridge in 1946, and *The Lyric Impulse* (1965) which contains the Charles Eliot Norton Lectures delivered at Harvard in 1965. The titles sufficiently indicate the contents, but they do not indicate the special grace of Day Lewis's criticism, which like all his work is personal and individual. Day Lewis was a master, and he speaks with a master's authority. The range of his reading is wide and his citations and quotations have that inevitability which is the mark of authority—they seem to have been originally written in order to support this text. Nor is this criticism academic, divorced from the common reader; consider the excellent sense of this, and its unexpressed implications:

> If some lyrical writing has aspired to the condition of music, some literary criticism of recent years has aspired to the condition of science. This aspiration tempts certain critics into the supercilious or brash bumptious-ness of tone, the complacence, the lack of humility, which can be heard in the utterances of the more mediocre nineteenth-century scientists. But what is to the point in the present context is the effect of our critical climate upon the lyric impulse. Irony, toughness, ambiguity—these are qualities the modern critic can get his teeth into; poems which contain them exercise his full resources. Upon the lyric, smoother, purer, simpler, he finds it difficult to get a purchase. Faced with 'O wert thou in the cauld blast' or
>
> > *He came all so still*
> > *Where his mother was,*
> > *As dew in April*
> > *That falleth on the grass*
>
> what on earth can the critic say that will not diminish the poem's effect by officiously enlarging upon it. He would do best to give it a silent nod and step out of the light: but critics are a voluble tribe, to whom silence does not come easily. One can well understand why they direct our attention to the less pure, more complex kinds of poetry where their guidance can be of great value. One may also suspect that the emphasis their criticism throws upon such poetry has contributed to the present decline of interest in the lyric.
>
> (*The Lyric Impulse*, pages 19-20)

There is much in the other critical essays, including a useful series addressed
to children; Day Lewis's full powers are well shown in 'The Lyrical Poetry
of Thomas Hardy' (1951) which was a Warton Lecture delivered at the
British Academy.

I shall not speak of Day Lewis's novels—beyond reminding the reader
that his series of crime stories under the non-de-plume Nicholas Blake are
among the most literate of their time, without sacrificing the special
excellence called for in fiction of this kind. But I do wish to invite attention
to his autobiography, *The Buried Day* (1960), which is the only work of
autobiography by any Laureate fit to stand with Masefield's *So Long to
Learn*. Many of the Laureates never ventured into this field, and the rise
of autobiography is a mainly nineteenth-century phenomenon in English.
Colley Cibber's *Apology* is a work of great historical interest, and it has
many passages of personal idiosyncrasy and charm; but it is chiefly of value
for reasons having nothing to do with the likeness Cibber draws of himself. Readers of *The Buried Day* may perhaps turn to it for information
about the poets of the thirties, but he will not find that it is a history in the
way that Cibber's narrative very nearly is. It is a conscious self-portrait,
where perhaps the truth of Cibber's portrait occurs where he is least conscious of the picture he is making. Masefield's *In the Mill*, and *New Chum*
are chapters of autobiography based on events; *So Long to Learn* (again to
use Wordsworth's phrase) is more nearly the record of the growth of a
poet's mind; and Day Lewis successfully combines both areas of study
into a single 'personal memoir'. He tells us where he was born, where he
went to school, and in general, 'what happened to him'; well, we can get
most of that out of the reference books. The reader's delight and refresh-
ment come as he sees the young Day Lewis growing not in years only, but
in stature as a person under now this stimulus, now that influence, now
these anxieties, challenges and dilemmas. Alas, the book is too short,
and it ends at a moment when the author had another thirty years to live:
there is so much more he might have told us, and we shall never hear
it now.

In his conception of the obligations of his office Day Lewis was the most
conscientious laureate since Tennyson. This is not to imply a criticism
of Masefield and Bridges, both of whom showed a wide awareness of their
position, not only by writing poems of an official nature from time to time,
but by public work in literature and the arts (and it is as a leader and
exemplar in this field that a modern laureate can perhaps best use the
authority of his office). But Bridges over seventeen years, and Masefield

over thirty-seven, gave poetry to the laureateship comparatively rarely; in his too-brief-term—less than six years—and over a period when he was often desperately ill, Day Lewis composed an impressive series of 'official' poems, some of them lengthy, taking as his terms of reference the practice of Tennyson and Bridges in using 'national' themes rather than themes personal to the sovereign. Among the poems which he felt lay within the scope of his official position was one on the amalgamation of six towns in Tees-side—'If I can make a verse out of that, it's a real challenge' was his comment, and an entirely adequate poem was the result. Some of this work was done with great courage when he was almost too ill to hold the pen.

C. Day Lewis was the most important English poet to be born in the years 1900-1914, which produced the generation of writers who composed the characteristic poetry of the mid-century. There may be readers who will question this, in particular with reference to W. H. Auden, whose influence was probably wider. I believe Auden's overall achievement as a poet—impressive as it is—is too much of its time to be wholly accepted as time passes. There is an essence of poetry in the work of Day Lewis which is as timeless as 'He came all so still' and the rest of that marvellous lyric heritage which the centuries have left us. He accepted the tradition, and enlarged it.

Pass, friend, and fare you well, and may all such travellers be speeded
Who bring us news we had almost forgot we needed.

18

Sir John Betjeman

SIR John Betjeman's appointment to the Laureateship was announced on October 10, 1972, rather more than four months after the death of C. Day Lewis. Betjeman, like Day Lewis, was a nationally known literary figure, seen frequently on television, so that his voice, appearance, personality, mannerisms even, were already familiar to a large public. After his appointment, Tennyson became a national figure; Betjeman was already a national figure when appointed. Accordingly, the appointment gave general satisfaction; people had no occasion to say to one another, 'Never heard of him', or 'Who's he?'. People had not only heard of Betjeman, many of them had read him. Most poets of his time counted themselves fortunate if their books sold five hundred copies, but Betjeman's sales reached not hundreds, but thousands; not thousands merely, but tens of thousands. It may be interesting in a moment to consider why.

John Betjeman was born in London in 1906, the son of a manufacturer of luxury personal goods—dressing cases, and the like—which were sold to Maharajahs (we are told in the autobiographical poem, *Summoned by Bells*) by the jewellers of Bond Street. The name Betjeman is of Dutch origin, but the poet's family had been established in London for a hundred years and more, and no-one (as his writings show) could be more English than he. Like Day Lewis, Betjeman was educated in the west country, but some miles east of Sherborne, at Marlborough; and he went on to Magdalen College, Oxford. Like Day Lewis also, Betjeman worked for a time as a schoolmaster (though not for so long as Day Lewis) and again like Day Lewis, in Government offices during the 1939-45 war. The two were roughly of the same age, and there are various other parallels in their careers as writers. They both began somewhat tentatively as poets, although Day Lewis published his first book at a younger age, his *Beechen Vigil* appearing when he was twenty-one; Betjeman was twenty-five when he published *Mount Zion*. but neither book made a large immediate impact. Indeed, Betjeman's astonishing success in terms of circulation was a late phenomenon, long after he had made a solid reputation in literary and cultured circles; and that reputation was first established by his prose essays.

From an early age, Betjeman's chief love was architecture, especially the architecture of churches, and more especially the church (and chapel) architecture of the nineteenth century, then largely despised or disregarded. As a young man he worked in journalism on the *Architectural Review*, and this gave him opportunities to meet leading members of the profession and to learn something of professional practice and politics from the inside. The first fruit in book form of these studies was *Ghastly Good Taste* (1933) an essay on the rise and fall (as he then saw it) of English architecture. The author was twenty-six, and in reissuing the book many years later he had the honesty and unusual humility to admit some of his errors of judgement—but these were slight enough in comparison with the trenchant freshness of the essay as a whole, and its engaging prose. Sir John writes an unpretentious, readable prose in the tradition of his Laureate predecessors Dryden and Southey, designed like theirs to convey precisely what he wishes it to convey, without the extraneous ornament which defaces so much bad prose—and bad architecture. He is a master of apposite quotation, and he draws extensively, but never obtrusively, on his wide reading among the lesser English poets, mentioning names probably unknown, and certainly unread by most of his readers; among contemporary writers, perhaps only Edmund Blunden might be found remembering two lines here, and half a dozen there, from such unlikely worthies as Sir Henry Taylor, N. T. Carrington, and James Hurdis. It would be amusing to discuss where else in the twentieth century one may find a passage quoted from Thomas Cooper's *The Purgatory of Suicides*, and to say this is not to make a mere passing comment on a minor aspect of Betjeman's work, because only by the vigilance of such writers as he do interesting and some-times important works remain in memory. What he says of Hurdis, for example, may send a handful of fit readers to a poet else entirely neglected, and they will not be unrewarded. When he adds to his own considerable authority the authority of the office of Poet Laureate, Sir John by citations such as these is doing English poetry a considerable service. There is, alas, far more of our poetry than any of us can ever read, and not everything that is forgotten deserves to be—it is well to remember the case of Robert Herrick, who fell out of sight for a hundred and fifty years and did not find general recognition until he had been in his grave for considerably longer than that.

Betjeman is not a copious writer—his admirers might echo Patmore and say, 'He has written little, but it is all of his best'. There is no long row of substantial volumes on the shelf to testify to Betjeman's forty and more years as an author. He brings to the Laureateship the slightest literary baggage of any holder of the office since Pye, and there are other areas in which he differs widely from most of his predecessors, especially in the specialised and relatively narrow range of his work in prose. With trivial exceptions, his prose essays are concerned with architecture or related matters, or are frankly topographical guides which do not pretend to be contributions to literature. Of course, the influence of these essays has been quite out of proportion to their length, and they have always been written in support of preservation and conservation in the environment. Sir John has no lengthy string of novels, as had Day Lewis and Masefield; no shelf of discursive causerie like Alfred Austin's *The Garden that I love* and its fellows; no literary criticism to match with Bridges and Warton; no drama to set beside Tennyson and the eighteenth-century laureates. At one point he touches Wordsworth, for that worthy also ventured on a Guide Book—not to mention an autobiography in blank verse. But *The Prelude* is an altogether different affair from *Summoned by Bells*. There is not the smallest parallel between the enormous professional output of such laureates as Dryden and Southey and the writings of John Betjeman. His *Collected Poems*, in the latest edition, offers under two hundred pieces, most of them relatively short; and to these may be added *Summoned by Bells*, which has about twenty-five hundred lines. To find out the best and worst about this poet a reader will need to examine perhaps a total of five thousand lines—not so much of a task as reading *The Purgatory of Suicides*, which contains around eight and a half thousand, or, for that matter, *The Prelude*, which contains about eight. But no-one ever said of Wordsworth's work, 'It is all of his best'. Undoubtedly a large part of Sir John's work has been for radio and television, and in day-to-day journalism, and perhaps we are already in an era when the printed books on a shelf do not necessarily sum up a writer's contribution to his time. Like Day Lewis, Betjeman, in his different way has been concerned with immediate issues where an influence can be exerted more effectively in the spoken word, or in the word written for some less apparently permanent piece of printing than a book. It would be interesting to know how much influence he has exerted by timely letters to newspapers drawing attention to neglect, abuse or mismanagement of our natural and architectural treasures. It may be proper also to record his generosity in introducing the works of others.

It is often hard to say just when a poet who has been publishing for many years first began to reach a wide public. In Betjeman's case, it would seem to be the first appearance of a collected edition of his poems in 1958 (for which John Sparrow's *Selected Poems of John Betjeman*, in 1952, paved the way). Lord Birkenhead's judicious and enthusiastic Introduction to the *Collected Poems*, and John Sparrow's earlier Introduction, invited the attention of readers who were inclined to look upon Betjeman as a humorous poet to other aspects of his work. In 1960 *Summoned by Bells* reinforced the impact of *Collected Poems* and established Betjeman as that phenomenon among poets, a best-seller.

The blank verse employed in *Summoned by Bells* may be characterised as 'conversational'. 'The author has gone as near prose as he dare', a prefatory note tells us, and the poem is often as pedestrian as a page from *The Course of Time*:

> That was the summer Audrey, Joc and I
> And all the rest of us were full of hope:
> 'Miss Usher's coming.' Who Miss Usher was
> And why she should be coming, no one asked.
> She came, a woman of the open air,
> Swarthy and in Girl Guide-y sort of clothes:
> How nice she was to Audrey and to Joc,
> How very nice to Biddy and to Joan . . .
> But somehow, somehow, not so nice to me.

But this deliberate flatness has a curious charm (so has *The Course of Time* although there the flatness is not deliberate) and the narrative catches unerringly the frustrations, apprehensions and uncertainties of youth; catches, too, youth's delight in sunshine, friendship, enthusiasms, excursions. 'We overtook a six-ton Sentinel, Our bike chains creaking with the strain . . .' The observation is the exact observation of a boy: even the business of labouring to overtake a lorry did not blind him to the kind of lorry it was. The poem tells us a great deal about boyhood and adolescence in general, and about one boy and adolescent in particular, and we may find here the first loves which a lifetime later were still the last loves—English lanes, village churches, sounding bells, clanking locomotives, a stormy sunset momentarily re-gilding weather vanes blackened by urban smoke. The poem traces Betjeman's life from early childhood to early manhood, when— like so many young hopefuls before him—he stood irresolute in the office of the scholastic agency of Gabbitas and Thring, applying—with the most rudimentary understanding of cricket—for a cricket-master's job.

The success of *Summoned by Bells*—the twentieth century has not produced many autobiographies in verse,[1] and the novelty secured appreciative attention—together with the success of the *Collected Poems*, served to establish Betjeman as the best-known living English poet, a position left untenanted by the death of Walter de la Mare.

The reason for this—the excellence of Betjeman's shorter poems apart —lies in the nature of his work. These poems appeal to the non-specialist reader, they are about aspects of life which he understands and shares, they are unpretentious, undemanding, without wilful obscurity or conscious superiority; and the general reader has been alieniated over the past fifty years by poetry too often written, as it seems to him, by clever people addressing others of comparable cleverness in accents which say little to the rest of us. The general reader, interested in poetry, might open the pages of the fashionable academic critics of the 'thirties and 'fifties and conclude that there was nothing memorable now to be had—perhaps that there never was much. In recent years, the contraction in popular literary journalism and the disappearance of popular literary weeklies like *John o' London's* and *Everybodys* deprived the enquiring reader of much helpful guidance. The highbrow critics who dismiss as trivial the criticism of writers like J. C. Squire and Arnold Bennett ignore the useful function they performed, in making widely known the names and writings of authors whose appeal embraced audiences who knew nothing of Oxford and even less of Cambridge.

A large part of Betjeman's work may be defined as 'light verse', and it is a mistake to suppose that this means 'funny verse', although there is certainly plenty of amusing stuff among the rest. Rather, in this context, light verse may be characterised as 'every-day verse'—verse about homely, human pleasures and common human predicaments and the every-day scene around us—a child to whom the competition means everything thrown from her pony to break her collar-bone right in front of the judges; or a young officer falling in love at a game of tennis; or a journalist sitting over a coffee cup in Fleet Street to be told he's redundant; or a housewife, taken ill at a bus stop: experiences we have all heard about, or shared in, in our trim suburban villas. But how far Betjeman is from a merely 'funny' poet may be judged by reference to such poems as 'Five o'Clock Shadow', 'On the Portrait of a Deaf Man', and the memorial lines to the Marquess of Dufferin; and there are many more, as any reader may see.

[1]   That delightful poem, *The Horoscope*, by Horace Horsnell (1934) remains almost wholly unknown.

Betjeman's interest in landscape and architecture is naturally a large element in his verse. His range across the countryside is wide—Cornwall, Ireland, East Anglia, the Home Counties, all come in for celebration, and he has an eye for beauty in unexpected places, in an ordinary colourless suburban street he can see colour, and also in a colourless suburban life. He records in terms everyone can follow the common delight we all feel in an afternoon in Epping Forest or a trip to the seaside:

> *O! thymy time of evening: clover scent*
> *And feathery tamarisk round the churchyard wall*
> *And shrivelled sea-pinks and this foreshore pale*
> *With silver sand and sharpened quartz and slate*
> *And brittle twigs, bleached, salted and prepared*
> *For kindling blue-flamed fires on winter nights.*

It is a poetry of suburbia, and the people of suburbia (who had not often been noticed by the poets before) took it to their hearts.

Perhaps the most familiar element in Betjeman's work is his love for London, and the many poems in which it figures. There is naturally already a large body of poetry about London, including some notable character sketches of London's inhabitants, and quite a few graphic scences in verse depicting the busy life of the streets—the *Trivia* of Gay, the 'City Shower' of Swift, and so on—but when Dunbar (if it was Dunbar) wrote of 'the flower of cities all' he was not thinking of Camden Town or Clapham. Sir John Betjeman is one of a group of later poets who have very much extended London's poetic boundaries: such poets as F. O. Mann, Douglas Goldring, James Elroy Flecker, John Davidson, and a whole series of nineteenth-century poets extending back from Egan Mew to James Smith. These are poets in whom there is an interest in Greater London as it spreads seemingly interminably outwards from the City; and a consciousness of the inexhaustible variety of human life drawn to London and spawned by London.

Thus, F. O. Mann in *London and Suburban* (1925) has poems on a city typist, a cockney funeral, a disastrous love affair and marriage between a clerk and a prostitute, and a whole gallery of other metropolitan characters against the familiar backdrop:

> *Flats, warehouses, stores and banks*
> *In brutal blocks and fuddled ranks,*
> *With here and there a lonely spire,*

> *Pathetic in the evening fire,*
> *And gaudy dome or gilded ball*
> *Of picture-house or music-hall;*
> *A million houses brick on brick,*
> *With fronts and backs to make you sick;*
> *Ten thousand streets in rows and rows,*
> *Where to or from or why, God knows.*

In *St. James's Park* (1930) Mann gathers another group of Londoners, the gas-man, the charwoman, the barmaid, and a chattering group of hop-pickers. In *Streets* (1920), Douglas Goldring ranged from Rotherhithe to Muswell Hill observing Londoners at work and at home. Such poems of Goldring's as 'In a Taxi' remind us of the tentative approaches Betjeman's lovers make in the Camberley dusk—

> *No one can hear! So now, good-bye!*
> *Darling, to crush you in the gloom,*
> *With kisses, would be ecstasy . . .*
> *'Shh, mother's moving in her room!'*

In his satire Goldring is generally closer to his contemporary Osbert Sitwell than to Betjeman, for these poets traffic more in contempt, and Betjeman in scorn. Sitwell's 'Mrs. Kinfoot' appeared in *Wheels* in the same year as Goldring's *Streets*, with 'Mrs. Skeffyngton Calhus', but Goldring again approaches Betjeman with 'Marveilleuses des nos Jours' which suggests Betjeman's 'Reproof Deserved', and with 'The Young Married Couple' he gives us something to set beside the domestic interior of Betjeman's 'How to Get on in Society' for contrast and emphasis.

The London poems of Flecker are less topographically exact than Betjeman's (or Mann's and Goldring's) but they add their mite to the tradition we are examining:

> *The great and solemn-gliding tram,*
> *Love's still mysterious car,*
> *Has many a light of gold and white,*
> *And a single dark red star.*

In John Davidson we find poems on London Bridge and Liverpool Street which complement Betjeman's prose essays on the London railway stations, and he also has verse vignettes complementing Betjeman:

> *Athwart the sky a lowly sigh*
> > *From west to east the sweet wind carried;*
> *The sun stood still on Primrose Hill;*
> > *His light in all the city tarried;*
> *The clouds on viewless columns bloomed*
> *Like smouldering lilies unconsumed.*

The famous *Fleet Street Eclogues*, of course, are conversation pieces having little to do directly with London, but other poems including 'The Thames Embankment', 'Fleet Street' and 'The Crystal Palace', are steeped in the atmosphere of their period, which is the period of Betjeman's infancy—

> *The daylight wears; twilight ends; the night comes down.*
> *A ruddy targetlike moon in a purple sky*
> *And the crowd waiting on the fireworks. Come:*
> *Enough of Mob for one while. This way out—*
> *Past Linacre and Chatham—the second Charles,*
> *Venus and Victory—and Sir William Jones*
> *In placid contemplation of a State!—*
> *Down the long corridor to the district train.*

So we may trace Betjeman's predecessors back: Egan Mew, *A London Comedy and other Vanities* (1897) among others offers a group of 'London Maids', one of whom lives in Camden Town somewhere near Betjeman's 'Business Girls' while another is a waitress in the very cafe, perhaps, of Betjeman's 'Caprice'—

> *She's pale and neat; she's dressed in black:*
> > *She comes to your table wearily,*
> *With pensive air, but a modern knack*
> > *Of hinting at life's vacuity.*

> *She carries no old-world courtesy,*
> *But the air is freighted odorously,*
> *For they give one excellent tea*
> *In the sober salons of 'A B C'.*

From this, with glances at J. L. Owen, Frederick Locker, James Thomson (I am not thinking of 'The City of Dreadful Night' so much as of lighter poems like 'Sunday at Hampstead'), we may trace the tradition back to James Smith, whose 'London Lyrics' include the well-known 'Poet of Fashion' and one of the earliest forerunners of Betjeman in architectural mood, 'The Church in Langham Place'. This is a critical examination of Nash's All Soul's (1822-24), a church which met with a good deal of ridicule at the time, though accepted now by familiarity:

> *This plan was Doric, ergo bad,*
> *   And that Ionic, ergo base;*
> *No proper model could be had*
> *   To shape this church in Langham-place.*

There is indeed a wealth of London poetry, and it is a measure of Sir John's success that he has added so much original matter in an area so extensively worked before him. Poems like 'The Sandemanian Meeting House', 'Parliament Hill Fields', 'Middlesex' and 'Business Girls' are a permanent addition to the literature of the metropolis, sometimes satirical, sometimes tender, sometimes graphic, sometimes impressionistic, sometimes factual, but evocative always.

> *Rumbling under blackened girders, Midland, bound for Cricklewood,*
> *Puffed its sulphur to the sunset where that Land of Laundries stood,*
> *Rumble under, thunder over, train and tram alternate go,*
> *Shake the floor and smudge the ledger, Charrington, Sells, Dale and Co.,*
> *Nuts and nuggets in the window, trucks along the tine below.*

Betjeman's highest achievement, surely (and it is no small achievement) is to make the commonplace 'not common' and to demonstrate that there is poetry in the bricks and mortar of endless streets, and in the everyday concerns of living and working and dying among them.

19

Epilogue

IN more than three hundred years the Laureateship has naturally seen many changes, in the nature of the office and in the personalities of its holders. When Dryden became the first 'official' Laureate there were no set duties, but as the appointment was in a measure political it followed that the Laureate was expected to write in support of the King and his Ministry—so that to this appointment we owe the greatest political satires in English poetry, satires which are perennially fresh long after the dust of their occasion has settled. Dryden's immediate successors began the custom of providing New Year and Birthday Odes which during the whole of the eighteenth century were recognised as an obligation on the Laureate, and led to the composition of a huge body of the worst poetry in the world, which must have been even more execrable when set to music and declaimed (one hardly cares to say, sung). It was the accident of George III becoming insane which interrupted this practice, and the public performances were never resumed, although, as we have seen, Robert Southey was still required to provide for them.

It was with the appointment of William Wordsworth in 1843 that the office took its modern form, in which there is no specific obligation laid upon the holder. This appointment, and Tennyson's which followed, might have established a tradition whereby the Laureateship would be reserved for the greatest poet of the day, as a mark of public recognition of his pre-eminence; but such a tradition would perhaps have been unworkable in practice, for it seldom happens that any one poet is universally acknowledged to be the greatest of his time; and in any event, the choice of Alfred Austin to succeed Tennyson effectively destroyed the tradition almost before it was born. Austin was nothing like so bad a poet as his present reputation suggests, but he was completely inadequate as a successor to Tennyson, and indeed the only poet of comparable stature with Tennyson then available was Swinburne. Perhaps Swinburne was then 'the greatest living poet' so far as Great Britain was concerned; perhaps also he was the least likely to commend himself to Queen Victoria.

When Wordsworth took office he acquiesced in the notion that nothing would be required of him, and for this we may be thankful. He was already an old man and he had long since ceased to produce the magnificent verse which had set him alongside Shakespeare and Milton among the English poets. It was right that the office should honour him, rather than he the office. But Tennyson—a much younger man, at the height of his powers— was a conscientious Laureate who added many noble verses to the body of Laureate poetry, and succeeding Laureates have taken the same view of their obligations, that although not required specifically to write on public occasions it was desirable that they should sometimes do so. As we have seen, this might in the event be an embarrassment, as Alfred Austin learned. But the practice itself is to be commended. When the nation rejoices or mourns with the Sovereign it is right that the Laureate should not always keep silent, even if he does not make verses for every occasion.

With the appointment of Robert Bridges the conception of the office again alters and is brought into line with twentieth-century thinking. Bridges wrote few 'royal' poems but (like Tennyson) he wrote what may be called 'public poems', for example the 'Ode on the Tercentenary Commemoration of Shakespeare, 1916' and a group of shorter pieces during the war. So far as the war was concerned Bridges made his principal contribution by compiling a notable anthology, *The Spirit of Man*, and like Dryden and Southey before him he had a natural talent for making an anthology which was more than merely a collection of short pieces. This small gathering is also a work of art, as the anthologies of Walter de la Mare were works of art. But the most important aspect of the Laureateship of Robert Bridges lay in his conception of the duty imposed upon the Laureate to take a lead in maintaining the standards of authorship. He would tolerate nothing shoddy or second-rate, and in particular he deplored the facile and the pretentious in poetry—Edward Thompson records some astringent remarks about Robert Browning's reference to the thrush's 'careless rapture' in singing, which Bridges said had nothing to do with the truth of the matter. The Society for Pure English, which Bridges was the prime mover in establishing, had an importance quite disproportionate to its comparatively brief history. By these and similar activities Bridges and the Laureates who have succeeded him have given the prestige of their office to literary causes and movements calculated to enlarge, enhance and preserve our literature. After Bridges, Masefield was active in the promotion of verse-speaking, and he did much for the re-establishment of verse drama in the theatre after a long period in which it was in decline as a respected art form in England. C. Day Lewis was active for many years—long before he became Laureate—in the same cause of verse-speaking which had engaged Masefield's interest, and the prestige of these poets helped to promote popular movements like the reading of poetry in pubs.

Robert Bridges took seriously the implied obligations of the Laureateship, and discharged them with dignity, but he was an aloof man and he never became a public figure. When Masefield took office he was much better known to the general reading public than ever Bridges had been, and it is possible that the public expected more from him as Laureate; but Masefield like Bridges was too dedicated a poet to put out 'verses to order', and his body of Laureate verse is comparatively slight. He wrote a significant footnote to his war-books of 1914-18 with *The Nine Days' Wonder* (1941), an account of the Dunkirk withdrawal, and—again, in the new conception of a Laureate lending the name of his office to literary causes—he was an active and influential supporter of the National Book League. Like Bridges, Masefield was a shy man, and although more in the public eye than Bridges he remained personally little-known beyond the circle of his family and friends; 'he was Chaucer's man' and a rare spirit whom we may approach more nearly when a full biographical assessment comes to be written.

The too-brief Laureateship of C. Day Lewis promised to bring the general public into an appreciative awareness of the office, for Day Lewis was familiarly known to thousands beyond the restricted confines of the lecture hall or even the printed book; he was the first Laureate to be at home with the vast audiences of radio and television. The cause of poetry was immeasurably advanced by the appointment of such a man, rather than of a retiring, academic figure such as Robert Bridges had been. Bridges was right for the Laureateship in 1913, when the prestige of the office needed restoring after the undistinguished tenure of Alfred Austin. In 1967, C. Day Lewis was an ideal choice, for he brought different qualities, suitable for a different time. The tragedy of his death within so few years, and after a long and distressing illness, robbed the literary scene in England of one of its most distinguished figures, and it robbed the history of the Laureateship of a significant chapter: for I believe that if Day Lewis had lived a further ten or fifteen years (as he might reasonably have done) he would have raised the Laureateship to a position in the public consciousness which it had not held since Tennyson, and such as before Tennyson it had hardly held at all. Moreover, Day Lewis brought poetry to the young, and there could hardly be a more valuable service in a Laureate. His widely known and helpful book, *Poetry for You* (published many years before he became Laureate) was supported by his anthologies, and by his personal appearances in schools. Only weeks before his death, towards the end of an illness of increasing severity which had lasted eight years, he was speaking at a big east-London school, and it would be difficult to over-value services such as this in bringing an awareness of what poetry is to impressionable minds. It is not true to suppose that every man of letters lives a sheltered, comfortable life, compared with the man of action; we may think of C. Day Lewis as we think of Captain Oates: he was a very gallant gentleman.

So, over the years, the Laureateship has changed, as the world has changed. It will continue to change so long as Laureate succeeds Laureate. We cannot yet see how the pattern will alter under the hand of Sir John Betjeman, for these words are written only short months since he was appointed. We know that Sir John, like Day Lewis, has been active in public affairs for many years, supporting causes, resisting abuses. Day Lewis's work with the Arts Council, the British Council, the Royal Society of Literature, the Royal Literary Fund—and all sorts of other committees and authorities—would make a chapter in itself. So, too, would a catalogue of Sir John Betjeman's public activities. But neither of these poets ever forgot that the prime business of a poet is poetry.

More than once in this book I have reminded the reader that the Poet Laureate is an official of the Sovereign's household. It is for the Sovereign alone to decide if the office is to continue in being, and under what conditions. But we may hope that the Laureateship will long continue, nor have we reason to suppose it will be otherwise. I said right at the beginning that the greatest poetry of the world has been written in English—although I hope this is not to ignore or undervalue the magnificent poetry of Greece, Rome, Italy, Germany, Russia, and of scores of splendid poets writing in languages other than English. It seems to me proper that our heritage should be supported and underlined by an office in which one eminent living poet may stand to represent all, whether living or dead, so that the recognition of the one is a recognition of the many: and at the same time a recognition by the Crown that among the qualities which have set this nation high in the muster-roll of mankind, poetry is not the least.

II

*Selections from the Works
of the Poets Laureate*

NOTE

IN these brief selections I have followed two main purposes: first, to represent each poet by the work he wrote officially as Laureate—which is to say, in most cases, by his least attractive work. Next, therefore, I have tried to let him redeem himself by specimens of his best work. In the case of such writers as Wordsworth and Tennyson, whose best work is already familiar to most readers, I have chosen lesser known poems. Few poets can be adequately represented by selections as brief as these that follow, but there is not space in the present book for more. I hope that the small taste here given of poets now seldom read will send at least a few readers to Warton, Southey, Austin . . . if not to Pye. For the pleasures of poetry include the pleasures of exploration along the by-ways.

In almost every case the source given for the poems quoted is the edition from which I have taken my text. It is not necessarily the source of the first publication of the poem.

Ben Jonson

TO KING JAMES

How, best of Kings, do'st thou a scepter beare!
  How, best of *Poets*, do'st thou laurell weare!
But two things, rare, the FATES had in their store,
  And gave thee both, to shew they could no more.
For such a *Poet*, while thy dayes were greene,
  Thou wert, as chief of them are said t'have beene.
And such a Prince thou art, wee daily see,
  As chiefe of those still promise they will bee.
Whom should my Muse then flie to, but the best
  Of Kings for grace; of *Poets* for my test?

from *Epigrammes* (1616)

Jonson first collected his shorter poems in the 1616 folio of his *Works*, but many of them had been written years earlier. This one no doubt was written about the time of James's accession (1603). It would be a poor outlook for the poetry lover if James were indeed the 'best of poets,' and a poor outlook for tobacco manufacturers if the rest of us shared his views on smoking.

AN EPIGRAM. TO K. CHARLES

FOR A 100. POUNDS HE SENT ME IN MY SICKNESSE 1629

Great Charles, among the holy gifts of grace
　　Annexed to thy Person, and thy place,
'Tis not enough (thy pietie is such)
　　To cure the call'd *Kings Evill* with thy touch;
But thou wilt yet a Kinglier masterie trie,
　　To cure the *Poets Evill*, Povertie:
And, in these Cures, do'st so thy selfe enlarge,
　　As thou dost cure our *Evill*, at thy charge.
Nay, and in this, thou show'st to value more
　　One Poet, then of other folke ten score.
O pietie! so to weigh the poores estates!
　　O bountie! so to difference the rates!
What can the *Poet* wish his *King* may doe,
　　But, that he cure the Peoples Evill too?

　　　　　　　　　　　From *Under-woods* (1640)

SONG

Slow, slow, fresh fount, keepe time with my salt teares;
　　Yet slower, yet, O faintly gentle springs:
List to the heavy part the musique beares,
　　'Woe weepes out her division, when shee sings.
　　　　Droupe hearbs, and flowres;
　　　　Fall griefe in showres;
　　　　Our beauties are not ours:
　　　　　　O, I could still
　　(Like melting snow upon some craggie hill,)
　　　　drop, drop, drop, drop,
　　Since natures pride is, now, a wither'd daffodil.'

　　　　　　　　　　　from *Cynthia's Revels* (1601)

This charming play was first produced at Blackfriars in 1600. One of
the players, says the first edition, was Salemon Pavy—of 'The Children
of Queen Elizabeth's Chapel,' upon whom Jonson wrote one of his
most celebrated epitaphs; beginning:

　　　　　　　Weepe with me all you. that read
　　　　　　　　This little storie:
　　　　　　　And know, for whom a teare you shed,
　　　　　　　　Death's selfe is sorry . . .

Another delightful song in *Cynthia's Revels* is that beginning

　　　　　Queen and Huntress, chaste and fair . . .

SONG

The faiery beame upon you,
The starres to glister on you;
  A Moone of light,
  In the Noone of night,
Till the Fire-Drake hath o're-gone you.
The Wheele of fortune guide you,
The Boy with the Bow beside you,
  Runne aye in the way,
  Till the Bird of day,
And the luckyer lot betide you.

from *A Masque of the Metamorphosed Gipsies* (1640)

This Masque was first played in 1621 and first printed in a pirated edition in 1640. It re-appeared with variant text in the 1641 folio of Jonson's *Works*.

This little song, and another in the same measure, in the manner of Tom o' Bedlam, is one of the most extraordinary little snatches of music Jonson—a master of curious music—ever wrote. It has the authentic magic and mystery of the 'mad songs' which abound in the earlier years of our literature, and of which the secret has apparently perished except for an occasional echo in Blake or more faintly yet, in Christina Rossetti, and notably in our own time, in Walter de la Mare.

Sir William Davenant

SONG

O Thou that sleep'st like Pigg in Straw,
   Thou Lady dear, arise;
Open (to keep the Sun in awe)
   Those pretty pinking eyes:
And having stretcht each Leg and Arme,
   Put on your cleane White Smock,
And then I pray, to keep you warme,
   A Petticote on Dock.
Arise, arise! Why should you sleep,
   When you have slept enough?
Long since, French Boyes cry'd Chimney-Sweep,
   And Damsels Kitching-stuffe.

The Shops were open'd long before,
   And youngest Prentice goes
To lay at's Mrs. Chamber-doore
   His Masters shining shooes.
Arise, arise; your Breakfast stayes,
   Good Water-grewell warme,
Or sugar-sops, which Galen says
   With Mace, will do no harme.
Arise, Arise; when you are up,
   You'l find more to your cost,
For Morning-draught in Caudle-cup,
   Good Nutbrown-Ale, and Tost.

from *News from Plimouth* (1635)

Perhaps Davenant borrowed his measure from Bishop Corbet, whose 'proper new ballad intituled The Faeryes Farewell' appeared a few years earlier. How pleasant it would be to go on and talk about the good Bishop. . . .

SONG

The Lark now leaves his watry Nest
  And climbing, shakes his dewy Wings;
He takes this Window for the East;
  And to implore your Light, he sings,
Awake, awake, the Morn will never rise,
Till she can dress her Beauty at your Eies.

The Merchant bows unto the Seaman's Star,
  The Ploughman from the Sun his Season takes;
But still the Lover wonders what they are,
  Who look for day before his Mistress wakes.
Awake, awake, break through your Vailes of Lawne!
Then draw your Curtains, and begin the Dawn.

from *Madagascar* (1638)

If in the former Davenant took a hint from Corbet, in this celebrated song he may perhaps have given one to Cleveland, whose wholly delightful 'Upon Phillis walking in a morning before sun-rising' in both thought and phrase sometimes recalls the above. I mention such an influence (it is no more) not to chide the influenced, but to praise him for the excellence of his model. The anthologies have seldom visited Cleveland; and are the worse for the omission.

I have given the foregoing specimens from Jonson and Davenant, although they do not properly come into the list of Laureates, so as to have the pleasure of copying them out; perhaps the reader will allow that the space is not ill-employed, without going on to cry for a passage or so from 'Andrew Bernard' as Warton calls his shadowy predecessor.

John Dryden

FROM ASTRAEA REDUX
A POEM
ON THE HAPPY RESTORATION AND RETURN OF HIS SACRED
MAJESTY CHARLES II. 1660

. . . And welcome now, great monarch, to your own;
Behold th' approaching cliffs of Albion:
It is no longer motion cheats your view,
As you meet it, the land approacheth you.
The land returns, and, in the white it wears,
The marks of penitence and sorrow bears.
But you, whose goodness your descent doth show,
Your heavenly parentage and earthly too;
By that same mildness, which your father's crown
Before did ravish, shall secure your own.
Not tied to rules of policy, you find
Revenge less sweet than a forgiving mind.
Thus, when the Almighty would to Moses give
A sight of all he could behold and live;
A voice before his entry did proclaim
Long-suffering, goodness, mercy, in his name.
Your power to justice doth submit your cause,
Your goodness only is above the laws;
Whose rigid letter, while pronounced by you,
Is softer made. So winds that tempests brew,
When through Arabian groves they take their flight,
Made wanton with rich odours, lose their spite.
And as those lees that trouble it, refine
The agitated soul of generous wine:
So tears of joy, for your returning, spilt,
Work out, and expiate our former guilt.
Methinks I see those crowds on Dover's strand,
Who, in their haste to welcome you to land,
Chok'd up the beach with their still growing store,

And made a wilder torrent on the shore:
While, spurr'd with eager thoughts of past delight,
Those, who had seen you, court a second sight;
Preventing still your steps, and making haste
To meet you often, wheresoe'er you past.
How shall I speak of that triumphant day,
When you renew'd th' expiring pomp of May!
(A months that owns an interest in your name:
You and the flowers are its peculiar claim.)
That star that at your birth shone out so bright,
It stain'd the duller Sun's meridian light,
Did once again its potent fires renew,
Guiding our eyes to find and worship you.

from *Astraea Redux* (1660) lines 250–291.

The Restoration found most of the poets ready with civil tributes, some from pleasure, some from policy. Dryden's suggestion above that the people were overjoyed is no exaggeration. Hume tells us in his *History* (and I rejoice to quote it in its bi-centenary year) that the King's return proved too much for some: 'Traditions remain of men who died for pleasure, when informed of this happy and surprizing event.' Charles landed at Dover on May 26th, 1660.

TO THE MEMORY OF MR. OLDHAM

Farewel, too little and too lately known,
Whom I began to think and call my own;
For sure our Souls were near ally'd; and thine
Cast in the same Poetick mould with mine.
One common Note on either Lyre did strike,
And Knaves and Fools we both abhorr'd alike:
To the same Goal did both our Studies drive,
The last set out the soonest did arrive.
Thus *Nisus*[1] fell upon the slippery place,
While his young Friend perform'd and won the Race.
O early ripe! to thy abundant store
What could advancing Age have added more?
It might (what Nature never gives the young)
Have taught the numbers of thy native Tongue.
But Satyr needs not those, and Wit will shine
Through the harsh cadence of a rugged line.
A noble Error, and but seldom made,
When Poets are by too much force betray'd.
Thy generous fruits, though gather'd ere their prime
Still shew'd a quickness; and maturing time
But mellows what we write to the dull sweets of Rime.
Once more, hail and farewel; farewel, thou young
But ah too short, Marcellus of our Tongue;
Thy Brows with Ivy, and with Laureals bound;
But Fate and gloomy Night encompass thee around.

from *The Remains of Mr. John Oldham* (1684)

John Oldham (1653-1683) was celebrated in his own time for his *Satires on the Jesuits* (1679) and in ours, alas, only by his name attached to Dryden's poem. He was well liked and sincerely mourned, for in addition to Dryden's tribute there are memorial verses by Nahum Tate, Durfey and others all of whom speak of him with something more than conventional regret.

Dryden takes the view then common, that satire needs a rugged style to clothe it, which is odd, for his own practice had already shown the added effectiveness of a polished line. He was probably nearer the mark when he hinted that Oldham had still much to learn of the exacting trade of poetry: but so have most of us who follow it.

---

[1] *Nisus,* famous in *Virgil* for his Friendship with *Euryalus,* with whom he lost his life; the moving Account of which see in *Virgil's* ninth Book of his *Aeneis.* (Dryden's note.)

A SONG OF THE RIVER THAMES

Old Father Ocean calls my Tyde:
Come away, come away;
The Barks upon the Billows ride,
The Master will not stay;
The merry Boson from his side,
His Whistle takes to check and chide
The lingring Lads delay,
And all the Crew alowd has Cry'd,
Come away, come away.

See the God of Seas attends Thee,
Nymphs Divine, a Beauteous Train:
All the calmer Gales befriend Thee
In thy passage o'er the Main:
Every Maid her Locks is binding,
Every *Triton's* Horn is winding,
Welcome to the watry Plain.

from *Albion and Albanius* (1685)

This unlucky opera was performed on June 3rd, 1685, but never met with much success, for reasons severally given as (i) the landing of the Duke of Monmouth about that time, which threw the nation into 'great Consternation;' (ii) the death not long before of Charles II—'it was all compos'd' (Dryden tells us) 'and was just ready to have been perform'd when he, in Honour of whom it was principally made, was taken from us . . .'; and (iii) because the music was not liked. With characteristic opportunism Dryden in dedicating the published work to the late King takes the opportunity of remarking what a fine fellow his successor is; and why not?—James II had excellent qualities along with various others.

Thomas Shadwell

ODE ON THE ANNIVERSARY OF THE QUEEN'S BIRTH

I

Now does the glorious Day appear
The mightiest Day of all the Year,
Not anyone such Joy could bring,
Not that which ushers in the Spring.
That of ensuing Plenty hopes does give,
This did the hope of Liberty retrieve;
This does our Fertile Isle with Glory Crown,
And all the Fruits it yields we now can call our own.
On this blest day was our Restorer born,
Farr above all let this the Kalendar Adorn.
Now, now with our united Voice
Let us aloud proclaim our Joys;
To Triumph *let us sing*
And make Heav'ns mighty concave ring.

2

It was a work of full as great a weight
And require the self-same Power,
Which did frail Humane kind Create,
When they were lost them to restore;
For a like Act, Fate gave our Princess Birth,
Which adding to the Saints, made Joy in Heaven,
As well as Triumphs upon Earth,
To which so great, so good a Queen was given.

3

By beauteous softness mixt with Majesty,
An Empire over every Heart she gains
And from her awful Power none could be free,
She with such Sweetness and such Justice Reigns:

Her Hero too, whose Conduct and whose Arms
The trembling Papal World their Force must yield.
Must bend himself to her victorious Charms,
And give up all the trophies of each Field
Our dear Religion, with our Laws defence,
To God her Zeal, to Man Benevolence;
Must her above all former Monarch raise
To be the everlasting Theme of Praise;
No more shall we the great *Eliza* boast,
For her Great Name in Greater *Mary's* will be lost.

I hope the reader will not be sorry that I have given, as a specimen of
Shadwell's Laureate poems, the shortest. If the story of the Laureates
could show nothing better than this, perhaps it would not be worth
writing. This poem abundantly testifies to Shadwell's dullness and if
the second stanza deviates into sense I do not detect it. The birthday
thus so strangely celebrated was that of 1689, when Queen Mary was
twenty-seven. She was a Queen who possessed many of the virtues
attributed to her, but no-one could receive such a poem as Shadwell's
without appearing somewhat ridiculous.

SONG

Thus all our life long we are frolic and gay,
And, instead of Court-Revels, we merrily play
At Trap, and at Keels, and at Barlibreak run,
At Goff, and at Stool-ball, and when we have done
These Innocent Sports, we laugh, and lie down,
And to each pretty Lass we give a green-Gown.

We teach little Dogs to fetch and to carry
The Partridge, the Hare, and the Pheasants our Quarry:
The nimble Squirrels with cudgels we chase,
And the little pretty Lark we betray with a Glass,
And when we have done, we laugh and lie down,
And to each pretty, &c.

About the *May-pole* we dance all around,
And with Garlands of Pinks, and of Roses are Crown'd;
Our little kind tributes we cheerfully pay
To the gay Lord, and to the bright Lady of the May.
And when we have done, &c.

With our delicate Nymphs we kiss and we toy,
What all others but Dream of, we daily enjoy;
With our sweet-hearts we dally so long till we find
Their pretty Eyes say that their hearts are grown kind:
And when we have done, we laugh and lie down,
And to each pretty Lass we give a green Gown.

from *The Royal Shepherdesse* (1669)

Shadwell was never completely happy in verse, and this song hardly
sings itself as do the best of Dryden's and the whole marvellous range
of songs in the Elizabethans. But it has charm and that little catalogue
of games is inviting. 'Trap' was a ball game in which the ball was
lodged in a sort of wooden cup and thrown up by a blow beneath the
cup with the bat; which was then employed in an attempt to hit the
ball itself. 'Keels' was a kind of skittles. 'Barlibreak' was a game in
which couples chased one another and 'Goff' was golf. 'Stool-ball' was
a form of cricket. It seems reasonable after so much activity to 'laugh
and lie down.'

SONG

Bright was the morning, cool the Air,
  Serene was all the Sky,
When on the waves I left my fair,
  The centre of my joy;
Heaven and Nature smiling were,
  And nothing sad but I.

Each rosy field its odour spread,
  All fragrant was the shore,
Each river God rose from his bed,
  And sigh'd and owned her power;
Curling their waves they deckt their head
  As proud of what they bore.

Glide on, ye waters, bear these lines
  And tell her how I am opprest;
Bear all my sighs, ye gentle winds,
  And waft them to her breast;
Tell her if ere she prove unkind
  I never shall have rest.

Conventional, but not less charming for that. Dryden, in *An Evening's Love* (1671) has a song beginning 'Calm was the Even, and cleer was the Skie,' but the spirit of Shadwell's song belongs to the time of Charles I.

This song is printed by Montague Summers, Shadwell's *Works*, 1927, Vol. V. 'from British Museum, MSS. Additional, No. 19,759.' I have not examined the original.

Nahum Tate

❦❦❦❦❦❦❦❦

AN ODE UPON THE NEW YEAR 1693

The Happy Happy Year is Born,
   That Wonders shall disclose;
That Conquest with fix'd Lawrells shall adorn
And give our lab'ring Hercules Repose.
   Ye Graces that resort
To Virtue's Temple, blest Maria's Court,
   With Incense and with Songs as Sweet
   The Long expected Season meet,
   The Long expected Season gently Greet.

Maria (thus devoutly say)
Maria—Oh appear! appear!
   Thy softest Charms Display,
   Smile and bless the Infant Year;
Smile on its Birth in Kindness to our Isle,
   For if this Genial Day
   You cheerfully Survey
Succeeding Years in just Return on you and Us shall Smile.

Thus, let Departing Winter Sing,
Approach, Advance, Thou promis'd Spring,
   And if for Action not designed
   Together, soon, together bring
Confederate Troops in Europe's Cause combin'd.
   A Busier Prospect Summer yields,
   Floating Navies harrass'd Fields.
   Far from the Gallick Genius spying
   (Of Unjust War the Just Disgrace)
   Their Broken Squadrons Flying,
And Britain's Caesar Lightning in the Chase.

But Autumn does Impatient grow
To crown the Victor's brow;
To wait him home triumphant from Alarms
To Albion and Maria's Arms.
Then to conclude the Glorious Scene,
To Europe's Joy let me return,
When Britain's Senate shall convene
To thank their Monarch and no more his Absence mourn.
Their kind supplies our fainting Hopes restored,
Their injur'd counsels shall sure means afford,
To fix the Gen'ral Peace won by our Monarch's Sword.

Chorus

While Tyrants their Neighbours and Subjects Oppress
All Nations the Pious Restorer Caress.
Securely our Hero prepares for the Field,
His Valour his Sword, his Virtue his Shield;
He Arms in Compassion for Europe's Release,
He Conquers to Save, and he Warrs to give Peace.

My choice has fallen on the same Ode as Professor Broadus re-printed, but—as he points out—there is little to choose between them. I was attracted by the curiously modern allusions—the 'confederate troops in Europe's cause combined' sound uncommonly like the army which now has its headquarters at Paris; the 'kind supplies' mentioned towards the end have also a twentieth century counterpart, as we have cause to know; and 'warrs to give peace' are still apt to crop up from time to time, though none in Tate's time or ours has had much success.

THE BANQUET

Dispatch, and to the myrtle grove convey
  Whatever with the natural palate suits,
The dairy's store with salads, roots, and fruits;
I mean to play the Epicure today!
    Let naught be wanting to complete
      Our bloodless treat;
But bloodless let it be, for I've decreed
The grape alone for this repast shall bleed.
    Sit worthy friends—but ere we feed,
      Let Love b'expell'd the Company;
Let no man's mirth here interrupted be
With thought of any scornful little She!
Fall to, my friends. Trust me the cheer is good!
    Ah! (if our bliss we understood)
      How should we bless th' indulgent Fates!
Indulgent Fates, that with content have stor'd
      Our rural board,
A rarity ne'er found amongst the cates
Of most voluptuous potentates.

                                              from *Poems* (1677)

ON SNOW FALL'N IN AUTUMN, AND DISSOLVED BY THE SUN

Nature now stript of all her summer dress,
  And modestly surmising, 'twere unmeet
For each rude eye to view her nakedness,
  Around her bare limbs wraps this snowy sheet.

The wanton Sun the slight-wrought shroud removes,
  T'embrace the naked dame, whose fertile womb
Admits the lusty paramour's warm loves,
  And is made big with the fair spring to come.

                                              from *Poems* (1677)

A pretty conceit. Tate has something in common with the lively muse
of his friend Thomas Flatman, a poet very unjustly left unread these
days.

SLIDING ON SKATES IN VERY HARD FROST

How well these frozen floods now represent
Those crystal waters of the firmament!
Though hurricanes should rage, they could not now
So much as curl the solid water's brow;
Proud fleets whose stubborn cables scarce withstood
Th' impetuous shock of the unstable flood,
In watry ligaments are restrain'd
More strict than when in binding ooze detain'd.
But though their services at present fail,
Ourselves without the aid of tide or gale
On keels of polisht steel securely sail;
From every creek to every point we rove,
And in our lawless passage swifter move
Than fish beneath us, or than fowl above.

from *Poems* (1677)

Skating was popular in the time of Charles II, but I do not recall
another contemporary poem on the subject.

THE HURRICANE

What cheer my Mates? Luff ho!—we toil in vain!
  That northern mist forebodes a hurricane.
  See how th' expecting ocean raves,
  The billows roar before the fray,
  Untimely night devours the day,
  I'th' dead eclipse we naught descry
But lightning's wild caprices in the sky,
And scaly monsters sparkling through the waves.
  Ply! Each a hand, and furl your sails.
  Port, hard a'port—the tackle fails.
  Sound ho!—five fathom and the most.
A dangerous shelf! sh'as struck, and we are lost.
Speak in the hold!—she leaks amain—give o'er;
  The crazy boat can work no more.
She draws apace, and we approach no shore.
A ring, my Mates: let's join a ring, and so
  Beneath the deep embracing go.
Now to new worlds we steer, and quickly shall arrive:
Our spirits shall mount as fast as our dull corpses dive.

from *Poems* (1677)

This piece is as graphic in its way as Swift's *City Shower*; it has that
'rich badness' called for by G. K. Chesterton—but it is not contemptible.

THE ROUND

How vain a thing is Man whom toys delight,
  And shadows fright!
  Variety of impertinence
  Might give our dotage some pretence;
  But to a circle bound
  We toil in a dull round:
  We sit, move, eat and drink,
  We dress, undress, discourse and think
  By the same passions hurried on,
  Imposing, or imposed upon:
  We pass the time in sport or toil,
  We plough the seas, or safer soil:
  Thus all that we project and do,
  We did it many a year ago.
  We travel still a beaten way,
And yet how eager rise we to pursue
  Th' affairs of each returning day,
As if its entertainments were surprising all and new.

from *Poems* (1677)

Nicholas Rowe

SONG,

FOR THE KING'S BIRTH-DAY,

28TH OF MAY, 1716

I

Lay thy flowry Garlands by,
Ever blooming gentle May!
Other Honors now are nigh;
   Other Honors see we pay.
Lay thy flow'ry Garlands by, &c.

2

Majesty and great Renown,
Wait thy beamy Brow to crown,
Parent of our Hero, thou,
GEORGE on *Britain* didst bestow.
Thee the Trumpet, thee the Drum,
With the plumy Helm, become:
Thee the Spear and shining Shield,
With ev'ry Trophy of the warlike Field.

3

Call thy better Blessings forth,
   For the Honor of his Birth:
Still, the Voice of loud Commotion,
   Bid the complaining Murmurs cease,
Lay the Billows of the Ocean;
   And compose the Land in Peace.
   Call thy better, &c.

4

Queen of Odors, fragrant *May*,
For this Boon, this happy Day,
Janus with the double Face
Shall to thee resign his Place,
Thou shalt rule with better Grace:
Time from thee shall wait his Doom,
And thou shalt lead the Year for ev'ry Age to come.

5

Fairest Month! In Caesar pride thee,
  Nothing like him canst thou bring,
Though the Graces smile beside thee:
  Tho' thy Bounty gives the Spring.

6

Tho' like *Flora* thou array thee,
  Finer than the painted Bow;
Carolina shall repay thee
  All thy Sweetness, all thy Show.
She herself a Glory greater
  Than thy golden Sun discloses;
And her smiling Offspring sweeter
  Than the Bloom of all thy Roses.

This is perhaps the least insupportable of Rowe's official poems. It was 'perform'd at the Royal Palace of St. James's' to music by John Eccles, Master of His Majesty's Music. In the other official poems there are occasional lines which please (not always in the way the poet intended) but they would not repay reprinting in their entirety; indeed, neither does the present one but as a specimen.

LINES FROM TAMERLANE, ACT 2 SCENE 2

AXALLA.   From this auspicious day the *Parthian* name
              Shall date its birth of empire, and extend
              Even from the dawning East to utmost *Thule*
              The limits of its sway.

PRINCE OF
TANAIS.   Nations unknown,
              Where yet the *Roman* eagles never flew,
              Shall pay their homage to victorious *Tamerlane*,
              Bend to his valour, and superior virtue,
              And own, that conquest is not giv'n by chance,
              But (bound by fatal and resistless Merit)
              Waits on his Arms.

TAMERLANE.   It is too much, you dress me
              Like an Usurper in the borrow'd attributes
              Of injur'd Heav'n: can we call conquest ours?
              Shall Man, this pigmy with a giant's pride,
              Vaunt of himself, and say, Thus have I done this?
              Oh! vain pretence to greatness! Like the Moon,
              We borrow all the brightness, which we boast,
              Dark in ourselves, and useless. If that Hand
              That rules the fate of battles strike for us,
              Crown us with fame, and gild our clay with honour:
              'Twere most ungrateful to disown the benefit,
              And arrogate a praise which is not ours.

AXALLA.   With such unshaken temper of the soul
              To bear the swelling tide of prosp'rous fortune,
              Is to deserve that fortune: in adversity
              The mind grows tough by buffetting the tempest;
              Which, in success dissolving, sinks to ease,
              And loses all her firmness.

TAMERLANE.   Oh! *Axalla*!
              Could I forget I am a Man, as thou art,
              Would not the winter's cold, or summer's heat,
              Sickness, or thirst, and hunger, all the train
              Of Nature's clamorous appetites (asserting
              An equal right in kings and common men)
              Reprove me daily?—No—If I boast of aught

Be it, to have been Heaven's happy instrument,
The means of good to all my fellow creatures;
This is a king's best praise.

from *Tamerlane* (1702)

This brief passage sufficiently indicates the difference between Rowe's king and Marlowe's. The elder poet's conception of the conqueror was nearer historical truth, but it would never have served as a portrait of Dutch William. There is a quiet strength in Rowe's use of blank verse which is here very effective although its absence of fine flights tend to monotony when the verse is read in bulk. The Prince's lines beginning

Nations unknown
Where yet the Roman *eagles never flew*

afford an interesting parallel with the well-known stanza of Cowper's 'Boadicea:'

'*Regions Caesar never knew,*
Thy posterity shall sway;
Where his eagles never flew,
None invincible as they.'

PROLOGUE TO *The Non-Juror,* A COMEDY, BY MR. CIBBER
As it was acted at the Theatre-Royal in Drury Lane
1718

To-night, ye Whigs and Tories both be safe,
Nor hope at one another's Cost to laugh,
We mean to souse Old Satan and the Pope;
They've no Relations here, nor Friends, we hope.
A Tool of theirs supplies the Comic Stage
With just materials for Satiric rage:
Nor think our colours may too strongly paint
The stiff Non-Juring Separation Saint.
Good breeding ne'er commands us to be civil
To those who give the Nation to the Devil;
Who at our surest, best Foundation strike,
And hate our Monarch and our Church alike;
Our Church,—which aw'd with reverential fear,
Scarcely the Muse presumes to mention here.
Long may She these her worst of foes defy,
And lift her mitred Head triumphant to the sky:
While theirs—but Satire silently disdains
To name, what lives not, but in Madmen's brains.
Like bawds, each lurking Pastor seeks the dark,
And fears the Justice's enquiring clerk.
In close back rooms his routed flocks he rallies,
And reigns the patriarch of blind lanes and allies.
There safe, he lets his thund'ring censures fly,
Unchristens, damns us, gives our laws the lie,
And excommunicates three stories high.
Why, since a Land of Liberty, they hate,
Still will they linger in this Free-Born State?
Here, ev'ry hour, fresh, hateful, objects rise,
Peace and Prosperity afflict their eyes:
With anguish, Prince and People they survey,
Their just obedience, and his rightful sway.
Ship off, ye Slaves, and seek some passive land,
Where Tyrants after your own hearts command.
To your transalpine Master's rule resort,
And fill an empty, abdicated Court:
Turn your possessions here to ready Rhino,
And buy ye Lands and Lordships at Urbino.

The practice of providing a Prologue and Epilogue to plays, which flourished for nearly two centuries in England, undoubtedly led to the composition of some of the dullest verse ever penned; but this mass of mediocrity contains a wealth of contemporary allusion which redeems it for the student without making it of general interest.

Rowe's prologue to the *Non-Juror*, however, is a vigorous piece which may be read with interest by anyone; for such phrases as 'excommunicates three stories high' have a life of their own apart from their context.

This piece is also of interest for the link it supplies between one Laureate and another; and Cibber himself afterwards claimed that he was given the Laureateship for the *Non-Juror*. The play is worth something, apart from its political intention.

The Non-Jurors were those clergy who refused to take the Oath of Allegiance to William and Mary in 1689; and the bitterness of the controversy may be measured by the fact that Cibber's play was first acted in 1718, almost thirty years after the original disputes. The play, which was an adaptation from the *Tartuffe* of Molière, ran for sixteen nights. Cibber received a gift of two hundred guineas from George I for the dedication.

SONG,

ON A FINE WOMAN WHO HAD A DULL HUSBAND

I

When on fair Celia's eyes I gaze,
  And bless their light divine;
I stand confounded with amaze,
  To think on what they shine.

2

On one vile clod of earth she seems
  To fix their influence;
Which kindles not at those bright beams
  Nor wakens into sense.

3

Lost and bewilder'd with the thought,
  I could not but complain,
That Nature's lavish hand had wrought
  This fairest work in vain.

4

Thus some who have the stars survey'd,
  Are ignorantly led,
To think those glorious lamps were made
  To light Tom Fool to bed.

from Rowe's *Works* (edition of 1747)

Laurence Eusden

ODE FOR THE KING'S BIRTHDAY, 1723

Recitativo

Hail to the lov'd, returning, glorious *Day*!
Let Phoebus gild it with a brighter Ray:
Long may we joy to see it smiling rise,
And long great BRUNSWIC want his kindred Skies.

Air

Breath the Hautboy, touch the Lyre,
Melting Harmony inspire;
Let no clouded Brow be found
In the glittering, pompous Round.
Music! gently fan Love's Fire,
Welcome *Mirth* and young *Desire*,
    Breath the Hautboy, touch the Lyre,
    Melting Harmony inspire!

Recitativo

To Him, what Numbers shall we bring,
In equal Numbers, whom no *Muse* can sing?
To Him, what deathless Trophy raise,
Who, all transending, nobly scorns all Praise?
In pleasing wonder lost we see,
How lovely Virtue shines in MAJESTY!

Air

Still let Nations, freed, resound Him,
Guardian Angels still surround Him,
Crown Him with the sweetest Pleasure,
Without End, and without Measure,
Let no treacherous Foe confound Him,
    Still let Nations, freed, resound Him,
    Guardian Angels still surround Him!

Recitativo

But hear! the yelling Furies rave;
How widely yawns th' Avernian cave!
See! *Treason* from the Realms of Night
Up-rears her Head, a hideous Sprite!
The Monster, pale with guilty Fears,
No sooner spy'd, but disappears.

Air

O! Traytors, odious Train!
Of public Bliss the Bane!
With pious Leer demure,
Fain would they stab secure.
An outward Ease they wear,
But pant with inward Care,
Their Dreams new Horrors bring,
They fly a vengeful KING.
O! Traytors, odious Train!
Of public Bliss the Bane!

Chorus

'Tis CAROLINA all their Hopes destroys,
The fruitful Mother of our Joys!
Still may the ROYAL PROGENY appear
Encreas'd by ev'ry circling Year;
Still let kind Heaven display each dark Design,
Shield BRUNSWIC, and his godlike LINE:
This we for Blessings on BRITANNIA pray,
BRITANNIA! ever blest, if THEY.

The Hautboy referred to in the first Air was perhaps grandfather to
the one in the first draft of the *Rejected Addresses* almost a century later
in which was originally written (we are told)

> . . . *one hautboy will*
> *Give, half-ashamed, a tiny flourish still,*

after the orchestra had finished tuning up. There are so few Hautboys
in English literature that I think the relationship is very probable.

AN ODE FOR THE NEW-YEAR AS IT WAS SUNG BEFORE HIS MAJESTY

Recitativo

Lift up thy hoary Head, and rise,
   Thou mighty Genius of this Isle:
Around thee cast thy wond'ring Eyes
   See all thy Albion smile.
Mirths Goddess her blest Pow'r maintains
In Cities, Courts, and rural Plains,
BRUNSWICK, the glorious BRUNSWICK reigns.

Air

Tho' thy king Eyes were once o'erflowing,
Our too impeding dangers knowing:
Tho' Days, tho' Nights, were spent in Groaning,
Poor BRITTANNIAS fate bemoaning:
Now forbear, forbear to languish,
Chearful rise from needless Anguish:
For pleasures now are ever growing,
Tho' thy kind Eyes were once o'erflowing.

Recitativo

Let the young dawning year a GEORGE resound,
A GEORGE'S Fame can fill its spacious Round,
Here ev'ry Virtue pleas'd thou may'st behold,
Which rais'd a Heroe to a God of Old,
To form this One the miz'd Ideas drew
From EDWARD, HENRY, and thy lov'd NASSAU.

Air

Such to BRITTANNIA is her King,
As the softly murmuring Spring,
To thirsty Travellers, who sweat
On Libyan Sands and die with Heat.
They view it with a glad Surprise
And drink the water with their Eyes.
Then with gay Hearts, refresh'd, they sing:
Such to BRITTANNIA is her King.

Recitativo

By thee contending nations are ally'd,
To thee *Hesperia* sinks her tow'ring Pride,
Moscovia's Prince begins his Bonds to know,
And roaring Volga silently to flow.
Thee GALLIA'S Regent with fix'd Eyes admires,
For thee *Germania* feels a Lover's Fires.
From Belgian moles thy praise is heard around,
Thy Albion's Cliffs return the pleasing Sound.
Janus again his iron doors must close,
A new *Augustus* seeks the World's Repose.

Air

With Rapture every Breast is fir'd,
  Loud Poeans ev'ry Tongue employ;
Thus while great Jove sometimes retir'd,
  The Court of Gods his Absence mourn'd,
  But when the Thunderer return'd,
The whole *Olympus* shook with Joy.

Chorus

GENIUS! now securely rest
We shall ever now be blest
Thou thy Guardianship mayst spare
BRITTANNIA is a BRUNSWICK'S Care.

Those critics who have thought Cibber the worst of the Laureates ought to have given more attention to Eusden.

FROM THE ROYAL FAMILY!—A LETTER TO
MR. ADDISON ON THE KING'S ACCESSION TO THE THRONE

> . . . We ev'ry Art industriously employ
> To paint our Passion, and describe our Joy.
> Each tuneful Son of Harmony prepares
> His sweetest Musick, and his softest Airs.
> Old Age, transported, feels a youthful Fire,
> And, trembling, strikes the long-neglected Lyre.
> Poetic Youths their Infant Pinions try,
> And every callow Muse attempts to fly.
> Ev'n those by Nature not design'd to Sing,
> Who never tasted the *Castalian* Spring,
> Forgetful of their unperforming Parts,
> In homely Doggrell vent their honest Hearts:
> At the high Theme they impotently aim,
> And sacrifice to Loyalty their Fame.
> While dextrous Virgins nobler Arts pursue,
> And with old Glories interweave the New:
> Watchful the Slumbers of the Night they break,
> And teach the curious Needle how to speak.
> Embroider'd Chiefs deal harmless Blows around,
> And Groupes of gasping Heroes strow the Ground.
> Here, *British* Ensigns are display'd on high,
> And Gallia's silken Squadron's seem to fly:
> There, Foreign Princes silently attend,
> And to one Warrior all submissive bend;
> The Warrior's Horse moves with a gracious Spring,
> And bounds, as conscious, that he bears the King.

This passage is a fair example of Eusden at his best. No doubt a great
many poets can do better, but that is no real condemnation; this poem,
the Cambridge verses, and some others by Eusden, are still able to give
pleasure, if not the highest pleasure. To me at least the picture of the
Virgins stitching away far into the night is an attractive one; and for the
'embroider'd Chiefs' I would forgive him a number of his alleged
indecencies.

Colley Cibber

❧❧❧❧❧❧❧❧❧

AN ODE FOR HIS MAJESTY'S BIRTHDAY, OCT. 30, 1731

When *Charles*, from Anarchy's Retreat,
  Resum'd the Regal Seat;
When (hence, by frantick Zealots driv'n)
  Our holy Church, our Laws,
  Returning, with the Royal Cause,
Rais'd up their thankful Eyes, to Heaven,
  Then Hand in Hand,
  To bless the Land,
Protection, with Obedience came,
And mild Oblivion wav'd Revenge,
  For wrongs of Civil Flame.

   Wild, and wanton, then, our Joys,
    Loud, as raging War before:
   All was Triumph, tuneful Noise,
    None, from Heaven, could hope for more.

   Brother, Son, and Father Foes,
    Now embracing, bless their Home:
   Who so happy, could suppose
    Happier days were still to come?

But Providence, that better knows
  Our wants, than we,
  Previous to those,
(Which human wisdom could not, then, foresee)
Did, from the pregnant former Day,
A Race of Happier Reigns, to come, convey.

   [1]The Sun, we saw precede,
   Those mighty Joys restor'd,
   Gave to our future Need,
From great PLANTAGENET a [1]Lord.

[1] *King* George I, *born* May 28th, 1660. (Cibber's note.)

From whose high Veins this greater Day arose,
A Second GEORGE, to fix our World's Repose,
From CHARLES restor'd, short was our Term of Bliss,
But GEORGE from GEORGE entails our Happiness.

> *From a Heart, that abhors the Abuse of high Pow'r,*
>   *Are our Liberties duly defended;*
> *From a Courage, inflam'd by the Terrors of War,*
>   *With his Fame, is our Commerce extended.*

> *Let our publick high Spirits be rais'd, to their Height*
>   *Yet our Prince, in that Virtue, will lead 'em.*
> *From our Welfare, he knows, that his Glory's more bright;*
>   *As Obedience enlarges our Freedom.*

What Ties can bind a grateful People more,
Than such diffus'd Benevolence of Pow'r?

> *If private Views could more prevail,*
> *Than Ardour, for the Public Weal,*
> *Then had his Native, Martial Heat,*
> *In Arms seduc'd him, to be Great.*

> *But Godlike Virtue, more inclin'd*
>   *To Save, than to destroy,*
>   *Deems it superior Joy,*
> *To lead, in Chains of Peace, the Mind.*

With Song, ye BRITONS, lead the Day!
  Sing! sing the Morn, that gave him Breath,
Whose Virtues never shall decay,
  No, never, never taste of Death.

Chorus
When Tombs, and Trophies shall be Dust,
Fame shall preserve the Great, and Just.

This extraordinary production is a fair sample of Cibber's official Odes. What it means—if indeed, meaning lurks within it—I have not learned.

SONG

Tell me, *Belinda*, prithee do,
  (The wanton Caelia said)
Since you'll allow no lover true,
  (Inform a tender Maid)
Are not we Women Fools then to be so?
Belinda smiling thus her sex betray'd:

  Men have their Arts, and we have Eyes,
  We both believe, and noth tell Lies;
  Tho' they a thousand Hearts pursue,
  We love to wound as many too.

Yet still with Virtue! Virtue! Virtue! keep a Pother,
  We look! We love!
  We like! We leave!
  We doth deceive!
And thus are Fools to one another.
      from *Woman's Wit, or the Lady in Fashion* (1697)

SONG

Lovers may talk of Joys
And pretty Toys
And Cooing;
I'm sure I only find
Bobs, Blows, and Noise,
In my poor Wooing.
      from *The Rival Fools* (1709)

SONG

What tho' they call me Country Lass,
  I read it plainly in my Glass,
  That for a Duchess I might pass:
  Oh, could I see the Day!
Would Fortune but attend my Call,
At Park, at Play, at Ring and Ball,
I'd brave the proudest of them all,
  With a *Stand-by—Clear the Way*.

Surrounded by a Crowd of Beaux,
With smart Toupees, and powder'd Clothes,
At Rivals I'd turn up my Nose;
  Oh, could I see the Day!
I'll dart such Glances from these Eyes,
Shall make some Lord or Duke my Prize;
And then, Oh! how I'll tyrannize,
  With a *Stand-by—Clear the Way*.

Oh! then for every new Delight
For Equipage and Diamonds bright,
Quadrille, and Plays, and Balls all Night;
  Oh, could I see the Day!
Of Love and Joy I'd take my Fill
The tedious Hours of Life to Kill,
In ev'ry thing I'd have my Will,
  With a *Stand-by—Clear the Way*.

from *The Provok'd Husband, or a Journey to London* (1728)

This play was written by Cibber from a draft left by Sir John Vanbrugh; this gay and arrogant song is too lively, perhaps, to be in
Cibber's share of the play. But I was so glad to find it among a lot of
dull prose that I could not resist copying it and passing it on—especially
as I think it has been overlooked in the anthologies.

MR COLLEY CIBBER'S EPITAPH ON MR POPE

Our pious praise on tombstones runs so high
Readers might think, that none but good men die!
If graves held only such: *Pope*, like his verse,
Had still been breathing, and escap'd the hearse?
Tho' *fell* to all men's failings, but his own,
Yet to assert his vengeance, or renown,
None ever reached such heights of *Helicon*!
E'en death shall let his dust this truth enjoy,
That not his errors can his fame destroy.

Prince Henry *on the Death of* Hotspur

Adieu! and take thy praise with thee to Heaven!
Thy *ignominy* sleep with thee in the grave
But *not remembered* in thy epitaph.

These lines are from the June issue of *The Gentleman's Magazine,* 1744.
Not all the verses in 18th century journals were written by the people
to whom they were attributed but Cibber may well have had a hand
in these. He told Pope early on in their controversy that he meant to
have the last word! The quotation is from the *First Part of King Henry
the Fourth*: I wonder if Cibber used Rowe's edition—or Pope's?

William Whitehead

❧❧❧❧❧❧❧❧❧

ON THE BIRTH OF THE YOUNG PRINCE[1]

Thanks, Nature, thanks; the finish'd piece we own,
And worthy Fred'ric's love, and Britain's throne.
Th' impatient goddess first had sketch'd the plan,
Yet, ere she durst compleat the wond'rous man,
To try her power a gentler task design'd,
And form'd[2] a pattern of the softer kind.
  But now, bright boy, thy more exalted ray
Streams o'er the dawn, and pours a fuller day.
Nor shall displeas'd to thee her realms resign
That earlier promise of the rising line.
'Tis hers a milder scepter to sustain,
'The world's fair light, *not* empress of the main.'
O'er hostile monarchs shall her charms prevail,
And beauty triumph where our arms would fail.

  This be the virgin's fame; for thee remains
The dang'rous wreath, which lab'ring Virtue gains.
For thee, unshock'd, with equal strength to bear
The flatt'ring calms of peace, the storms of war:
With Num's prudence blend Hostilius' fire,
And strike with terror, as with love inspire.

  And see, what signs his future worth proclaim!
See our Ascanius boast a nobler flame!
On the fair form let vulgar fancies trace
Some fond presage in every dawning grace,
More unconfin'd poetic transport roves,
Sees all the soul, and all the soul approves.
Sees regal pride but reach th' exterior part,
And big with virtue beat the little heart;
Whilst from his eyes soft gleams of mercy flow,
And Liberty supreme smiles on his infant brow.

---

[1] Now Prince of Wales.   [2] Lady Augusta. (Whitehead's note.)

> Thus the small seed contains, by Nature wove,
> The embryo texture of its future grove.
> Soft, by degrees, as genial suns and skies,
> Warm their green blood, th' unfolding branches rise;
> Wide and more wide their verdant honors spread,
> An age's wonder, and a nation's shade.

from *Poems on Several Occasions* (1754)

These verses were written, of course, many years before Whitehead became Laureate. The young prince, born in 1738, eventually became George III. The Lady Augusta (1737–1813) married the Duke of Brunswick, that model General and thus passes out of this footnote into the pages of Prussian history.

I give the above instead of a complete official Laureate Ode because I have made several extracts from Whitehead's Odes in the text, and this serves to show his manner of treating a royal occasion just as well as would verses from his laborious attempts to pass off the war in America with a carefree insouciance that the outcome hardly justified.

IN A HERMITAGE

The man, whose days of youth and ease
   In nature's calm enjoyments pass'd,
Will want no monitors, like these,[1]
   To torture and alarm his last.

The gloomy grot, the cypress shade,
   The zealot's list of rigid rules,
To him are merely dull parade,
   The tragic pageantry of fools.

What life affords he freely tastes,
   When nature calls resigns his breath;
Nor age in weak repining wastes,
   Nor acts alive the farce of death.

Not so the youths of folly's train,
   Impatient of each kind restraint
Which parent nature fix'd, in vain,
   To teach us, man's true bliss, content.

For something still beyond enough
   With eager impotence they strive,
'Till appetite has learn'd to loath
The very joys by which we live.

Then, fill'd with all which sour disdain
   To disappointed vice can add,
Tir'd of himself, man flies from man,
   And hates the world he made so bad.

from *Poems on Several Occasions* (1754)

A skull, hour-glass, etc. (Whitehead's note.)

SONG FOR RANELAGH

Ye belles, and ye flirts, and ye pert little things,
   Who trip in this frolicsome round,
Pray tell me from whence this impertinence springs,
   The sexes at once to confound?
What means the cock'd hat, and the masculine air,
   With each motion design'd to perplex?
Bright eyes were intended to languish, not stare,
   And softness the test of your sex.

The girl, who on beauty depends for support,
   May call every art to her aid;
The bosom display's, and the petticoat short,
   Are samples she gives of her trade.
But you, on whom fortune indulgently smiles,
   And whom pride has preserved from the snare,
Should slyly attack us with coyness and wiles,
   Not with open, and insolent war.

The Venus, whose statue delights all mankind,
   Shrinks modestly back from the view,
And kindly should seem by the artist design'd
   To serve as a model for you.
Then learn, with her beauty, to copy her air,
   Nor venture too much to reveal:
Our fancies will paint what you cover with care,
   And double each charm you conceal.

The blushes of morn, and the mildness of May,
   Are charms which no art can procure:
O be but yourselves and our homage we pay,
   And your empire is solid and sure.
But if, Amazon like, you attack your gallants,
   And put us in fear of our lives,
You may do very well for sisters and aunts,
   But, believe me, you'll never be wives.

                from Whitehead's *Works* (1774)

ON THE BIRTHDAY OF A YOUNG LADY,
FOUR YEARS OLD

Old creeping Time, with silent tread,
Has stol'n four years o'er Molly's head.
The rose-bud opens on her cheek,
The meaning eyes begin to speak;
And in each smiling look is seen
The innocence which plays within.
Nor is the fault'ring tongue confin'd
To lisp the dawnings of the mind,
But fair and full her words convey
The little all they have to say;
And each fond parent, as they fall,
Finds volumes in that little all.
   May every charm, which now appears,
Increase, and brighten with her years;
And may that same old creeping Time
Go on till she has reach'd her prime,
Then, like a master of his trade,
Stand still, nor hurt the work he made.

from Whitehead's *Works* (1774)

Thomas Warton

꩜꩜꩜꩜꩜꩜꩜꩜

ODE ON HIS MAJESTY'S BIRTH-DAY,
June 4, 1787

I

The noblest Bards of Albion's choir
Have struck of old this festal lyre.
Ere Science, struggling oft in vain,
  Had dared to break her Gothic chain,
Victorious Edward gave the vernal bough
Of Britain's bay to bloom on Chaucer's brow:
Fir'd with the gift, he chang'd to sounds sublime
His Norman minstrelsy's discordant chime;
  In tones majestic hence he told
  The banquet of Cambuscan bold;
  And oft he sung (how'er the rhyme
  Has moulder'd to the touch of time)
  His martial master's knightly board,
  And Arthur's ancient rites restor'd;
The prince in sable steel that sternly frown'd,
And Gallia's captive king, and Cressy'd wreath renown'd.

II

Won from the shepherd's simple meed,
The whispers wild of Mulla's reed,
Sage Spenser wak'd his lofty lay
  To grace Eliza's golden sway:
O'er the proud theme new lustre to diffuse,
He choose the gorgeous allegoric Muse,
And call'd to life old Uther's elfin tale,
And roved thro' many a necromantic vale,
  Pourtraying chiefs that knew to tame
  The goblin's ire, the dragon's flame,
  To pierce the dark enchanted hall,
  Where Virtue sate in lonely thrall.

From fabling Fancy's inmost store
A rich romantic robe he bore;
A veil with visionary trappings hung,
And o'er his virgin-queen the fairy texture flung.

III

At length the matchless Dryden came,
To light the Muses' clearer flame;
To lofty numbers grace to lend,
And strength with melody to blend;
To triumph in the bold career of song,
And roll th' unwearied energy along
Does the mean incense of promiscuous praise,
Does servile fear, disgrace his regal bays?
I spurn his panegyric strings,
His partial homage, tun'd to kings!
Be mine, to catch his manlier chord,
That paints th' impassioned Persian lord,
By glory fir'd, to pity su'd,
Rouz'd by revenge, by love-subdu'd;
And still, with transport new, the strains to trace,
That chant the Theban pair, and Tancred's deadly vase.

IV

Had these blest Bards been call'd, to pay
The vows of this auspicious day,
Each had confess'd a fairer throne,
A mightier sovereign than his own!
Chaucer had made his hero-monarch yield
The martial fame of Cressy's well-fought field
To peaceful prowess, and the conquests calm,
That braid the sceptre with the patriot's palm;
His chaplets of fantastic bloom,
His colourings, warm from Fiction's loom,
Spenser had cast in scorn away,
And deck'd with truth alone the lay;
All real here, the Bard had seen
The glories of his pictur'd Queen!
The tuneful Dryden had not flatter'd here,
His lyre had blameless been, his tribute all sincere!

Like many lesser authorities, the historian of English Poetry promotes
Chaucer to the laurel—perhaps here by poetic license, for in the History
itself he is silent upon the subject. In the matter of the comparative
merits of Edward III, Elizabeth I, Charles II and George III, no doubt
every reader will take sides for himself.

ODE TO SLEEP

On this my pensive pillow, gentle Sleep!
Descend, in all thy downy plumage drest:
Wipe with thy wing these eyes that wake to weep,
And place thy crown of poppies on my breast.

O steep my senses in oblivion's balm,
And sooth my throbbing pulse with lenient hand;
This tempest of my boiling blood becalm!—
Despair grows mild at thy supreme command.

Yet ah! in vain, familiar with the gloom,
And sadly toiling through the tedious night,
I seek sweet slumber, while that virgin bloom,
For ever hovering, haunts my wretched sight.

Nor would the dawning day my sorrows charm:
Black midnight and the blaze of noon alike
To me appear, while with uplifted arm
Death stands prepar'd, but still delays, to strike.

SONNET
TO THE RIVER LODON

Ah! what a weary race my feet have run,
Since first I trod thy banks with alders crown'd,
And thought my way was all through fairy ground,
Beneath thy azure sky, and golden sun:
Where first my Muse to lisp her notes begun!
While pensive Memory traces back the round,
Which fills the varied interval between;
Much pleasure, more of sorrow, marks the scene.
Sweet native stream! those skies and suns so pure
No more return, to cheer my evening road!
Yet still one joy remains, that not obscure,
Nor useless, all my vacant days have flow'd,
From youth's gay dawn to manhood's prime mature;
Nor with the Muse's laurel unbestow'd.

SONNET

WRITTEN AT STONEHENGE

Thou noblest monument of Albion's isle!
Whether by Merlin's aid from Scythia's shore,
To Amber's fatal plain Pendragon bore,
Huge frame of giant-hands, the mighty pile,
T'entomb his Britons slain by Hengist's guile:
Or Druid priests, sprinkled with human gore,
Taught mid thy massy maze their mystic lore:
Or Danish chiefs, enrich'd with savage spoil,
To Victory's idol vast, and unhewn shrine,
Rear'd the rude heap: or, in thy hallow'd round,
Repose the kings of Brutus' genuine line;
Or here those kings in solemn state were crown'd:
Studious to trace thy wondrous origine,
We muse on many an ancient tale renown'd.

Warton was prominent among eighteenth century pioneers of the study of antiquities. If modern archaeologists smile at some of his fancied solutions to Stonehenge's mystery, they should remember that they have yet to establish anything more authentic.

SONNET

WRITTEN IN A BLANK LEAF OF DUGDALE'S MONASTICON

Deem not, devoid of elegance, the Sage,
By Fancy's genuine feelings unbeguil'd,
Of painful pedantry the poring child;
Who turns, of these proud domes, th' historic page,
Now sunk by Time, and Henry's fiercer rage.
Thinkst thou the warbling Moses never smil'd
On his lone hours? Ingenuous views engage
His thoughts, on themes, unclassic falsely styl'd,
Intent. While cloister'd Piety displays
Her mouldering roll, the piercing eye explores
New manners, and the pomp of elder days,
Whence culls the pensive bard his pictur'd stores.
Nor rough, nor barren, are the winding ways
Of hoar Antiquity, but strown with flowers.

This celebrated sonnet is a remarkable link between the formal diction of Milton (whose influence is everywhere in Warton) and the romantic feeling of Wordsworth—who might indeed have written the last line, in an interval perhaps from writing bits into the poems of Coleridge.

THE PROGRESS OF DISCONTENT
(Written at Oxford in the year 1746)

When now mature in classic knowledge,
The joyful youth is sent to college,
His father comes, a vicar plain,
At Oxford bred—in Anna's reign,
And thus, in form of humble suitor,
Bowing accosts a reverend tutor:
'Sir, I'm a Glo'stershire divine,
And this my eldest son of nine;
My wife's ambition and my own
Was that this child should wear a gown:
I'll warrant that his good behaviour
Will justify your future favour;
And, for his parts, to tell the truth,
My son's a very forward youth;
Has Horace all by Heart—you'd wonder—
And mouth's out Homer's Greek like thunder'
If you'd examine—and admit him,
A scholarship would nicely fit him;
That he succeeds 'tis ten to one;
Your vote and interest, Sir!'—'Tis done.

Our pupil's hopes, tho' twice defeated,
Are with a scholarship completed:
A scholarship but half maintains,
And college-rules are heavy chains:
In garret dark he smokes and puns,
A prey to discipline and duns;
And now, intent on new designs,
Sighs for a fellowship—and fines.

When nine full tedious winters past,
That utmost wish is crown'd at last:
But the rich prize no sooner got,
Again he quarrels with his lot:
'These fellowships are pretty things,
We live indeed like petty kings:
But who can bear to waste his whole age
Amid the dullness of a college,
Debarr'd the common joys of life,
And that prime bliss—a loving wife!
O! what's a table richly spread,
Without a woman at its head!

Would some snug benefice but fall,
Ye feasts, ye dinners! farewell all!
To offices I'd bid adieu,
Of Dean, Vice Praef.—of Bursar too;
Come joys, that rural quiet yields,
Come, tythes, and house, and fruitful fields!'

Too fond of freedom and of ease
A Patron's vanity to please,
Long time he watches, and by stealth,
Each frail incumbent's doubtful health;
At length, and in his fortieth year,
A living drops—two hundred clear!
With breast elate beyond expression,
He hurries down to take possession,
With rapture views the sweet retreat—
'What a convenient house! how neat!
For fuel here's sufficient wood:
Pray God the cellars may be good!
The garden—that must be new plann'd—
Shall these old-fashioned yew-trees stand?
O'er yonder vacant plot shall rise
The flow'ry shrub of thousand dies:—
Yon wall, that feels the southern ray,
Shall blush with ruddy fruitage gay:
While thick beneath its aspect warm
O'er well-rang'd hives the bees shall swarm,
From which, ere long, of golden gleam
Metheglin's luscious juice shall stream:
This awkward hut, o'ergrown with ivy,
We'll alter to a modern privy:
Upon yon green slope, of hazels trim,
An avenue so cool and dim
Shall to an harbour, at the end,
In spite of gout, entice a friend.
My predecessor lov'd devotion,
But of a garden had no notion.'

Continuing this fantastic farce on,
He now commences country parson.
To make his character entire,
He weds—a Cousin of the 'Squire;
Not over weighty in the purse,
But many Doctors have done worse:

And tho' she boasts no charms divine,
Yet she can cerve and make birch wine.

Thus fixt, content he taps his barrel,
Exhorts his neighbours not to quarrel;
Finds his Church-wardens have discerning
Both in good liquor and good learning;
With tythes his barns replete he sees,
And chuckles o'er his surplice fees;
Studies to find out latent dues,
And regulates the state of pews;
Rides a sleek mare with purple housing,
To share the monthly club's carousing;
Of Oxford pranks facetious tells,
And—but on Sundays—hears no bells;
Sends presents of his choicest fruit,
And prunes himself each sapless shoot;
Plants colliflowers, and boasts to rear
The earliest melons of the year;
Thinks alteration charming work is,
Keeps bantam cocks, and feeds his turkies;
Builds in his copse a fav'rite bench,
And stores the pond with carp and tench.—

But ah! too soon his thoughless breast
By cares domestic is opprest;
And a third Butcher's bill, and brewing,
Threaten inevitable ruin:
For children fresh expenses yet,
And Dicky now for school is fit.
'Why did I sell my college life
(He cries) for benefice and wife?
Return, ye days, when endless pleasure
I found in reading, or in leisure!
When calm around the common room
I puff'd my daily pipe's perfume!
Rode for a stomach, and inspected,
At annual bottlings, corks selected:
And din'd untaxed, untroubled, under
The portrait of our pious Founder!
When impositions were supply'd
To light my pipe—or sooth my pride—
No cares were then for forward peas,
A yearly longing wife to please;

My thoughts no christening dinners crost,
No children cried for butter'd toast;
And ev'ry night I went to bed,
Without a Modus in my head!'

Oh! trifling head, and fickle heart!
Chagrin'd at whatsoe'er thou art;
A dupe to follies yet untry'd,
And sick of pleasures, scarce enjoy'd!
Each prize possess'd, thy transport ceases,
And in pursuit alone it pleases.

This tale well shows Warton as the poet of transition by contrast with the sonnets; here there is nothing changed from Swift or Prior, and in the sonnets a temper entirely alien to theirs.

This, and all the poems quoted, comes from Warton's *Poetical Works* (1802).

Henry James Pye

ODE FOR HIS MAJESTY'S BIRTHDAY 1807

I

Still does the trumpet's brazen throat
  Pour forth a martial sound,
Still do the notes of battle float
  In warlike clangour round;
Nor rural pipe, nor past'ral lay,
  In peaceful descant hail the day
    To grateful Britain ever dear;
The thunder of embattled plains,
The shouting Conquest's choral strains;
  Burst on the listening ear.

II

Yet, while Bellona's iron car
  Whirls o'er th'ensanguined plains,
'Mid Hyperborean climes afar
  Stern War terrific reigns;
While, with colossal power endow'd
The ruthless minister of blood
  Calls to his scatter'd naval host,
Go forth and bid the bolts of fate
On Britain's trembling harbours wait,
  Shut commerce from her coast;

III

Behold, the sovereign Queen of Isles,
  The Empress of the Waves,
Meeting the vaunt with scornful smiles,
  The empty menace braves;
And see, on Plata's sea-broad stream
Her banners wave, her bright arms gleam;

While ploughing seas of classic fame,
Nile yields once more to Albion's powers,
And Alexandria vails her towers
To George's mightier name.

IV

Firm are the sons that Britain leads
  To combat on the main,
And firm the hardy race that treads
  In steady march the plain:
And proudly may her bards record
The victor arm, the victor sword,
  That drives the foe from Ocean's tide;
And loudly too, with fond acclaim,
Chaunt trophied Maida's deathless fame,
  With military pride.

V

Be hush'd awhile each ruder sound,
  While Britain's grateful voice
Bids all her echoing vales resound
  The Monarch of her choice.
Though round the tyrant's hated throne
Arm'd legions form an iron zone,
  They cannot blunt guilt's scorpion sting;
While Virtue's sacred shield is spread
O'er George's heav'n-protected head,
  The Parent and the King.

1807 was a varied year with Napoleon generally doing rather well, which was no help to H. J. Pye in his labours. He glances appreciatively at Sir John Stuart's victory of Maida (which was won in the previous year) and makes what he can of the capture of Alexandria, without going so far as to admit that it was evacuated immediately after. No doubt the seas of classic fame are those which wash the Dardanelles where, in that year, Admiral Sir Thomas Duckworth took a fleet that failed to achieve much. As for Plata, the less said about that the better; neither Buenos Ayres nor Monte Video remained long enough in British hands to make a respectable appearance in a birth-day Ode.

from ALFRED, *an Epic Poem*

. . . Fierce Coelph views the field with fiery eye,
And marks where haughty Oswald's banners fly:
Then swift and dreadful as the whirlwind's force
Speeds o'er the ruin'd fields its fatal course,
Through all the horrors of the raging fray
He cuts with furious arm his eager way;
Before the Danish chief his circling train
Their spears and sheltering shields oppose in vain:
Breathless and bleeding onward still he press'd
Through groves of iron pointed at his breast,
'Gainst Oswald's heart his rapid sword he drives,
The thundering stroke the solid corselet rives;
Prone falls the injurious tyrant on the ground,
His lifeblood streaming from the fatal wound;
Pierced by a thousand spears, on earth laid low
The expiring victor spurns his prostrate foe,
O'er the warm corse in fatal triumph lies
And sated with revenge exulting dies!

from *Alfred* (1801)—Book V

If it does nothing more, this passage demonstrates the great stride taken
by Scott, whose battle scenes really stir the blood; Pye's hero is pierced
by a thousand spears without any reader being in the smallest degree
moved, except perhaps to surprise that anybody in the heat of battle
had time to count them.

ON MRS. BOSCAWEN'S VILLA AT RICHMOND WHICH
FORMERLY BELONGED TO JAMES THOMSON, AUTHOR
OF 'THE SEASONS'

Ye seats, where oft, in pensive Rapture laid,
  The Bard of Nature wak'd the rural Reed,
  And as the Months in circling lapse succeed
Her varying form in glowing tints pourtrayed
Or, to Britannia's listening ear conveyed
  The exulting Praise of Freedom's sacred meed;
  Or taught the sympathetic Breast to bleed,
As Tragedy her shadowy woes displayed:

Still Fancy's train your verdant Paths shall trace
  Tho' closed her fav'rite Votary's dulcet lay,
Each wonted Haunt their footsteps still shall grace,
  Still Genius thro' your green Retreats shall stray
Far from the scene Boscawen loves to grace
  The attendant Muse shall ne'er be long away.

from FARINGDON HILL

. . . His country freed, discerning ALFRED saw
How vain the civil bond of social law;
Of crowds untrain'd how weak the hasty aid,
When force prevails, and barbarous hosts invade.
That policy which guards each modern throne
Was then to Europe's bounded kings unknown,
No artful statesman then with treacherous breast,
Arm'd half a people to enslave the rest,
A tyrant's call while ready troops attend,
If foes attack, or subjects dare offend.
With milder care a rampart firm he plan'd
To save from future foes the happy land,
The noblest rampart liberty can find,
When freedom guard, the freedom of mankind.
He taught each sturdy labourour of the field,
The sickle, and the sword by turns to wield:
With chearful industry the generous swains,
Till for their wealthy lords the peaceful plains;
Or roused from rural toil by wars alarms
Beneath their well known banners rush to arms.
Let other realms where freedom never smiled,
O'er-awaed by rigor, or by fraud beguiled,
See mercenary bands surround the throne,
Of safety seek from alien arms alone:
But shall not ENGLAND blush for every son
Too proud to guard the rights his sires have won?

from *Faringdon Hill* (1774) Book II

Robert Southey

from AN ODE FOR ST. GEORGE'S DAY

. . . But thou, O England! to that sainted name
Hast given its proudest praise, its loftiest fame.
Witness the field of Cressy, on that day,
When vollying thunders roll'd unheard on high,
    For in that memorable fray
Broken, confused, and scatter'd in dismay,
France had ears only for the Conqueror's cry,
St. George, St. George for England! St. George and Victory!
    Bear witness Poictiers! where again the foe
From that same hand received his overthrow.
    In vain essay'd, Mont Joye St. Denis rang
        From many a boastful tongue,
    And many a hopeful heart in onset brave;
Their courage in the shock of battle quail'd
His dread response when sable Edward gave,
And England and St. George again prevail'd.
    Bear witness Agincourt, where once again
    The bannered lilies on the ensanguin'd plain
    Were trampled by the fierce pursuers' feet;
        And France, doom'd ever to defeat
    Against that foe, beheld her myriads fly
        Before the withering cry,
St. George, St. George for England! St. George and Victory!

        That cry in many a field of Fame
    Through glorious ages held its high renown;
Nor less hath Britain proved the sacred name
        Auspicious to her crown.
    Troubled too oft her course of fortune ran
        Till when the Georges came
        Her happiest age began.
    Beneath their just and liberal sway,
    Old feuds and factions died away;

270

One feeling through her realms was known,
One interest of the Nation and the Throne.
Ring, then, ye bells upon St. George's Day,
From every tower in glad accordance ring;
And let all instruments, full, strong, or sweet,
With touch of modulated string,
And soft of swelling breath, and sonorous beat,
The happy name repeat,
While heart and voice their joyous tribute bring
And speak the People's love for George their King.

from *The Poetical Works of Robert Southey* Vol III (1838)

Southey's Laureate poems are all somewhat long; this is a fair specimen, composed in 1820.

LINES

WRITTEN UPON THE DEATH OF THE PRINCESS CHARLOTTE

'Tis not the public loss which hath imprest
This general grief upon the multitude,
And made its way at once to every breast,
The young, the old, the gentle, and the rude;
'Tis not that in the hour which might have crowned
The prayers preferred by every honest tongue;
The very hour which should have sent around
Tidings wherewith all steeples would have rung,
And all our cities blazed with festal fire,
And all our echoing streets have peeled with gladness;
That then we saw the high-raised hope expire,
And England's expectation quenched in sadness.
It is to think of what thou wert so late
O thou who now liest cold upon thy bier!
So young, and so beloved: so richly blest
Beyond the common lot of royalty;
The object of thy worthy choice possest;
And in thy prime, and in thy wedded bliss,
And in the genial bed,—the cradle drest,
Hope standing by, and Joy, a bidden guest!
'Tis this that from the heart of private life
Makes unsophisticated sorrow flow;
We mourn thee as a daughter and a wife,
And in our human nature feel the blow.

from *The Poetical Works of Robert Southey* (Paris, 1829)

These lines Southey did not collect into his ten-volume edition; they are from Galignani's edition. There is a sincerity in their informality which is not so readily recognised in the 'official' *Funeral Song for the Princess Charlotte of Wales*, though that is a noble thing. Although Southey had been spared such a sorrow as this, he had known what it was to lose a child in infancy, and another, his son Herbert, when just coming to adolescence, only a few months before the tragic death of the Princess Charlotte.

Princess Charlotte was the only child of the Prince Regent, and was heiress-presumptive of the throne of Britain; she had married Prince Leopold (afterwards King of the Belgians) in 1816, and died in child-bed on November 6th, 1817. The nation's consternation and grief found expression in scores of poems and orations.

Among the most extraordinary of these is *A Cypress Wreath, for the Tomb of her late Royal Highness the Princess Charlotte of Wales* (1817) which is a literary curiosity occasionally to be met with on the tuppenny tray. It contains 'original tributes to her memory by J. Gwilliam and others.' No less than nine of the original tributes are from the pen of Mr. J. Gwilliam and of the rest some that wear a familiar air are found on examination to be by Milton, Herrick, and others, with the name Charlotte inserted here and there to fit the occasion.

SONNET

A wrinkled, crabbed man they picture thee,
Old Winter, with a rugged beard as grey
As the long moss upon the apple-tree;
Blue-lipt, and ice-drop at thy sharp blue nose,
Close muffled up, and on thy dreary way,
Plodding alone through sleet and drifting snows.
They should have drawn thee by the high-heapt hearth,
Old Winter! seated in thy great arm'd chair,
Watching the children at their Christmas mirth;
Or circled by them as thy lips declare
Some merry jest, or tale of murder dire,
Or troubled spirit that disturbs the night,
Pausing at times to rouse the mouldering fire,
Or taste the old October brown and bright.

SONNET TO A GOOSE

If thou didst feed on western plains of yore;
Or waddle wide with flat and flabby feet
Over some Cambrian mountain's plashy moor;
Or find in farmer's yard a safe retreat
From gypsy thieves, and foxes sly and fleet;
If thy grey quills, by lawyer guided, trace
Deeds big with ruin to some wretched race,
Or love-sick poet's sonnet, sad and sweet,
Wailing the rigour of his lady fair;
Or if, the drudge of housemaid's daily toil,
Cobwebs and dust thy pinions white besoil,
Departed Goose! I neither know nor care.
But this I know, that we pronounced thee fine,
Season'd with sage and onions, and port wine.

from THE CURSE OF KEHAMA

from XIX Mount Calasay

. . . So saying, up he sprung,
And struck the Bell, which self-suspended hung
Before the mystic Rose.
From side to side the silver tongue
Melodious swung, and far and wide
Soul-thrilling tones of heavenly music rung.
Abashed, confounded,
It left the Glendoveer; . . . yea all astounded
In overpowering fear and deep dismay;
For when that Bell had sounded,
The Rose, with all the mysteries it surrounded,
The Bell, the Table, and Mount Calasay,
The holy Hill itself with all thereon,
Even as a morning dream before the day
Dissolves away, they faded and were gone.

from XXIII Padalon

. . . There rolls the fiery flood,
Girding the realms of Padalon around.
A sea of flame it seem'd to be,
Sea without bound;
For neither mortal nor immortal sight,
Could pierce across through that intensest light.
A single rib of steel,
Keen as the edge of keenest scymitar,
Spann'd this wide gulf of fire. The infernal Car
Roll'd to the Gulf, and on its single wheel
Self-balanced, rose upon that edge of steel.
Red-quivering float the vapours overhead,
The fiery gulf beneath them spread,
Tosses its billowing blaze with rush and roar;
Steady and swift the self-moved Chariot went,
Winning the long ascent,
Then, downwards rolling, gains the farther shore.

from *The Curse of Kehama* (1810)

These two little pictures are from the most readable of Southey's epics —which can be read throughout with unfailing interest. To readers of Science Fiction the poem would be a revelation, giving yet one more confirmation that there is nothing new under the sun, even though one may travel through several light-years looking for it.

William Wordsworth

LINES
INSCRIBED IN A COPY OF HIS POEMS SENT TO THE QUEEN
FOR THE ROYAL LIBRARY AT WINDSOR

Deign, Sovereign Mistress! to accept a lay,
  No laureate offering of elaborate art;
But salutation taking its glad way
  From deep recesses of a loyal heart.

Queen, Wife and Mother! may All-judging Heaven
  Shower with a bounteous hand on Thee and Thine
Felicity that only can be given
  On earth to goodness blest by grace divine.

Lady! devoutly honoured and beloved
  Through every realm confided to thy sway;
May'st thou pursue thy course by God approved,
  And he will teach thy people to obey.

As thou art wont, thy sovereignty adorn
  With woman's gentleness, yet firm and staid;
So shall that earthly crown thy brows have worn
  Be changed for one whose glory cannot fade.

And now by duty urged, I lay this Book
  Before thy Majesty, in humble trust
That on its simplest pages thou wilt look
  With a benign indulgence more than just.

Nor wilt thou blame the Poet's earnest prayer
  That issuing hence may steal into thy mind
Some solace under weight of royal care,
  Or grief—the inheritance of humankind.

For know we not that from celestial spheres,
   When Time was young, an inspiration came
(Oh were it mine!) to hallow saddest tears
   And help life onward in its noblest aim.

                    your Majesty's
                           devoted Subject and Servant
                                 William Wordsworth.

I do not give here Wordsworth's *Ode on the Installation of His Royal Highness Prince Albert as Chancellor of the University of Cambridge, July, 1847,* partly because it is very long, and partly because it was not written by Wordsworth, anyway.

ON THE DEATH OF HIS MAJESTY
(George the Third)

Ward of the Law!—dread Shadow of a King!
Whose realm had dwindled to one stately room;
Whose universe was gloom immersed in gloom,
Darkness as thick as life o'er life could fling,
Save haply for some feeble glimmering
Of Faith and Hope—if thou, by nature's doom,
Gently hast sunk into the quiet tomb,
Why should we bend in grief, to sorrow cling,
When thankfulness were best?—Fresh-flowing tears,
Or, where tears flow not, sigh succeeding sigh,
Yield to such after-thought the sole reply
Which justly it can claim. The Nation hears
In this deep knell, silent for threescore years,
An unexampled voice of awful memory!

King George III died on January 28th, 1820. In another sonnet,
'November, 1813'—'Now that all hearts are glad, all faces bright,'
Wordsworth speaks sadly of the king's affliction, unable to rejoice at
victory when all his people rejoice. Napoleon had recently—mid-
October, 1813—been heavily defeated at Leipzig.

SUGGESTED AT NOON ON LOUGHRIGG FELL

So fair, so sweet, withal so sensitive,
Would that the little Flowers were born to live,
Conscious of half the pleasure which they give;

That to this mountain-daisy's self were known
The beauty of its star-shaped shadow, thrown,
On the smooth surface of this naked stone!

And what if hence a bold desire should mount
High as the Sun, that he could take account
Of all that issues from his glorious fount!

So might he ken how by his sovereign aid
These delicate companionships are made;
And how he rules the pomp of light and shade;

And were the Sister-power that shines by night
So privileged, what a countenance of delight
Would through the clouds break forth on human sight!

Fond fancies! wheresoe'er shall turn thine eye,
On earth, air, ocean, or the starry sky,
Converse with Nature in pure sympathy;

All vain desires, all lawless wishes quelled,
Be Thou to love and praise alike impelled,
Whatever boon is granted or withheld.

Wordsworth was walking near Loughrigg Tarn with several friends when he stopped and drew their attention to the shadow of a daisy cast upon a stone. 'I remember saying at the time, "We shall have a sonnet upon it",' one of the party, Julius Hare afterwards wrote to Wordsworth. But in length at least the lines make a sonnet and a half. They were written in 1844.

TO SLEEP

A flock of sheep that leisurely pass by,
One after one; the sound of rain, and bees
Murmuring; the fall of rivers, winds and seas,
Smooth fields, white sheets of water, and pure sky;
I have thought of all by turns, and yet do lie
Sleepless! and soon the small birds' melodies
Must hear, first uttered from my orchard trees;
And the first cuckoo's melancholy cry.
Even thus last night, and two night more, I lay,
And could not win thee, Sleep! by any stealth:
So do not let me wear tonight away:
Without Thee what is all the morning's wealth?
Come, blessed barrier between day and day,
Dear mother of fresh thoughts and joyous health!

INSCRIPTION
FOR A MONUMENT IN CROSSTHWAITE CHURCH, IN THE VALE OF KESWICK

Ye Vales and hills whose beauty hither drew
The poet's steps, and fixed him here, on you
His eyes have closed! And ye, lov'd books, no more
Shall Southey feed upon your precious lore,
To works that ne'er shall forfeit their renown,
Adding immortal labours of his own—
Whether he traced historic truth, with zeal
For the State's guidance, or the Church's weal,
Or Fancy, disciplined by studious art,
Informed his pen, or wisdom of the heart,
Or judgments sanctioned in the Patriot's mind
By reverence for the rights of all mankind.
Wide were his aims, yet in no human breast
Could private feelings meet for holier rest.
His joys, his griefs, have vanished like a cloud
From Skiddaw's top; but he to heaven was vowed
Through his industrious life, and Christian faith,
Calmed in his soul the fear of change and death.

This is the inscription as published; as cut in Southey's monument there are slight but unimportant modifications.

COMPOSED BY THE SEA-SIDE, NEAR CALAIS, AUGUST 1802

Fair Star of evening, Splendour of the west,
Star of my Country!—on the horizon's brink
Thou hangest, stooping, as might seem, to sink
On England's bosom; yet well pleased to rest,
Meanwhile, and be to her a glorious crest
Conspicuous to the Nations. Thou, I think,
Shouldst be my Country's emblem; and shouldst wink,
Bright Star! with laughter on her banners, drest
In thy fresh beauty. There! that dusky spot
Beneath thee, that is England; there she lies.
Blessings be on you both! one hope, one lot,
One life, one glory!—I, with many a fear
For my dear Country, many heartfelt sighs,
Among men who do not love her, linger here.

This is the first of the Poems Dedicated to National Independence and Liberty.

The foregoing is perhaps a strange selection; but such a poet as Wordsworth could not in any case be represented adequately by any three or four short poems. I have therefore chosen a group of lesser known pieces, rather than copy again any of the famous ones.

Alfred, Lord Tennyson

❧❧❧❧❧❧❧❧

A WELCOME TO ALEXANDRA
March 7, 1863

Sea-Kings' daughter from over the sea,
              Alexandra!
Saxon and Norman and Dane are we,
But all of us Danes in our welcome of thee,
              Alexandra!
Welcome her, thunders of fort and of fleet!
Welcome her, thundering cheer of the street!
Welcome her, all things youthful and sweet,
Scatter the blossom under her feet!
Break, happy land, into earlier flowers!
Make music, O bird, in the new budded bowers!
Blazon your mottoes of blessing and prayer!
Welcome her, welcome her, all that is ours!
Warble, O bugle, and trumpet, blare!
Flags, flutter out upon turrets and towers!
Flames, on the windy headland flare!
Utter your jubilee, steeple and spire!
Clash, ye bells, in the merry March air!
Flash, ye cities, in rivers of fire!
Rush to the roof, sudden rocket, and higher
Melt into stars for the land's desire!
Roll and rejoice, jubilant voice,
Roll as a ground-swell dashed on the strand,
Roar as the sea when he welcomes the land,
And welcome her, welcome the land's desire,
The sea-kings' daughter as happy as fair,
Blissful bride of a blissful heir,
Bride of the heir of the kings of the sea—
O joy to the people and joy to the throne,
Come to us, love us, and make us your own:
For Saxon or Dane or Norman we,
Teuton or Celt, or whatever we be,
We are each all Dane in our welcome of thee,
              Alexandra!

This princess married the future Edward VII and became one of the most widely loved of Britain's queens.

IDYLLS OF THE KING
DEDICATION

These to His Memory—since he held them dear,
Perchance as finding there unconsciously
Some image of himself—I dedicate,
I dedicate, I consecrate with tears—
These Idylls.

      And indeed He seems to me
Scarce other than my king's ideal knight,
'Who reverenced his conscience as his king;
Whose glory was, redressing human wrong;
Who spake no slander, no, nor listen'd to it;
Who loved one only, and who clave to her—'
Her—over all whose realms to their last isle,
Commingled with the gloom of imminent war,
The shadow of His loss drew like eclipse,
Darkening the world. We have lost him: he is gone:
We know him now: all narrow jealousies
Are silent; and we see him as he moved,
How modest, kindly, all-accomplish'd, wise,
With what sublime repression of himself,
And in what limits, and how tenderly;
Not swaying to this faction or to that;
Not making his high place the lawless perch
Of wing'd ambitions, nor a vantage ground
For pleasure; but thro' all this tract of years
Wearing the white flower of a blameless life,
Before a thousand peering littlenesses,
In that fierce light which beats upon a throne,
And blackens every blot: for where is he
Who dares foreshadow for an only son
A lovelier life, a more unstain'd, than his?
Or how should England, dreaming of *his* sons
Hope more for these than some inheritance
Of such a life, a heart, a mind as thine,
Thou noble Father of her Kings to be,
Laborious for her people and her poor—
Voice in the rich dawn of an ampler day—
Far-sighted summoner of War and Waste
To fruitful strifes and rivalries of peace—
Sweet nature gilded by the gracious gleam

Of letters dear to Science, dear to Art,
Dear to thy land and ours, a Prince indeed,
Beyond all titles, and a household name,
Hereafter, thro' all times, Albert the Good.

Break not, O woman's-heart, but still endure;
Break not, for thou art Royal, but endure,
Remembering all thy beauty of that star
Which shone so close beside Thee that ye made
One light together, but has past and leaves
The Crown a lonely splendour.

May all love,
His love, unseen but felt, o'ershadow Thee
The love of all Thy sons encompass Thee,
The love of all Thy daughters cherish Thee,
The love of all Thy people comfort Thee
Till God's love set Thee at his side again!

This Dedication first appeared in the 1862 edition of *Idylls of the King*.
The Prince Consort had died on December 14th, 1861.

THE CHARGE OF THE HEAVY BRIGADE AT BALACLAVA
October 25, 1854

I

The charge of the gallant three hundred, the Heavy Brigade!
Down the hill, down the hill, thousands of Russians,
Thousands of horsemen, drew to the valley—and stay'd;
For Scarlett and Scarlett's three hundred were riding by
When the points of the Russian lances arose in the sky;
And he call'd 'Left wheel into line!' and they wheel'd and obey'd.
Then he look'd at the host that had halted he knew not why,
And he turn'd half round, and he bad his trumpeter sound
To the charge, and he rode on ahead, as he waved his blade
To the gallant three hundred whose glory will never die—
'Follow,' and up the hill, up the hill, up the hill,
Follow'd the Heavy Brigade.

II

The trumpet, the gallop, the charge, and the might of the fight!
Thousands of horsemen had gather'd there on the height,
With a wing push'd out to the left, and a wing to the right,
And who shall escape if they close? but he dash'd up alone
Thro' the great gray slope of men,
Sway'd his sabre, and held his own
Like an Englishman there and then;
All in a moment follow'd with force
Three that were next in their fiery course,
Wedged themselves in between horse and horse,
Fought for their lives in the narrow gap they had made—
Four amid thousands! and up the hill, up the hill,
Gallopt the gallant three hundred, the Heavy Brigade.

III

Fell like a cannonshot,
Burst like a thunderbolt,
Crash'd like a hurricane,
Broke thro' the mass from below,
Drove thro' the midst of the foe,
Plunged up and down, to and fro,
Rode flashing blow upon blow,
Brave Inniskillens and Greys

Whirling their sabres in circles of light!
And some of us, all in amaze,
Who were held for a while from the fight,
And were only standing at gaze,
When the dark-muffled Russian crowd
Folded its wings from the left and the right,
And roll'd them around like a cloud,—
O mad for the charge and the battle were we
When our own good redcoats sank from sight,
Like drops of blood in a dark-gray sea,
And we turn'd to each other, whispering, all dismay'd,
'Lost are the gallant three hundred of Scarlett's Brigade!'

IV

'Lost one and all' were the words
Mutter'd in our dismay;
But they rode like Victors and Lords
Thro' the forest of lances and swords
In the heart of the Russian hordes,
They rode, or they stood at bay—
Struck with the sword hand and slew,
Down with the bridle-hand drew
The foe from the saddle, and threw
Underfoot there in the fray—
Ranged like a storm or stood like a rock
In the wave of a stormy day;
Till suddenly shock upon shock
Staggered the mass from without,
Drove it in wild disarray,
For our men gallopt up with a cheer and a shout,
And the foemen surged, and waver'd, and reel'd
Up the hill, up the hill, up the hill, out of the field,
And over the brow and away.

V

Glory to each and to all, and the charge that they made;
Glory to all the three hundred, and all the Brigade!

The 'three hundred' of the 'Heavy Brigade' who made this famous
charge were the Scots Greys and the 2nd squadron of Inniskillings; the
remainder of the 'Heavy Brigade' subsequently dashed up to their
support. (Tennyson's note.)

The 'three' were Scarlett's aide-de-camp, Elliot, and the trumpeter and Shegog the orderly, who had been close behind him. (Tennyson's note.)

As the present book will appear in the centenary month of Balaclava it seems appropriate for the occasion to be thus represented. 'The Charge of the Heavy Brigade' suffers neglect by comparison with its companion piece, the 'Light Brigade.'

SONG

To sleep! to sleep! The long bright day is done,
And darkness rises from the fallen sun.
To sleep! to sleep!
Whate'er thy joys, they vanish with the day;
Whate'er thy griefs, in sleep they fade away;
To sleep! to sleep!
Sleep, mournful heart and let the past be past!
Sleep, happy soul, all life will sleep at last.
To sleep! to sleep!

from *The Foresters* (1892)

SONG

Shame upon you, Robin,
  Shame upon you now!
Kiss me would you? with my hands
  Milking the cow?
  Daisies grow again,
  Kingcups blow again,
And you came and kiss'd me, milking the cow.

Robin came behind me,
  Kiss'd me well I vow;
Cuff him could I? with my hands
  Milking the cow?
  Swallows fly again,
  Cuckoos cry again,
And you came and kiss'd me milking the cow.

Come, Robin, Robin,
  Come and kiss me now;
Help it can I? with my hands
  Milking the cow?
  Ringdoves coo again
  All things woo again.
Come behind and kiss me milking the cow!

from *Queen Mary* (1875)

Alfred Austin

ᗢᗢᗢᗢᗤᗤᗤᗤ

from VICTORIA
May 24, 1819–January 22, 1901

Dead! and the world feels widowed! Can it be
That she who scarce but yesterday upheld
The dome of empire, so the twain seemed one,
Whose goodness shone and radiated round
The circle of her still expanding rule,
Whose sceptre was self-sacrifice, whose throne
Only a loftier height from which to scan
The purpose of her people, their desires,
Thoughts, hopes, fears, needs, joys, sorrows, sadnesses,
Their strength in weal, their comforter in woe—
That this her mortal habitation should
Lie cold and tenantless! Alas! Alas!
Too often life has to be taught by death
The meaning and the pricelessness of love,
Not understood till lost. But she—but she
Was loved as monarch ne'er was loved before
From girlhood unto womanhood, and grew,
Fresh as the leaf, and fragrant as the flower,
In grace and comeliness until the day
Of happy nuptial, glad maternity,
More closely wedded to her people's heart,
By each fresh tie that knitted her to him,
Whose one sole thought was how she still might be
Helpmate to England; England then, scarce more,
Or bounded by the name of British realm,
But by some native virtue broadening out
Into an empire wider than all names,
Till, like some thousand-years' out-branching oak,
Its mildness overshadowed half the globe
With peaceful arms and hospitable leaves.

from *Victoria the Wise* (1903)

This is the opening of a long and not unimpressive poem. Austin collected everything he had ever written about Queen Victoria into a handsome quarto volume, *Victoria the Wise*, which although it does not contain a great deal of first-rate poetry, is a real convenience to any historian of the Laureates, for it is a dusty business tracking their ephemeral productions through the files of newspapers.

A MEETING
November 19, 1888

Queen, widowed Mother of a widowed child,
Whose ancient sorrow goeth forth to meet
Her new-born sorrow with parental feet,
And tearful eyes that oft on hers have smiled,
Will not your generous heart be now beguiled
From its too lonely anguish, as You greet
Her anguish, yet more cruel and complete,
And, through her woe, with woe be reconciled?
Or if this may not be, and all the years
Of love's bereavement be withal too brief
To bring slow solace to still lengthening grief
For loss of One whom distance but endears,
Surely to Both will come some sad relief,
Sharing the comfort of commingled tears.

The Princess Royal had married Prince Frederick William of Prussia
in 1858 and now, a few weeks after he had succeeded to the throne, as
Emperor Frederick III, he had died from a disease of the throat—on
June 15th. Austin's sonnet was on the occasion of the widowed
Empress's return to England.

LOVE'S UNITY

How can I tell thee when I love thee best?
In rapture or repose? how shall I say?
I only know I love thee every way,
Plumed for love's flight, or folded in love's nest.
See, what is day but night bedewed with rest?
And what the night except the tired-out day?
And 'tis love's difference, not love's decay,
If now I dawn, now fade, upon the breast.
Self-torturing sweet! Is't not the self-same sun
Wanes in the west that flameth in the east,
His fervour nowise altered nor decreased?
So rounds my love, returning where begun,
And still beginning, never most nor least,
But fixedly various, all love's parts in one.

This is not wholly unworthy of the *Sonnets from the Portuguese* which may well have influenced it. Austin thought highly of Mrs. Browning's work and called her 'the world's greatest poetess.' which, however, seems not to have turned aside her husband's wrath against 'such vermin as little Austin.'

AN AUTUMN PICTURE

Now round red roofs stand russet stacks arow:
Homeward from gleaning in the stubbly wheat,
High overhead the harsh rook saileth slow,
And cupless acorns crackle 'neath your feet.
No breeze, no breath, veereth the oasthouse hoods,
Whence the faint smoke floats fragrantly away;
And, in the distance, the half-hazy woods
Glow with the barren glory of decay.
Vainly the bramble strives to break the hedge,
Whose leafless gaps show many an empty nest:
The chill pool stagnates round the seeded sedge;
And, as the sunset saddens in the west,
Funereal mist comes creeping down the dale,
And widowed Autumn weeps behind her veil.

WRITTEN IN MID-CHANNEL

Now upon English soil I soon shall stand,
Homeward from climes that fancy deems more fair;
And well I know that there will greet me there
No soft foam fawning upon smiling strand,
No scent of orange-groves, no zephyrs bland,
But Amazonian March, with breast half bare
And sleety arrows whistling through the air,
Will be my welcome from that burly land.
Yet he who boasts his birthplace yonder lies,
Owns in his heart a mood akin to scorn
For sensuous slopes that bask 'neath Southern skies,
Teeming with wine, and prodigal of corn,
And gazing through the mist with misty eyes,
Blesses the brave bleak land where he was born.

This is one of three sonnets linked together, dated March, 1882. So long as there are people left who are not ashamed to love England—and who even persist in not calling it Britain—such thoughts as these of Austin's will be shared by Channel-travellers. For a poet almost universally condemned as execrable Austin does comparatively well; I could easily find a dozen sonnets no worse than those I have printed, and some other very readable verse in his works. The critical shibboleths that abound in the reading of English poetry are innumerable—that Browning was an optimist, that Southey is unreadable, that Coleridge by accident wrote three good poems and nothing else . . . etc. But I won't say people should read the poets instead of reading about the poets—or where would my book be?

Robert Bridges

༄༅༅༅༄

NOEL: CHRISTMAS EVE, 1913
Pax hominibus bonae voluntatis

A Frosty Christmas Eve
   when the stars were shining
Fared I forth alone
   where westward falls the hill,
And from many a village
   in the water'd valley
Distant music reached me
   peals of bells aringing:
The constellated sounds
   ran sprinkling on earth's floor
As the dark vault above
   with stars was spangled o'er.

Then sped my thought to keep
   that first Christmas of all
When the Shepherds watching
   by their folds were the dawn
Heard music in the fields
   and marvelling could not tell
Whether it were angels
   or the bright stars singing.

Now blessed be the tow'rs
   that crown England so fair
That stand up strong in prayer
   unto God for our souls:
Blessed be their founders
   (said I) an' our country folk
Who are ringing for Christ
   in the belfries tonight

With arms lifted to clutch
   the rattling ropes that race
Into the dark above
   and the mad romping din.

But to me heard afar
   it was starry music
Angels' song, comforting
   as the comfort of Christ
When he spake tenderly
   to his sorrowful flock:
The old words came to me
   by the riches of time
Mellow'd and transfigured
   as I stood on the hill
Heark'ning in the aspect
   of th' eternal silence.

This was sent to the King just before Christmas, 1913, and published in *The Times* 'at his Majesty's express desire.' The metre, Bridges tells us, is on the model of Milton's *Samson Agonistes* with slight modification. This is one of many poems in which Bridges experimented with the possibilities of new music in English metres—with some extremely happy successes.

from ODE ON THE TERCENTENARY COMMEMORATION
OF SHAKESPEARE. 1916

Thee SHAKESPEARE to-day we honour; and evermore,
Since England bore thee, the master of human song,
   Thy folk are we, children of thee,
     Who knitted in one her realm
   And strengthening with pride her sea-borne clans,
   Scorns't in the grave the bruize of death.
   All thy later-laurel'd choir
     Laud thee in thy world-shrine:
     London's laughter is thine:
   One with thee is our temper in melancholy or might,
And in thy book Great-Britain's rule readeth her right.

   Her chains are chains of Freedom, and her bright arms
   Honour Justice and Truth and Love to man.
     Though first from a pirate ancestry
       She took her home on the wave,
     Her gentler spirit arose disdainful,
     And smiting the fetters of slavery
     Made the high seaways safe and free,
       In wisdom bidding aloud
       To world-wide brotherhood,
     Till her flag was hailed as the ensign of Liberty,
And the boom of her guns went round the earth in salvoes of peace.

   And thou, when Nature bow'd her mastering hand
   To borrow an ecstasy of man's art from thee,
     Thou her poet secure as she
       Of the shows of eternity,
     Didst never fear thy work should fall
     To fashion's craze or pedant's folly
     Nor devastator whose arrogant arms
       Murder and maim mankind;
     Who when in scorn of grace
   He hath batter'd and burn'd some loveliest dearest shrine,
Laugheth in ire and boasteth aloud his brazen god.

SONNET

I heard great Hector sounding war's alarms,
Where thro' the listless ghosts chiding he strode,
As tho' the Greeks besieged his last abode,
And he his Troy's hope still, her king-at-arms.
But on those gentle meads, which Lethe charms
With weary oblivion, his passion glow'd
Like the cold night-worm's candle, and only show'd
Such mimic flame as neither heats nor harms.

'Twas plain to read, even by those shadows quaint,
How rude catastrophe had dim'd his day,
And blighted all his cheer with stern complaint:
To arms! to arms! what more the voice would say
Was swallow'd in the valleys, and grew faint
Upon the thin air, as he passed away.

from *The Growth of Love* (the edition
called *LXXIX Sonnets,* 1889)

FORTUNATUS NIMIUM

I have lain in the sun
I have toil'd as I might
I have thought as I would
And now it is night.

My bed full of sleep
My heart of content
For friends that I met
The way that I went.

I welcome fatigue
While frenzy and care
Like thin summer clouds
Go melting in air.

To dream as I may
And awake when I will
With the song of the birds
And the sun on the hill.

Or death—were it death—
To what should I wake
Who loved in my home
All life for its sake?

What good have I wrought?
I laugh to have learned
That joy cannot come
Unless it be earned;

For a happier lot
Than God giveth me
It never hath been
Nor ever shall be.

John Masefield

ⓈⓈⓈⓈⓈⒸⒸⒸⒸⒸ

ON THE PASSING OF KING GEORGE V

When Time has sifted motives, passions, deeds,
  Now complex to results and made appear
The unexpected fruits of scattered seeds,
  And scattered dust in the expected ear,
Then watchers of the life of man will know
  How spirits quickened in this ended reign,
Till what was centuries stagnant 'gan to flow
  And what was centuries fettered moved again;
How with this Ruler entered into rest
  The country's very self from slumber stirred
Took charity as guide and hope as guest,
  And ventured to a nobler marching word.

AT THE PASSING OF A BELOVED MONARCH
OUR SOVEREIGN LORD
KING GEORGE THE SIXTH
OF BLESSED MEMORY

The everlasting Wisdom has ordained
That this rare Soul, His earthly service done
Shall leave the peoples over whom he reigned
For other service at a higher Throne,
Where Life's rewarders sing at Triumph won
In nobleness attempted and attained
Through years more terrible than any known.

What is a Nation's love? No little thing:
A vast dumb tenderness beyond all price;
Surely a power of prayer upon a wing;
The living anguish of a hope to heal
Offered by all hearts here in sacrifice
To spirits bowed in sorrow for the King
That it may touch, to comfort or anneal.

May this devotion help them in their grief.
May the devotion kindle to resolve
To make this stricken country green with leaf
Glad with another hope to be again
A Sun about which singing orbs revolve
A Kingdom grown so worthy of her Chief
That millions yet unborn shall bless her reign.

A PRAYER FOR A BEGINNING REIGN

HE who is Order, Beauty, Power, Glory,
HE the All-Wise, who made the eterne abyss,
The Splendour, without Presence, without Story,
Maker and Arbiter of all that is,
HE set within Man's mind
All thought and image of a kingly kind:
In serving earthly kingship, we serve HIS.

Therefore, to THEE, All-Glorious, let us pray
For Her, THY Destined, consecrate today.

We, then, beseech THEE, Everlasting Power,
That This, THY dedicated Soul, may reign
In peace, in wisdom, for her mortal hour
In this beloved Land.
So guide Her with THY ever-giving Hand
That she may re-establish standards shaken
Set the enfettered Spirit free again,
With impulse green again in hearts forsaken,
With light to gladden as men reawaken
That they, after such winter-time, may flower.

Grant, KING OF KINGS, All-Merciful, All-Knowing,
That in Her reign Her people may advance
In all fair knowledges of starry sowing
In all arts that rejoice,
In beauty of sound of instrument and voice,
In colour and form that leave the soul befriended,
In ancient joy, our Land's inheritance
For light of THINE to make our living splendid
In service to the Queen who guides our going.

We, as a people, have been split in sunder
By all a century of thoughtless greed.
What glory in that time has been kept under?
What stunted hopes allowed?
What miles of squalid city under cloud?
Let us forget all this as done for ever;
This is a season of the springing seed
Of all a People one in an endeavour
To make our Sovereign Lady Queen indeed
Over a Kingdom worthy, the world's wonder.

THE CHIEF CENTURIONS

Man is a sacred city, built of marvellous earth.
Life was lived nobly here to give this body birth.
Something was in this brain and in this eager hand,
Death is so dumb and blind, Death cannot understand.
Death drifts the brain with dust and soils the young limbs' glory.
Death makes women a dream and men a traveller's story,
Death drives the lovely soul to wander under the sky,
Death opens unknown doors. It is most grand to die.

from *The Tragedy of Pompey the Great* (1910)

The young Commander, Valerius Flaccus lies dead after the battle. The Chief Centurions bear the body from the presence of Pompey the Great, speaking these sentences as they pass.

DUST TO DUST

Henry Plantagenet, the English King,
Came with Fair Rosamond, for monkish picks
Had lifted flaggings set in Roman bricks
And cleared a Latin-carven slab which told
That Arthur and his Queen were buried there . . .

They watched: the diggers raised the covering . . .
There lay those great ones placid under pyx;
Arthur enswathed as by a burning wing
Or wave of Gwenivere's undying hair,
Which lit the vaulty darkness with its gold.

Seeing such peace the living lovers knelt
And sought each other's hands: those dead ones lay
Untouched by any semblance of decay,
Liker to things immortal than things dead,
Manhood's undying glory, beauty's queen.

The crimson rose in Rosamunda's belt
Dropped, on the dead, one petal, soft as may.
Like ice that unseen April makes to melt,
Those bodies ceast, as though they had not been;
The petal lay on powder within lead.

from *Midsummer Night* (1928)

C. Day Lewis

Today bells ring, bands play, flags are unfurled,
 Anxieties and feuds lie buried
Under a cermonial joy. You, sir, inherit
 A weight of history in a changing world,
Its treasured wisdom and its true
 Aspirings the best birthday gift for you.

Coming of age, you come into a land
 Of mountain, pasture, cwm, pithead,
Steelworks. A proud and fiery people, thoroughbred
 For singing, eloquence, rugby football, stand
Beneath Caernarvon's battlements
 To greet and take the measure of their prince.

But can they measure his hard task—to be
 Both man and symbol? With the man's
Selfhood the symbol grows in clearer light, or wanes.
 Your mother's grace, your father's gallantry
Go with you now to nerve and cheer you
 Upon the crowded, lonely way before you.

May your integrity silence each tongue
 That sneers or flatters. May this hour
Reach through its pageantry to the deep reservoir
 Whence Britain's heart draws all that is fresh and young.
Over the tuneful land prevails
 One song, one prayer—God bless the Prince of Wales.

OLD VIC, 1818–1968

Curtain up on this dear, honoured scene!
A South-bank Cinderella wears
The crown tonight of all our country's theatres.
The stage where Kean
Enthralled and Baylis wove dazzling tradition
On a shoestring, makes good the vision
Of a hundred and fifty years.

Old Vic, your roof held generations under
A magic spell. And we have known
So many incandescent nights flash past and flown
Away—no wonder,
Where the young dreamed their dreams and learned their trade,
Stars come home to celebrate
Their nursery's renown.

Here everyman buys at a small price
An audience with Shakespeare, gleans
Self-knowledge from the hero's fall, the heroine's
Love-sacrifice.
This stage is all the world; in all our hearts
Rosalind smiles, Iago hates,
Lear howls, Malvolio preens.

Old cockney Vic, with what strange art you bring
Us strollers into one family
That learns through discipline, patience, tears and gaiety
'The play's the thing'.
We mirror old and new in serious play,
Man's worst and best, and what he may
Yet crave, yet come to be.

SONNET

If love means exploration—the divine
Growth of a new discoverer first conceived
In flesh, only the stranger can be loved:
Familiar loving grooves its own decline.

If change alone is true—the ever-shifting
Base of each real or illusive show,
Inconstancy's a law: the you that now
Loves her, to otherness is blindly drifting.

But chance and fretting time and your love change her
Subtly from year to year, from known to new:
So she will always be the elusive stranger,
If you can hold her present self in view.

Find here, in constant change, faithful perceiving,
The paradox and mode of all true loving.

From "Moods of Love", a sequence of sonnets in *Pegasus and other poems.*

ON A DORSET UPLAND

The floor of the high wood all smoking with bluebells,
Sap a-flare, wildfire weed, a here-and-gone wing,
Frecklings of sunlight and flickerings of shadowleaf—
How quick, how gustily kindles the spring,
Consumes our spring!

Tall is the forenoon of larks forever tingling:
A vapour trail, threading the blue, frays out
Slowly to a tasselled fringe; and from horizon
To horizon amble white eternities of cloud,
Sleepwalking cloud.

Here in this niche on the face of the May morning,
Fast between vale and sky, growth and decay,
Dream with the clouds, my love, throb to the awakened
Earth who has quickened a paradise from clay,
Sweet air and clay.

Now is a chink between two deaths, two eternities.
Seed here, root here, perennially cling!
Love me today and I shall live today always!
Blossom, my goldenmost, at-long-last spring,
My long, last spring!

Sir John Betjeman

ᗎᗎᗎᗎᗘᘓᘓᘓᘓᘓ

DEATH OF KING GEORGE V

"New King arrives in his capital by air. . . ."
Daily Newspaper.

Spirits of well-shot woodcock, partridge, snipe
   Flutter and bear him up the Norfolk sky:
In that red house in a red mahogany book-case
   The stamp collection waits with mounts long dry.

The big blue eyes are shut which saw wrong clothing
   And favourite fields and coverts from a horse;
Old men in country houses hear clocks ticking
   Over thick carpets with a deadened force.

Old men who never cheated, never doubted,
   Communicated monthly, sit and stare
At the new suburb stretched beyond the run-way
   Where a young man lands hatless from the air.

MONODY ON THE DEATH OF A PLATONIST BANK CLERK

This is the lamp where he first read Whitman
Out of the library large and free.
Every quarter the bus to Kirkstall
Stopped and waited, but on read he.

This was his room with books in plenty:
Dusty, now I have raised the blind—
Fenimore Cooper, Ballantyne, Henty,
Edward Carpenter wedged behind.

These are the walls adorned with portraits,
Camera studies and Kodak snaps;
'Camp at Pevensey'—'Scouts at Cleethorpes'—
There he is with the lads and chaps.

This is the friend, the best and greatest,
Pure in his surplice, smiling, true—
The enlarged Photomaton—that's the latest,
Next to the coloured one 'August Blue'.

These are his pipes. Ah! how he loved them,
Puffed and petted them, after walks,
After tea and a frowst with crumpets,
Puffed the smoke into serious talks.

All the lot of them, how they came to him—
Tea and chinwag—gay young lives!
Somehow they were never the same to him
When they married and brought their wives.

IN A BATH TEASHOP

"Let us not speak, for the love we bear one another—
Let us hold hands and look."
She, such a very ordinary little woman;
He, such a thumping crook;
But both, for a moment, little lower than the angels
In the teashop's ingle-nook.

SUNDAY MORNING, KING'S CAMBRIDGE

File into yellow candle light, fair choristers of King's,
Lost in the shadowy silence of canopied Renaissance stalls
In blazing glass above the dark glow skies and thrones and wings
Blue, ruby, gold and green between the whiteness of the walls
And with what rich precision the stonework soars and springs
To fountain out a spreading vault—a shower that never falls.

The white of windy Cambridge courts, the cobbles brown and dry,
The gold of plaster Gothic with ivy overgrown,
The apple-red, the silver fronts, the wide green flats and high,
The yellowing elm-trees circled out on islands of their own—
Oh, here behold all colours change that catch the flying sky
To waves of pearly light that heave along the shafted stone.

In far East Anglian churches, the clasped hands lying long
Recumbent on sepulchral slabs or effigies in brass
Buttress with prayer this vaulted roof so white and light and strong
And countless congregations as the generations pass
Join choir and great crowned organ case, in centuries of song
To praise Eternity contained in Time and coloured glass.

PARLIAMENT HILL FIELDS

Rumbling under blackened girders, Midland, bound for
    Cricklewood,
Puffed its sulphur to the sunset where that Land of Laundries
    stood.
Rumble under, thunder over, train and tram alternate go,
Shake the floor and smudge the ledger, Charrington, Sells,
    Dale and Co.,
Nuts and nuggets in the window, trucks along the lines below.

When the Bon Marché was shuttered, when the feet were hot
    and tired,
Outside Charrington's we waited, by the "STOP HERE IF
    REQUIRED",
Launched aboard the shopping basket, sat precipitately down,
Rocked past Zwanziger the baker's, and the terrace blackish
    brown,
And the curious Anglo-Norman parish church of Kentish Town.

Till the tram went over thirty, sighting terminus again,
Past municipal lawn tennis and the bobble-hanging plane;
Soft the light suburban evening caught our ashlar-speckled spire
Eighteen-sixty Early English, as the mighty elms retire
Either side of Brookfield Mansions flashing fine French-window
    fire.

Oh the after-tram-ride quiet, when we heard a mile beyond,
Silver music from the bandstand, barking dogs by Highgate Pond;
And my childish wave of pity, seeing children carrying down
Sheaves of drooping dandelions to the courts of Kentish Town.

INDEX

To keep this index within limits titles are listed only under author's names and references not to books, poems or persons are reduced to a minimum.